P9-BHU-386

Rabbi Shear Yashuv Cohen

MODERN JEWISH LIVES • VOLUME 5

Rabbi
SHEAR YASHUV COHEN

BETWEEN WAR AND PEACE

Yechiel Frish
and
Yedidya HaCohen

Translated by
Dr. Irene Lancaster

URIM PUBLICATIONS
Jerusalem • New York

Chief Rabbi Shear Yashuv Cohen:
Between War and Peace
by Yechiel Frish and Yedidya HaCohen
Translation by Dr. Irene Lancaster

Series: Modern Jewish Lives – Volume 5
Series Editor: Tzvi Mauer

Copyright © 2017 by Yechiel Frish and Yedidya HaCohen

All rights reserved.
No part of this book may be used
or reproduced in any manner whatsoever
without written permission from the copyright
owner, except in the case of brief quotations
embodied in reviews and articles.

Typeset by Ariel Walden

Printed in Israel.
First Edition.
ISBN: 978-965-524-253-9

Urim Publications
P.O. Box 52287, Jerusalem 91521 Israel
www.UrimPublications.com

Cover photo of Rabbi Cohen, Chief Rabbi of Haifa,
against the backdrop of his home city (photo courtesy of the family)

Library of Congress Cataloging-in-Publication Data

Names: Frish, Yechiel, author. | HaCohen, Yedidyah, author.
Title: Rabbi Shear Yashuv Cohen : between war and peace / Yechiel Frish and
    Yedidya HaCohen ; translated by Dr. Irene Lancaster.
Other titles: Ha-ish 'al ha-'edah. English
Description: Jerusalem ; New York : Urim Publications, [2017] | Series: Modern
    Jewish lives ; volume 5
Identifiers: LCCN 2016039021 | ISBN 9789655242539 (hardback)
Subjects: LCSH: Cohen, Shear-Yashuv. | Rabbis—Israel—Biography. | Rabbis—
    Israel—Haifa—Biography. | Chief Rabbinate—Israel—Haifa. | BISAC: RELIGION
    / Judaism / General. | BIOGRAPHY & AUTOBIOGRAPHY / Religious.
Classification: LCC BM755.K598 F7513 2017 | DDC 296.8/32092 [B] —dc23 LC
    record available at https://lccn.loc.gov/2016039021

OSKAR OLINER *z"l*
עוזר בן שאול ז"ל
נפטר י"ג מנחם אב תשנ"ח

SEYMOUR SUMNER *z"l*
הרב שמעון בן זכריה ז"ל
נפטר ז' מר חשון תשנ"ט

HENA OLINER *a"h*
הענא בת מרדכי מענדל ע"ה
נפטרה ב' דראש השנה תשס"ד

MARGIE SUMNER *a"h*
מלכה יטא בת צבי הרש הכאן ע"ה
נפטרה כ"ג אדר תשס"ח

❧

*O*ur parents, OSKAR and HENA OLINER, of blessed memory, and SHIMON and MARGIE SUMNER, of blessed memory, were devout and righteous Jews. They led exemplary lives of meticulous observance of ritual with generous displays of *Chessed* and *Tzedokah*, with an honest and wholesome lifestyle.

❧

*T*he Oliner door was always open to family and friends. The kitchen counter held HENA's famous sponge cake that was happily offered to everyone who graced their home. Sunday night dinners were a constant stream of honored guests who traveled from far and near to delight in scrumptious stuffed cabbage, brisket, and heavenly desserts. OSKAR was quiet and deep, clever and thoughtful, grateful and gracious, accepting whatever hand he was dealt. His work ethic was never compromised – no short cuts, no short change. His *emunah* was his partner in protecting his family through the horrors of war, with the struggles of an immigrant's life, and the challenges of a debilitating illness. OSKAR never questioned, never complained, only strived to achieve.

❧

*S*himmy and Margie were loved by all. SHIMMY had the widest smile and the biggest heart. His humor, countless jokes, and dancing feet were pure sunshine. MARGIE's list of friends was endless. Her engaging personality and uncanny ability to always push the right buttons was magnetic. Her daily phone calls are still sorely missed.

REVA & MARTY OLINER
Lawrence, NY
2017

Contents

Photos

Preface

The English translation of the original Hebrew version of this book was completed while our dear saintly Rabbi Shear (pronounced She'ar) Yashuv Cohen was yet living. To our tremendous sorrow, Rabbi Shear Yashuv Cohen passed away while this work was in its final stages, and he did not merit to see our English literary tribute to him in print. The day of his death was – how fittingly – the 3rd of Elul – the same date on which his renowned teacher and exemplar Chief Rabbi Avraham Yitzchak HaCohen Kook passed away precisely 81 years earlier. Though he is no longer with us, this English work refers to Rabbi Shear Yashuv Cohen as if he were still with us, in keeping with the format of the original Hebrew work.

For many years, Rabbi Shear Yashuv Cohen has played a pivotal role in the life of the Jewish people. He has been rabbi and spiritual leader for decades. He was Deputy Mayor of Jerusalem, helping to oversee the unification of the city. A devoted family man, he continues to be President of the Harry Fischel Institute for Research in Talmud and Jewish Law, most popularly known by its Hebrew name, Machon Harry Fischel, or simply, "Harry Fischel." He also continues in his role as President of the Ariel Institutes.

In addition, Rabbi Cohen was a member of the Underground in the period of the Mandate, serving in the Haganah and in other organizations. In the Israel Defense Forces (IDF), he eventually became Chief Rabbi of the Israel Air Force. He thus played a major role in helping establish *Medinat Yisrael* (The State of Israel) in her rightful place on the Land.

These are only some of the roles carried out over the years by Rabbi Cohen. Not many people are aware of the full story of his life. From the home of his father, Rabbi David Cohen (1887–1972) the legendary and holy *Nazir* of Jerusalem, also known as *HaRav HaNazir*, he grew up at the knee of the legendary Chief Rabbi Abraham Isaac HaCohen Kook

(1865–1935), and was himself destined to be a *Nazir* from birth, which status lasted until he reached the age of sixteen.

After that, Rabbi Cohen studied at Yeshivat Merkaz HaRav with Rabbi Yaakov Moshe Charlap (1882–1951) and Rav Kook's son, Rabbi Tzvi Yehudah HaCohen Kook (1891–1982). All three shared a vision of setting up the first *Hesder* Yeshiva, which would combine Torah learning with fighting in defense of the Old City of Jerusalem. Rabbi Cohen continued to fight during the 1948 War of Liberation until he was severely wounded and taken to Jordan as a prisoner of war.

However, the greatest achievement in his life of public service and Torah teaching was to serve as Chief Rabbi of Haifa and President of the Rabbinical Courts, Haifa District, for 36 years, from 1975 until 2011. And even though he has officially retired, Rabbi Cohen is still regarded as spiritual leader of Haifa.

The life of Rabbi Cohen is therefore not merely personal, but encapsulates the story of *Eretz Yisrael* and how it was liberated after 19 centuries of foreign yoke. This book focuses to a great extent on the historically spiritual city of Jerusalem and the historically secular city of Haifa which gradually became less secular, to a great extent as a result of the impact of Rabbi Cohen.

For the first time, this book enables us to read excerpts of a rare historical document, Rabbi Cohen's own diary, written during the fight for besieged Jerusalem and his imprisonment during the War of Liberation. He depicts his own personal history as a religious soldier who fought in this war, and his writings shine through with the clear insight of pure faith. The diary tells of the first *Hallel* prayer recited within the walls of the Old City at the moment when the State was resurrected, as well as the many prayers that accompanied the battles for the Old City. All these details are brought to life most vividly in the diary.

The diary also recalls, however, the loud cries for help broadcast by the soldiers stranded in the Jewish Quarter of the Old City during the grueling battles of 1948, which went unheeded at the time. This subject continues to be controversial even today.

This work is based on scores of interviews with Rabbi Cohen himself, as well as with members of his family, and close friends. Many of the pictures and much of the historic, literary and archival material appear in this book for the first time.

It gives us great pleasure to acknowledge the assistance of Rabbi Cohen's family and in particular, Rabbi Cohen's lifelong partner, Rabbanit Dr. Naomi Cohen, who worked with us during the writing of this book, and made important comments and suggestions both on the archival material and on the photographs that they placed at our disposal.

Many thanks are due also to Rabbi David Tabachnik, Director of the Ariel Institutes, as well as to Rabbi Harel Cohen, Director of the Nezer David Institute, for their generous assistance. We would also like to acknowledge the assistance of the National Library of Israel. Finally, many thanks to everyone who read through the manuscript and added significant comments or suggestions.

After the great success of the first Hebrew edition of the book, first published in 2013, and the extremely positive reactions that we received, resulting in a second printing of the book within a very short space of time, we are very pleased to announce the publication of a new and expanded English edition of the book.

We would like to thank our English translator, Dr. Irene Lancaster, who has worked tirelessly with great love and devotion on the translation of this book, and made our dream come true. We are most indebted to Canon Guy Wilkinson who carefully went over the manuscript as a labor of love and admiration. Finally, many thanks and great appreciation to Rabbi Hillel Fendel for devotedly reviewing and editing the nuances of the English version.

A special thank you also to Rabbi Aaron Reichel, who first suggested that the life and work of his uncle, Rabbi Shear Yashuv Cohen *shlita*, should be made available to the English-speaking world. Rabbi Reichel has worked with the translator and made many helpful editing suggestions. He also interviewed dozens of Americans for the chapter he wrote about Rabbi Cohen's activities outside of Israel for the English edition of the book. The roles were then reversed, with Dr. Lancaster editing his work after condensing it and adding the material furnished by the British personalities cited.

We would also like to acknowledge the role of Tzvi Mauer of Urim Publications, for the part he has played in publishing the English edition of the book and in general publishing books of interest of the highest caliber to the Jewish reading public.

Yechiel Frish and Yedidya HaCohen
Shaanan Academic College, Haifa 5775

Rabbi Shear Yashuv Cohen (1927–2016)
(Courtesy of the family.)

Between War and Peace

It gives me great pleasure to acknowledge the help and support received from many friends and colleagues in the course of translating this splendidly scholarly, yet readable, Hebrew biography about a towering figure in the history of *Medinat Yisrael* (the State of Israel), Emeritus Chief Rabbi Shear Yashuv Cohen of Haifa.

I had the privilege of getting to know the Chief Rabbi and his wife, Rabbanit Dr. Naomi Cohen, when I lived up the road in Einstein Street, Ahuza, from August 2006 until February 2008. I had arrived just two days after the end of the Second Lebanon War. Much of Haifa had been evacuated, but the Chief Rabbi and his wife chose to stay put.

A few days after Sukkot, I received a phone call from Rabbanit Naomi. I will never forget those soft, melodic New York tones:

"Welcome to Haifa. Please come around for *Shabbat*."

In anticipation, I walked down the road that Friday afternoon to make the acquaintance of a lively and most unusual couple, whose first words were: "What do you know about the Church of England?"

We never looked back.

During my time in Haifa, not only did we talk at length about inter-religious dialogue in all its aspects, but I was also invited to join the Israel Translators' Association, for whom I translated and edited approximately 30 books, articles and websites.

These ranged from the highly academic, including the latest material on biblical research from the Israeli Academy of Sciences and Humanities, to information from the Haifa Tourist Board, the Tel Aviv Stock Exchange, and scholarly articles from *Michlelet Shaanan* (Shaanan Academic Religious Teachers' Training College), which has commissioned the translation of this book.

And, in addition, I helped to edit Rabbanit Naomi's own scholarly publication for Brill on Philo of Alexandria.

I would like to thank my Broughton Park neighbors, Anne and Dovzi Lopian, who, in summer 2013, introduced me to the original book in Hebrew. Many thanks also to Danny Nissan, my accountant in Haifa, who acted as "go-between" with *Michlelet Shaanan.*

The book itself is a detailed, highly academic piece of research scholarship, written in a variety of literary genres, with a very extensive set of notes for the Hebrew reader.

However, the English-language version needed to take account of Jews in the Diaspora, and also the non-Jewish world, which features a great deal throughout the book, especially toward the end.

The book is also based on eye-witness reports, starting in 1927 during the British Mandate period, up until the present day. It therefore takes in the British occupation, the Arab riots, the internal struggles between all the Jewish factions, the special role of the Old City of Jerusalem especially during the War of Liberation, Rabbi Cohen's desire to bring modern thinking into the "Torah" world, in order to enhance both, and most of all, to do his utmost to preserve *Am Yisrael, Torat Yisrael* and *Eretz Yisrael*, while retaining the unity of *Klal Yisrael.*

In this translation, I have tried to retain the flavor of the original, and not offered up a "polished" or "sanitized" version. The challenge has been to work in so many different literary genres and languages.

In the course of translation, I translated a poem written in classical-modern Hebrew by the young Shear Yashuv Cohen, during his time as a POW in Jordan. I have also had to translate from Biblical Hebrew, Mishnaic Hebrew, Talmudic Hebrew, Talmudic Aramaic, medieval Hebrew, Yiddish, classical-modern Hebrew, modern Hebrew (Ivrit) and Arabic. I have also had to bear in mind the American readership for which this book is primarily aimed. I would like to thank Rabbi Aaron Reichel of New York for constantly guiding me on this path. And if the result is transatlantic, so much the better!

The difficulties were not only those of language. The book also contains many branches of Jewish thought and culture. There are references to the Hebrew Bible, Biblical commentaries, Talmudic Law, Midrash, Aggada, medieval thought, poetry, philosophy, mysticism, history, biblical archaeology, Jewish Law and contemporary Israeli law. There is also a great deal on modern global history, ideas, international law and politics.

I am lucky that my academic background has prepared me for this plethora of Jewish inventiveness and culture. And I was also able to call on the assistance of many friends and colleagues in Broughton Park, Cambridge, Haifa, Jerusalem, London and New York, to name but a few!

I alone am responsible for all the translations, having occasionally consulted with others and much appreciated their opinions. I hope that any "arguments" have been for the sake of heaven, but at all times the goal was to reproduce the words in context, while bearing in mind the contemporary reader – no easy task!

In addition, I did extensive background research on every person or event mentioned in the book, adding dates and extra historical or biographical material where necessary, in order to assist the reader.

Transliteration is mostly according to modern Hebrew (Ivrit) usage.

Some chapters have been expanded. This is particularly true of Chapter 14, *A Light Unto the Nations*, which deals exclusively with inter-religious dialogue. I felt that in addition to the sterling work done with the Vatican and the Roman Catholic Church, a short extract should be included about the first steps taken by the Church of England toward rapprochement.

This book has been written over a nine-month period, starting in early January 2014 and culminating in September, just before Rosh HaShanah 5775.

In the course of translation, I found that art often mirrored life. When I came to the chapter detailing all the institutions founded by Rabbi Cohen, I myself found in our synagogue library the "Practical Talmudic Dictionary of Aramaic, Hebrew and English," published by Ariel Institutes, with a foreword by Chief Rabbi Cohen!

When, in July, I reached the chapter on the Disengagement Plan from Gaza (2005), Operation "Protective Edge" had just started. And I wrote that chapter to the sound of rocket fire coming from Gaza, which could be heard daily on our radios, together with the invective of anti-Semitism emanating from religious leaders, politicians, the media and other pundits.

I have already thanked the people who helped me at the start of this "adventure." In addition I would like to thank Canon Steve Williams and Iain Duffus for technical assistance.

Marian Daintree initiated me into the different types of guns, rifles and other armoury in use during the Second World War and beyond, many of which were adopted by the Jewish Underground Groups under the Mandate, as well as by the fledgling Israel Defense Force.

Shimon Shapiro is equally knowledgeable about vintage cars and other vehicles, which proved invaluable when describing the many trucks and lorries which travelled to and from the Jordanian POW camp in 1948, bearing gifts for the Jewish New Year from the new Jewish State to its first POWs!

Martin Stern provided invaluable information about some of the more obscure Talmudic concepts. Shoshana Stern's knowledge of classical-modern Hebrew and Arabic is "beyond rubies." To both of you, many thanks.

Canon Dr. Andrew Shanks, Canon Guy Wilkinson CBE and former Archbishop of Canterbury, Dr. Rowan Williams, made very helpful suggestions regarding the language of inter-religious dialogue and authentic faith.

And to Rabbi Benjy Simmonds and librarian Joe Lazarus of Stenecourt Synagogue, thank you so much for the generous long loan of at least a dozen technical dictionaries and rabbinic commentaries.

To Rabbi Simmonds, especially, thank you so much for lending me your "Jastrow" when I really needed it, and also books about the life of the great Rabbi Aryeh Levin. Thanks also for your inspiring *shiurim* on Rav Abraham Isaac Kook, the first Chief Rabbi of *Eretz Yisrael* under the Mandate – poet, musician and seer without equal – who was such an inspiration for the young Shear Yashuv Cohen.

I would like to acknowledge in addition the very positive encouragement received from Chief Rabbi Ephraim Mirvis, a graduate of Ariel Institutes, and the first UK Chief Rabbi to have been awarded *semicha* (rabbinical ordination) in Israel, of which he is very proud. Dayan Isaac Berger, the *Av Bet Din* of Greater Manchester, also discussed with me Rabbi Cohen's huge contribution to *Klal Yisrael*.

It is with great pleasure that I reserve the bulk of my thanks for Rabbanit Dr. Naomi Cohen. Thank you for inviting me into your home and for your encyclopaedic knowledge. You have provided a wealth of extra information about all manner of subjects to do with the social, political, legal and religious life of *Eretz Yisrael* during the Mandate Period, as well as the early years of *Medinat Yisrael*.

All the Chief Rabbis, Prime Ministers and Presidents of this amazing young-old country have come to life in our numerous phone conversations. And many of your supplementary, and often hilarious, titbits have been incorporated into the book.

This book covers the history of Israel from 1927 until the present day. What I have translated is a seminal work about this hugely important period in the history of the Jewish people and their nation.

Just as my earlier work on our great Bible Commentator, Abraham ibn Ezra (1089–1164), was not merely about him, but also about his influence on posterity, so this book about Chief Rabbi Cohen of Haifa – who has lived all his life preparing for War, while genuinely seeking Peace – is also about the continuing existence of *Medinat Yisrael*, "the beginning of the flowering of our redemption." May it come speedily in our own day!

Dr. Irene Lancaster
Broughton Park, Salford, Greater Manchester
Elul 5774/September 2014

At Home

"Wonderful moments of chesed and inspiration in the early morning hours: these are our precious childhood memories from home. After the very early morning Tikkun Chatzot prayers, Father would sit surrounded by the books of his library immersed in the Upper Worlds and the realm of mystery and mysticism. From his lips would go forth the most amazing melodies that were not of this world; niggunim full of devotion and yearning from the depths of his soul. Sometimes Mother would stand behind the door and listen, with wonderment, awe and a hint of tears. We would occasionally notice a few people, early risers on their way to morning services, crowding together at our windows to listen, entranced by the prayerful melody emanating from the voice of the Nazir."

(Shear Yashuv Cohen: "My Parents' Home")

At Home

⇥ *NAZIR* FROM BIRTH

Rabbi Shear Yashuv Cohen was born on 9th Heshvan (4th November) 1927. His father was Rabbi David Cohen, *HaRav HaNazir* (1887–1972), the famous Nazirite, and his mother was Sarah (née Etkin). Rabbi David was the only *Nazir* of recent times. He lived a spiritual life, and was a unique and special personality known for his devotion. An accomplished scholar in his own right, he became one of the closest pupils of Rabbi Abraham Isaac HaCohen Kook. As a young man, he withdrew from all worldly pleasures and conducted himself with piety and abstinence.

Rabbi David took upon himself the obligations of *Nezirut* for life. From shortly after his meeting with Rav Kook until his death, no razor touched his hair or beard. Neither grapes nor wine were served at his table. On the Pesach Seder evening, he and his family would pour out four cups of apple wine for themselves, specially prepared by his wife. For guests they would, however, pour out traditional grape wine.

The *Nazir* was not only a Torah scholar, but was also well versed in philosophy and science, as well as in Kabbalistic wisdom. His wife, Rabbanit Sarah Cohen, together with Rabbanit Sarah Ostrovsky HaMeiri and Rabbanit Sarah Herzog, wife of Chief Rabbi Yitzchak Herzog, founded Emunah, the largest religious Zionist women's organization, first known as Omen. Rabbanit Cohen also helped found some of the earliest women's circles devoted to Torah study, focusing on both Bible study and Jewish thought.

The *Nazir* and his family lived first in the Nahalat Ahim neighborhood of Jerusalem, and later on Amos St. in what was then the modern neighborhood of Kerem Abraham (now, Geulah). The house was small, like its neighbors, and even old and drab from the outside – but inside, the house was full of light. Rabbanit Sarah had studied agriculture and botany in

HaRav HaNazir recites a blessing under the chupah at the wedding of his grand-daughter Tchiya Shapira (daughter of Rabbi Goren and currently a Tel Aviv District Court judge). Rav Shear Yashuv stands right behind him. Also in the picture are Rabbi Shlomo Yosef Zevin, Rabbi Yehoshua Bachrach, and Rabbi Shlomo Goren, holding the goblet of wine instead of the Nazir.

Russia before she came to Palestine, and she made use of her knowledge to beautify her home. She had an emotional bond with plants, and was devoted to their cultivation. Thus, the *Nazir's* home was always full of greenery. In every possible corner stood a flower pot, and the balcony was also full of plant pots and flowering saplings. This is how Ephraim Yair, a member of religious Kibbutz Tirat Tzvi, remembers their home in those days:

> "From the outside, the *Nazir's* house did not stand out particularly. It had neither looks nor charm. Inside, however, was a different story. The interior was imbued with light. Upon entering, we were accosted by flowers and plant-pots, bedecking all four walls. This was almost unheard of in the home of a Torah scholar in the Jerusalem of those days.
>
> "The whole room exuded a special vividness of its own, with vibrant greenery and vegetation. The old, worn-out furniture – tables and chairs from the 1920s; the decrepit, antiquated couch – the last word in simplicity. Not an ounce of elegance, no hint of luxury. The furniture was obviously not there to be beautiful. But all the same, the room was shrouded in a very special kind of

Rabbi Zecharia Mendel Katz, rabbi of Radin, grandfather of HaRav HaNazir.

charm. For you just couldn't take your eyes off it! An incomparable beauty of its own. All four walls were lined with book cabinets. Anywhere that wasn't a window, door, or plant pot, there was a book cabinet. Even the tops of windows and doors were crammed with books, all arranged according to category. Some cabinets had glass panels. These contained Written and Oral Torah, *Shas*, the six orders of the Talmud, and *Poskim*. Other cabinets were open to all, with no glass partition. These contained books on Jewish thought, Kabbalah, and the like. They seemed to cry out: 'Anyone who wants, come and take! Come and take in this veritable Garden of Eden!' On each and every shelf you could find a name-plate with an inscription designating the type of books there. Each book was marked; everything in its place. Order, beauty and grace.

"This room also served as a synagogue. For many years, the *Nazir* hardly set foot outside of his own home. Here he sat and

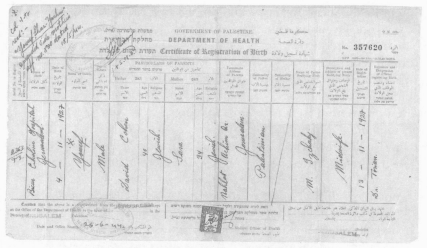

Rav Shear Yashuv's birth certificate

ב"ה. עיה"ק ירושלם ת"ו   ✡

מתכבדים בזה להזמין את כבו'
לבוא ולהשתתף בשמחת הכנסת בננו
בבריתו של אברהם אבינו
שתהי' אי"ה בר' עש"ק וירא ט"ז חשון תרפ"ח
בבקור חולים הוספיטל, בשעה 8 בבקר,
בהדרת הכבוד
דוד כהן ורעיתו

שאר ישוב שאר יעקב אל ✡ גבור

דפוס סלומון

Invitation to the brit milah of the son of the Nazir

learned, and here he meditated thoughts of holiness, here he prayed, here he taught his *shiurim* (lectures) on Jewish thought, and especially on the teachings of HaRav Kook. The *Aron Kodesh* (holy ark containing holy scrolls) and the prayer lectern completed the picture, underlining the ambience of sanctity."

It was into this special environment that Rabbi Shear Yashuv Cohen was born, a sibling for his older sister who was destined to become Rabbanit Tzefiyah Goren (1925–2007), wife of Chief Rabbi Shlomo

Goren. Rabbi Shear Yashuv was to be the first *Nazir*-from-birth since days of yore. Just as his sister's name referred to our "anticipation" of the Redemption, her little brother's name, too, had similar significance of national rebirth. For his *brit milah* (circumcision), which took place at the Bikkur Holim Hospital in Jerusalem in the presence of many leading rabbis, the *Nazir* alluded to his son's names by adorning the invitation with a quote from Isaiah 10:21: "*A remnant will return* (Shear yashuv), *the remnant of Jacob unto the mighty God*."

Rav Kook acted as honored *sandek*, holding the baby boy on his knees while the *mohel* carried out the circumcision. The *mohel*, as was customary, wanted to give the baby a drop of wine after the *brit*. But the *Nazir* did not allow this, in order to keep intact his son's *Nezirut*. Rav Kook indicated to the *mohel* that he should respect the father's wishes.

The baby was named "Yosef Shear Yashuv" – Yosef in honor of the *Nazir*'s father, and Shear Yashuv in reference to the above quotation from the Prophet Isaiah. Many years later, the *Nazir* taught his son Isaiah 10:22, where the name Shear Yashuv is again mentioned: "*For if thy people Israel shall be like the sand of the sea, the remnant of those that return shall wash away with righteousness the decreed destruction.*" The *Nazir* explained that he had always had the feeling that only a small part of the Nation of Israel would survive and return to Israel. So great were his fears regarding the calamity facing Diaspora Jewry that, according to Rabbanit Sarah, the *Nazir* sent her on a special mission to the religious Zionist leader, Rabbi Meir Berlin (Bar-Ilan). The objective was to persuade Rabbi Berlin to give every support to the highly controversial program led by the ideological leader of the Revisionist movement, Zeev Jabotinsky, on the eve of the Shoah, advocating the immediate evacuation of the Jews from Europe, whatever the price.

Baby Shear Yashuv began to utter his first words already at nine months. The *Nazir* describes in his diary that his son's first words were "Eliyahu the Tishbi" – for even as an infant, before he could enunciate the words *abba* and *imma* (father, mother), he would lie in his cradle singing "Eliyahu ha-bibi" to the tune of "Eliyahu haNavi." His ear had registered the sounds from the *zemirot* of *Motzaei* Shabbat (post-Shabbat hymns).

Some years later, the *Nazir* told his son that he had uttered these first sounds when they had all been staying with his teacher HaRav Kook on holiday on Mount Carmel – precisely where the Prophet Eliyahu overcame the prophets of Baal.

The Nazir with his face pressed to the Western Wall after the Six Day War

⇒ THE MIRACLE OF DELIVERANCE AND AN ADDITIONAL NAME

In 1929, when young Shear Yashuv was two years old, he came down with a severe case of pneumonia. His temperature was so high that he lost consciousness (this was before the days of penicillin) and the child's condition was very grave. The doctors were helpless and told the *Nazir*, "Your only hope is prayer," to the sounds of the relatives' weeping and wailing.

On hearing this, the *Nazir* chose ten students from Merkaz HaRav

*One of the first photos of Rav Shear Yashuv Cohen, when he
was about two years old*

(Rabbi Kook's Yeshiva) and walked with them to the *Kotel*, the Western
Wall of the Holy Temple Mount. He describes in his diary what happened
next: "I faced the *Kotel*, the Wall of our Holy Sanctuary, and with warm
tears rolling down my cheeks, I whispered a silent prayer from the depths
of my heart to the God of Israel Who cures all flesh and in Whose hands
I entrust my son's spirit."

As the Yeshiva students recited Psalms for his recovery, amidst weeping
and supplications, the *Nazir* consulted with Rav Kook, and they decided
to give the boy another name: Eliyahu. Usually in these circumstances,
it is customary to give an additional name symbolizing life. However,
"Eliyahu" had been the first sound that Shear Yashuv had uttered as a
baby, and therefore the *Nazir* felt that the prophet's merit would protect
him at this critical time.

After praying at the *Kotel*, the *Nazir* returned to the hospital. That

*The Nazir's two children:
Daughter Tzefiyah and son Shear
Yashuv.*

night turned out to be crucial. In the morning the doctors noticed that the child's condition had improved. After two more days, on *Motzaei* Shabbat, the baby woke up and even recognized his father when he entered his room.

This is how the *Nazir* described it: "I said to him, 'You know, you are *Eliyahu haNavi*,' and the child smiled happily and replied, 'But he is old.' In a short time, we brought the boy home, and for us it was a great miracle. From then on he was known as Eliyahu Yosef Shear Yashuv."

Rabbi Shear Yashuv himself relates:

> "Nearly 50 years after this incident, when I was chosen to serve as Rabbi of Haifa, together with Rabbi Eliyahu Bakshi Doron, many noted the special connection with the Prophet Eliyahu, whose life and work is associated with Mount Carmel and the city of Haifa. They said, 'Let us choose two Eliyahu's as joint rabbis of Haifa.' And I said to myself: 'Now it is known why my father and teacher chose this particular additional name for me.'"

CHAPTER TWO

Childhood

Rabbi Shear Yashuv's first childhood memory is associated with Rav Abraham Isaac HaCohen Kook, known simply as HaRav, the first Chief Rabbi of *Eretz Yisrael* under the British Mandate. He relates:

"In the month of Menachem Av 5689 (August 1929), at the time of the murderous anti-Jewish riots in Jerusalem and Hebron, we were staying in a house in Jerusalem that belonged to Rabbi Amram Abu-Rabiyeh, in the Nachalat Achim neighborhood, bordering on Shaarei Hesed. Fearing Arab attacks, the women and children were taken to safer quarters in the city center.

"My father and mother of blessed memory took my sister and me to the home of Chief Rabbi Abraham Isaac Kook in the center of Jerusalem, where we stayed for a few days. This was the time of the anti-Jewish riots in Hebron, culminating in the dreadful slaughter of the members of the Hebron Yeshiva. Naturally, as a small boy, I didn't really know what was going on, but one thing I *do* recall:

"Rav Kook always paid me a great deal of attention and would often sit me on his knees. So when Shabbat had concluded, after the evening prayer and the *Havdalah* ceremony, I tried, in my child-like way to engage with the Rav again, but this time I failed. For his face was aflame, and his amazing eyes were full of tears. He began to pace the room from one end to another, moving agitatedly in a zig-zag fashion. A sound like a great roar erupted from his throat, while he burst out with this heart-felt cry: '*O nations, sing the praises of His people, for He will avenge the blood of His servants: He will bring retribution upon His foes, and He will appease His land His people*' (Deuteronomy 32:43).

"Without stopping, the Rav kept on reiterating this biblical verse, with tears pouring down his cheeks, pacing back and forth in agitation, rushing from wall to wall. We were all left standing and watching; my father and Rabbi Natan Raanan, the Rav's son-in-law, and the others were distressed by the Rav's outburst of emotion.

"After some time, the Rav's wife, Rabbanit Raiza Rivka, came in and pleaded with him to stop: 'Come now,' she said. 'It's time for *Melava Malkah*' (the meal which accompanies the end of Shabbat). The Rav stopped and left the room with his wife. We didn't see the Rav again that evening.

"It was only when I had matured a bit that I learned both from my father the *Nazir*, as well as from Rav Kook's son-in-law, my teacher Rav Natan, that during that Shabbat the dreadful news about the massacre in Hebron had reached Hadassah Hospital. On hearing the news, the Rav had fainted and had needed medical attention. Later, he made every effort to assist the life-saving operations.

"In honor of Shabbat, the Rav had managed to restrain himself from venting his feelings. But as soon as the Sabbath was over, he could no longer hold in his pent-up emotions, and his heart simply erupted. The Rav's anger at the murderers and their British Mandate aiders and abettors knew no bounds. So much so, that he even refused to shake hands with Sir Charles Luke, High Commissioner of the Mandatory Government, telling him that they were 'stained with blood.'

"I also recall that the very words that he repeated, '*O nations, sing the praises of His people . . .*' were the opening lines to the *hakafot* dancing which took place a short time afterwards in his Yeshiva on the joyful festival of *Simchat Torah*. On this Simchat Torah, the Rav introduced a new, very special melody to that biblical verse. The crowd that gathered for the festival was deeply depressed because of the Hebron massacre, but they rallied around him in song, dancing and weeping at the same time. During these *hakafot*, Rav Kook took hold of me and together we danced.

"The dreadful spectacle of the Rav groaning '*in mourning because of the oppression of the enemy*' (Psalms 43:2), when he had always seemed to radiate such utter cheerfulness to me – this I will never forget!"

POVERTY AND DEPRIVATION

The special spiritual atmosphere cultivated by Rav Kook went hand in glove with poverty and deprivation. This was the lot of all Yeshiva teachers in those days. During his lifetime, and especially after his death, Yeshivat Merkaz HaRav suffered great financial stress. The teachers often did not receive remuneration and therefore had to endure poverty and deprivation.

Three-year-old Shear Yashuv Cohen

Sometimes the *Nazir* didn't even have two coins to rub together, while his wife, the Rabbanit, had to endure many hours of mental torment and humiliation outside the office of the director of the Yeshiva where she would wait patiently for the meager allowance he would dole out. But she never complained. The most she did was to occasionally let out a sigh and simply remark: "I am very worried about the director's health. I hope his heart does not give out, seeing as so many people need his help, which he is unable to give. May God send him salvation from heaven quickly!"

But even during these times of hardship, Rabbanit Cohen's own door continued to be open to the even more destitute, who were treated as members of the family. There was always at least a morsel of bread for those crowded around her table. Rabbi Shmuel Avidor HaCohen (1926–2005) remembers:

> "During the Shoah and later the War of Liberation, the Yeshiva was in severe financial difficulties. There was no food for the students, nor did the rabbis who taught them receive their payments. I recall Rabbanit Cohen, wife of the *Nazir*, coming to the Yeshiva and, with tears in her eyes, imploring the director, Rabbi Raanan, to give her some money. The pants of her son, Shear Yashuv, were torn and getting too small for him, and she didn't have the money to buy him new ones. Rabbi Raanan turned pale, but he simply couldn't do anything about it."

An even grimmer story is told by Rabbi Yehoshua Bachrach (1914–2002):

> "Facing the *Nazir's* family home on Amos St. was a grocery store. In those difficult days, the Rabbanit was frugal in her shopping habits, and the grocer noted down every item in his ledger. He himself, as well as his customers, found it very hard to make a living. He told us the following story himself, knowing how close we were to the *Nazir's* family, and in an attempt to alleviate his own guilt feelings. This is his story:
> "One Friday, the Rabbanit came to buy only two *challot* for

Shabbat, because she couldn't afford anything else. She took the *challot*, placed them on the counter and asked me to note the purchase in my ledger. I saw, though, that her account was full; she had been in the red for quite some time. I don't know what came over me that day, but I suddenly couldn't control myself. I picked up the *challot* and threw them onto the floor. The Rabbanit paused a second, and then bent down slowly, picked up the *challot*, put them in her basket, said 'Shabbat Shalom'

HaRav HaNazir, zatzal

and left. She crossed the road and slowly walked home. I am certain that when she came home, no one could tell what had happened to her.'"

Despite this severe poverty, the *Nazir's* home stood out in the Jerusalem landscape as a beacon of kindness. Rabbi Cohen tells this story:

"Our home was frequented by countless people who were down-and-out. I remember the years of my childhood in our small apartment. One room was used as a synagogue and study hall. This was where my father taught Torah to his pupils and which he used for every-day living. My parents rented out the second room to two young yeshiva students in order to ease their financial situation. And the third room was for the family.

"Despite the crowded conditions, there was always room for one guest in particular: a woman who lived alone, from a prominent religious Zionist family in Galicia. She needed help and support – not because she had no money, but because she had no home.

"During the summer months, a unique person, one of a kind, slept outside on the veranda. He came from a wealthy family in Kovno, Lithuania. He was a vegetarian, an eccentric in many ways, an astronomer who studied mathematics, a genius and misfit all in one. No one would take him in, but he felt at home with us, even though there was no room. Our home was open 24 hours a day. The Rabbi (the *Nazir*) would sit and learn, and the Rabbanit would perform *chesed* – acts of kindness – to a great variety of people. And there were also other people who came looking for help and support, such as uninvited guests who considered themselves semi-*Nazirites* on account of their thick manes of hair, and people with various problems who came for counsel and aid. They all enjoyed the special dishes prepared by the Rabbanit: vegetarian 'chopped liver' and vegetarian 'gefilte fish,' foods whose fame spread far and wide in the Jerusalem of those days."

Six-year-old Shear Yashuv Cohen

This education in *chesed* was imprinted on the psyche of young Shear Yashuv and had a lasting influence on him. Many poor and lonely people today can attest to the emotional and financial support they received from him. Even today, despite his age, Rabbi Cohen can occasionally be found sitting inside the Bnei Brit Home for the Elderly in Haifa, listening to their troubles and offering them his support.

EARLY CHILDHOOD EDUCATION

The *Nazir* started to educate baby Shear Yashuv while he was still in his cradle. The *Nazir* replaced the customary baby toys with letters of the alphabet, which he hung over the child's bed. Indeed, he learned to read and write at a very early age.

The *Nazir's* diary is full of descriptions of his children's childhood. By the age of six, young Shear Yashuv was well versed in Bible stories, including those from the Prophets. He also knew the Talmud Tractate *Berachot* by heart. His entire childhood environment – the childhood of a *Nazir* from birth – was centered on Torah learning and spiritual advancement. An interesting example of this phenomenon is the description of a children's game invented by the two Cohen children, Shear Yashuv and Tsefiyah. Together they studied, and acted out, the first *mishnah* of the Talmudic Tractate *Baba Metzia*, which describes two men claiming the same item. This is how the *Nazir* describes it in his diary:

He: One person says: 'I found it.'
She: And the other says: 'I found it.'
He: The first says: 'It all belongs to me.'
She: And the other says: 'It belongs to me.'
He: The first one takes an oath that no less than half belongs to him.
She: And the other one takes an oath that no less than half belongs to him.
The charade then concludes with them both singing the final ruling in a drawn-out melody: '*ve-yach-lo-ku* (they are to divide it between them).'

Former Knesset Member Menachem Porush (1916–2010) relates:

Shear Yashuv Cohen as a young boy

"I often attended services at the Batei Rand Synagogue in Jerusalem. One day the *Nazir* appeared in the synagogue with his little long-haired son. The *Nazir* was very keen to have his son by his side throughout the entire service, even before he knew how to pray or even to read. At the very least, the *Nazir* wanted him to say the Shema Yisrael prayer and occasionally look into the prayer book. Those were the days when the bitter disputes between the followers of Rav Kook and those of [haredi] Rav Sonnenfeld were at their height. It was therefore not exactly taken for granted that the *Nazir* and his son would come to pray in the very heart of the 'Old Yishuv.' But all those present were in awe of *HaRav HaNazir*."

CHESED TIMES

As we have seen above, it was ingrained in the children to set aside "hours of favor," as they nostalgically referred to them years later. As soon as dawn rose, the sound of the wonderful voice of the *Nazir* would wake up the children as he sat in his synagogue/*bet midrash* room, delving into mystical texts. His studies were accompanied by devotional melodies of yearning for the appearance of the Divine Presence; this also drew many Jerusalemites, who rose especially for the early-morning *Vatikin* prayers. They would stand outside the window and listen to the sacred melodies bursting forth from the lips of the *Nazir*. The heads of his children, Tsefiyah and Shear Yashuv, would peek into the room. And while all this was going on, the *Nazir* sat and studied Torah, to the accompaniment of

Attending a wedding as a young boy. Holding the cup of wine and reciting the blessing is Rabbi Yechezkel Sarna, Rosh Yeshivat Hebron. Behind are Rabbi Shalom Epstein and Rabbi Yitzchak Hutner.

supernal melodies and spiritual preparations for the morning prayers, totally oblivious to everything going on around him.

Here is an example of one of these "wonders" experienced by Rabbi Cohen in his father's house:

> "When I was about five, there was a drought in Jerusalem. It was announced in our neighborhood that there would be fasting and prayers. While we were all praying at home, the Holy Ark was opened and my father, wrapped in a *tallit* (prayer shawl) and accompanied by the entire *minyan* (prayer quorum), began to sing verses from the Song of the Sea (Exodus 15). He repeated the verses over and over and over again – until pouring rain began to fall."

⇒   AT SCHOOL

At a very young age Shear Yashuv was enrolled into a new kind of *Talmud Torah*, or *Heder*, one that taught in Hebrew rather than in Yiddish. This nationalist-haredi school was the brainchild of the famed educationalist Rabbi Shalom Friedman, and had just opened in the Geulah neighborhood. This is how young Shear Yashuv's first day is described in the *Nazir's* diary:

> "We wrapped the boy in a *tallit*, covering his face so that he would not see anything impure on the way, and led him through the city from south to north. The teacher opened a textbook entitled

HaShachar HaRishon (First Dawn). On the first page was a picture of a horse and the letters that spelled the Hebrew word for horse. I said to the teacher: 'Don't begin teaching him with something impure; even on the way here we covered him with a *tallit* to prevent him from encountering such creatures.' The principal was the well-known and inspired educator Rabbi Shalom Friedman, a native of Jerusalem. Rabbi Friedman was kind enough to oblige, and removed the first page of the book. The second page featured the word 'candle', with an appropriate accompanying picture. I said: 'May his first words give out light' (based on Psalms 119,130)."

Rabbanit Sarah Cohen baked a cake on which she sprinkled in sugar the letters of the verse, *Moshe commanded us the Torah* (Deuteronomy 33:4). The child licked up the letters while the cake itself was shared by the teachers and other pupils. But even after he had sent his son to school, the *Nazir* – who himself had been a teacher in his youth – continued to show a close interest in the boy's educational progress, as we learn from the following story:

The principal decided that after studying the Biblical portion of *Mishpatim*, in Exodus, the class should skip all the complicated portions dealing with the Tabernacle vessels and the sacrifices, and should move directly to *BaMidbar*, Numbers. Although the *Nazir* understood the educational motivation for skipping these passages, he felt that gifted pupils should be able to study the more intricate parts of the Torah. He therefore wrote a letter to the school principal: "Remember this general rule: Anything that is adequately clear to me, can also be explained to gifted pupils." He added that he recalled from his own childhood at *cheder* that the teacher had made a cloak and *ephod* (an elaborate garment worn by the High Priest) out of colored paper to teach the children about the appurtenances of the *Mishkan*.

⇒   EDUCATIONAL METHODS IN THE *NAZIR*'S HOME

In his second school year, young Shear Yashuv began to study Talmud in school – while in addition, his father sat with him every day to study an additional tractate. For example, when they studied Tractate *Baba Kama* in school, he and his father would study Tractate *Baba Metzia*, with commentaries by the *Rishonim* (11th-15th centuries) and the *Aharonim* (dating from the late 15th century). Thus, as a small boy, Rabbi Cohen already studied tractates that are normally taught in Yeshivot when a boy approaches Bar Mitzvah age.

Before the Jewish festivals, father and son would break from the fixed

Title page of young Shear Yashuv's notebook of novellae on Tractate Gittin.

curriculum and study the relevant tractate for the festival. In addition, every year between Purim and Pesach, they would study the entire Shulchan Arukh (*The Code of Jewish Law*) from the first printed edition (1565) of the work, a copy of which was in the *Nazir's* private library, divided into 30 daily study sections.

The *Nazir* felt that the building of one's spiritual character also requires the study of secular studies, so as to create the completeness that includes both Torah and general education. To this end, and despite the family's dire financial situation, he hired private teachers for the boy's general education: grammar, languages, math and other secular subjects. When he completed this curriculum, the boy stood successfully for the British matriculation certificate. We can see that the *Nazir* dedicated many hours of each day to the education of his beloved son.

Rabbi Cohen himself notes that in addition to the great love bestowed upon him at home, his education was "most exacting and uncompromising." He was tested in every subject both by his father the *Nazir* and by experts in the various disciplines.

⇥   *NIGGUN* – RELIGIOUS MELODY

Love of song and *niggun* (religious melodies) was central to the *Nazir*'s
way of life. "*Niggun* has always been, and always will be, the spiritual life
and core of my soul," he wrote in his diary; he even wrote some *niggunim*
himself. It is this love that led him to hire a special teacher, Dr. Yechiel
Vultz, who taught his two children to play the violin. Under the direction of the *Nazir*, Dr. Vultz also taught them sacred *niggunim*, including
a special melody written by Rav Kook to a *piyyut* (religious poem) by
the great Spanish-Jewish poet R. Yehudah HaLevi (1075–1140), entitled
Ye'iruni Ra'yonai ('*My idea wells up inside me*'), as well as compositions
by their own father, the *Nazir*. Dr. Vultz commented many years later:
"The young Shear Yashuv did not regard music simply as an art, but actually considered it to be something holy. For him music was an instrument
for the worship of God."

A fascinating tale lies behind the composition of one of the *Nazir*'s
very special *niggunim*, the devotional *Duvkah* melody, which he called
the "melody of my spirit and soul". The whole being of the *Nazir* was
imbued with yearning to come close to God. He longed to be worthy of
attaining the gift of prophecy. He felt that the return of the Jewish people
to *Eretz Yisrael* would also bring in its wake the return of the spirit of
prophecy which had ceased at the time of the Second Exile. He would
therefore occasionally slip out of Rav Kook's *bet hamidrash*, where he
taught, for a day or more, and would head for places where prophets had
walked, such as Ramat Shmuel, close to Mitzpeh, or the River Prat, near
Anatot.

One of these journeys, during which he composed *Duvkah*, is especially well-known. It took place in the summer of 1926 during the nine
solemn days leading up to the Fast of 9th Av (*Tisha B'Av*). The *Nazir* was
accompanied on his journey by two very close friends, who were also his
pupils: Rabbi Shalom Natan Raanan, the future son-in-law of Rav Kook,
and Rabbi Moshe Gurewitz.

The three of them left Jerusalem in the direction of Wadi Prat, not
planning to stay long. However, they lost their way in the vicinity of Wadi
Kelt and ended up wandering around the Judean Desert. Eventually their
meager rations of food and drink ran out. For three days the *Nazir* and
his companions tried in vain to find their way back. They had no choice
but to quench their thirst by sipping the last drops of water left over in
the rock crannies from the winter rains. This water was not fresh, which
damaged their health even more.

On the fourth day the *Nazir* harbored no further illusions about the
gravity of their situation. He therefore decided to write down in his note-

book his name and address, in both Hebrew and English, in case they did not manage to find their way out of the desert. This was so that if he were to be found, his wife could be informed, so that at least she would not remain an *agunah* and would be able to remarry.

It was during these difficult few days that the *Nazir* composed his devotional *niggun*, based on Psalm 63:1–2: "*A song of David when he was in the Judean desert: 'O God You are my God. My soul thirsts for You. My flesh longs for You in an arid and weary land, without water.'*" Thus, despite the hardships of these days in the desert, the *Nazir* used this time to concentrate his energy on how to come closer to God and achieve prophetic revelation.

On the fourth day, by which time the *Nazir* was down to his last ounce of strength, a group of Bedouins chanced upon them. In exchange for *baksheesh*, the Arabs agreed to lead the *Nazir* and his comrades back to Jerusalem, and they managed to get home before Shabbat.

The *Nazir's* children, Tsefiyah and Shear Yashuv, were understandably very fond of this special *niggun* composed by their father in the desert. Every year, at the climax of the Torah study of *Hoshanah Rabba* night, young Shear Yashuv would produce his violin and perform the devotional melody in his father's Sukkah. And not only then: Every *Motzaei* Shabbat, Shear Yashuv and Tsefiyah would perform a post-*Havdalah* musical program of special songs. These included *Eliyahu haNavi* and other favorite *niggunim* of the *Nazir*, such as *Yibaneh HaMikdash* ("*Let the Holy Sanctuary be rebuilt*") and *Zacharti Lach Chesed Ne'ura'yich* ("*I remember you, the kindness of your youth*").

⇒   FIRST COMPOSITIONS

Another unusual feature of the *Nazir's* educational approach was an emphasis on the writing of *chiddushim* (novellae, original comments on the Torah), even at a very young age. The *Nazir* used to interpret the Mishnah in *Pirkei Avot (Ethics of the Fathers)* 2:2) as follows: "All Torah study that is not accompanied by work, will cease in the end" – Torah study that is not accompanied by the work of writing it down, with original comments, will end up being completely forgotten.

And so by the time young Shear Yashuv was just six and a half years old, he had already written original thoughts on the Torah, the Prophet Isaiah and the Scroll of Esther, and the Talmud Tractate *Baba Metzia*. He called these original commentaries *Or Hadash* (*New Light*). By the age of eight, he had also added commentaries on *Yebamot, Gittin, Ketubot, Kiddushin, Baba Kama, Baba Batra, Sanhedrin* and *Rosh HaShanah*, as well as on the Haggadah for Pesach. He called these new, more advanced

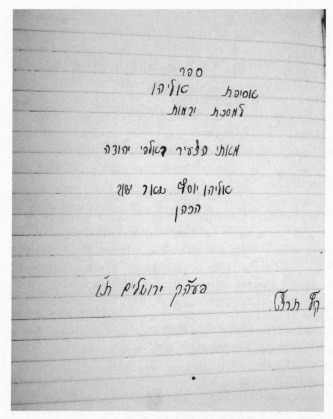

Title page of 11-year-old Shear Yashuv's notebook of novellae on Tractate Yebamot.

commentaries *Asifat Eliyahu* (*The Collected Works of Eliyahu*). All these original commentaries, written when Shear Yashuv was very young, are still extant in manuscript form today.

In his diary, the *Nazir* wrote about his son: "His questions were wonderful and his original comments both beautiful and brilliant." The young child also demonstrated similar flair for writing essays, which were subsequently published in contemporary children's magazines.

AT RAV KOOK'S KNEE

Chief Rabbi Abraham Isaac Kook was not only very close to the *Nazir*, but also felt a deep affinity with the *Nazir's* son, young Shear Yashuv. For example, in one of Rav Kook's letters to the *Nazir* which he sent from the Arza Convalescent Home in the Judean Hills, he added, "Don't forget to

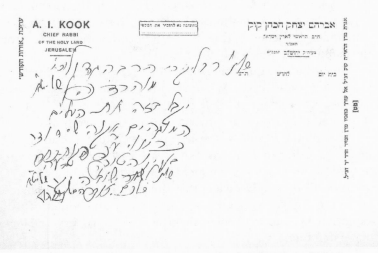

A letter from Rav Kook to the Nazir, the editor of his writings –
with regards to "dear Shear Yashuv."

say hello for me to dear Shear Yashuv, may he live long and happily." The young child was only about six years old at the time.

Occasionally, the *Nazir* would take his son to Rav Kook to be tested on his Talmudic learning. These sessions would usually take place on a Thursday evening or on Friday before the onset of Shabbat. On one such Sabbath Eve that became forever etched in the child's memory, the Rav asked him how well he knew *Bereshit,* the first portion of Genesis, which he had just been studying in school. Many years later, Rabbi Cohen gave an account of that conversation:

> "The Rav was sitting in his small room on his rocking chair, pondering over a book. When we arrived, the Rav called me to him, sat me on his knee and asked: 'What have you learned this week?' I answered, '*Chumash*' (the Pentateuch). 'Which *parasha* (weekly portion)?' he asked. '*Bereshit*,' I answered. Then the Rav asked: 'Did you understand everything? Maybe you have a question?' I replied: 'There are many things that I don't yet understand, and I do have some questions.' The Rav responded: 'Go on then, my son. Ask away!' I don't know where I got my courage from, but love just poured out of the Rav, so I went right up to him and asked:
>
> "In the Yigdal prayer, we say that God 'has no semblance of a body nor is He corporeal.' But this is contradicted by the verse

'*God created humanity in His image*' (Genesis 1:27). If according to the Yigdal prayer, God has no image, how do we understand this verse referring to God's image?" The truth is that I myself don't remember the details of this story, but I heard it many times from my parents, and this is what they told me:

"'You asked the question in all innocence. Silence reigned, and then the Rav answered: 'When you are playing a game and want to produce the image of a doll, child, or animal, you need not only the material, but also the pattern or mold. The mold is made from wood or metal, and the material is poured into it, producing the image according to the mold. The phrase '*in Our image, according to Our likeness*' refers to the mold that God made. The verse '*the image of God*' simply means that humanity's image belongs to God.' The Rav gazed upon you benevolently and added: 'This is all I can tell you today. When you grow up, you will have a deeper understanding.'"

"All present were overwhelmed by both question and answer. I received a kiss from the Rav, and a hug and kiss from my father. Rabbanit Raiza Rivkah, wife of the Rav, who had been present throughout, said under her breath in Yiddish, 'May the Evil Eye not rule over him,' to which all present responded Amen."

"At a later date, Rav Kook commented to my father, 'Sometimes a child asks in all innocence a question that even we adults find difficult to answer.' After many years I realized that the Rav's response had been based on Rashi's commentary to Genesis 1:26, where he interprets the phrase '*in Our image*' as '*in Our imprint.*'"

In his diary, the *Nazir* describes another similar occasion in 1935, the year of Rav Kook's death. The text they were studying on the Sukkot festival was Tractate *Sukkah* with commentaries by the *Rishonim*:

"Rav Kook tested the young boy on Tractate *Sukkah*. When the Rav heard him give all the commentaries of the *Rif* [Rabbi Isaac Alfasi, 1013–1103] and the *Raavad* [Rabbi Abraham ben David, ca.1125–1198], his eyes lit up in amazement at the child's deep knowledge and understanding of complex matters."

Another event recalled by Rabbi Shear Yashuv took place at the home of Rav Kook during the difficult period when the Rav publicly proclaimed the innocence of those accused of the murder of Chaim Arlosoroff [1899–1933]. During the trial Jerusalem was in turmoil, while Rav Kook led the campaign in support of the accused. The Rav's closest friends were most concerned, and begged him to desist: "How can you fight against the entire *Yishuv*?" An example of the problems with which the Rav had to contend in this context was when a young man came up to the *Nazir* and gave him a leaflet on which written, *"Woe to the generation whose priests cover up for murderers."*

Rabbi Cohen relates:

> "An event took place then which I remember very well. During the course of the trial, one of the accused was set free: Tzvi Rosenblatt. Naturally, Rosenblatt went to visit the Rav in his home on the first Shabbat after his release. Students from Merkaz HaRav were praying in the house. The Rav had stood by the accused and had never for one moment believed the false charges against them. Rosenblatt was received warmly, but no differently than the Rav treated any guest – even though the Rav's home was crowded with people waiting for a celebratory welcome for the freed man.
>
> "However, once the prayers were over, the Rav sent me, a small boy, to tell the Rabbanit that guests had arrived; he then organized a *Kiddush* and special Shabbat meal for the freed man. I was later told that the Rav had apparently had reservations about the irreligious conduct of the accused men. This did not prevent him from defending their innocence fiercely, in fulfillment of Leviticus 19:15, 'Do not stand by the blood of another' – but he did not want to identify with their secular behavior and secular Zionism. He thus offered them suitable hospitality befitting any guest."

EDITING *OROT HAKODESH* (RAV KOOK'S *"LIGHTS OF HOLINESS"*)

The *Nazir* spent many years of his life editing the writings of Rav Kook, which were collected in dozens of hand-written notebooks. These had not been arranged according to subject-matter, as the Rav's ideas covered many different areas which he would note down as soon as they came to him, rather than in any specific order. He entrusted the editing of his book *Orot HaKodesh* (Lights of Holiness) to his favorite pupil, the *Nazir*. And it was the *Nazir* who organized the words of his rabbi according to subject-matter.

When the Rav reviewed the edited edition of his writing, he became very emotional and said, "I am learning about myself from the edited book." He even went on to give his lectures from the edited proofs of the book. But he did not himself participate in the process of the editing.

Whenever the *Nazir* asked for advice and information regarding the chapter headings and their meanings, the Rav would refuse to respond, saying that he did not know how to organize and edit books. Only very rarely would the Rav give the *Nazir* guidance as to how to proceed.

Thus, during the Rav's lifetime, and even more so after his death, whenever the *Nazir* wanted to amend various turns of phrase and other aspects of Rav Kook's style, he consulted with the Rav's other outstanding students, as well as with experts in linguistics. And it was the *Nazir's* son, the young Shear Yashuv, whom he would send to them with sheets of paper full of supplementary questions. Many years later Rabbi Cohen wrote:

> "The care and respect given to the editing and ordering of the writings of Rav Kook was inestimable. Not a letter was removed, nor an expression edited, without lengthy consultation. When my father, the *Nazir*, wished to alter a specific word, or turn a sentence around in a way that differed from Rav Kook's original structure, he would send me to Rabbi Charlap and to Rav Kook's son, Rabbi Tzvi Yehudah Kook, and himself consult with Rabbi Shalom Natan Raanan, Rabbi Moshe Gurewitz, and Rabbi Yisrael Herling.
>
> "I recall arriving at Rabbi Charlap's house one Friday afternoon, after the Rabbi had finished writing his comments on the Torah portion of the week and had immersed in the *mikveh*. He would be in his chair, dressed in white, waiting for Shabbat to begin, and I would then present the questions to him. After that I would be sent to Rabbi Dr. Moshe Zeidel, an expert in linguistics and grammar; if the matter remained doubtful, I would make another stop, this time to Hanoch Yalon, a researcher into Rabbinic literature and language who lived then in Geulah, and he would give the final verdict. On subjects having to do with Jewish thought and philosophy, the *Nazir* would consult Professor Shmuel Hugo Bergman [1883–1975] and Professor Natan Rotenstreich [1914–1993], both of the Hebrew University."

⇒   "*TORAT YERUSHALAYIM*" AND THE DEATH OF RAV KOOK

At the age of eight, young Shear Yashuv was transferred from elementary school to the *Torat Yerushalayim* preparatory school for Merkaz HaRav. He also continued studying Torah with his father two hours a day. At *Torat Yerushalayim* he studied with Rabbis Chaim Bernstein, Moshe Bulebin and Menachem Lifschitz. Here, too, he was regarded as an outstanding pupil, being rapidly promoted until he reached the highest class. Sadly, however, his dream of studying Torah as a pupil of Rav Kook was never realized. For, just before Shear Yashuv enrolled at Merkaz HaRav itself, Rav Kook passed away, in the summer of 1935.

Shortly before, it was discovered that Rav Kook was afflicted with cancer, which caused him tremendous pain. The Rav travelled north to Mount Carmel for rest and recuperation. The young Shear Yashuv, concerned for his rabbi, wrote him a letter full of childlike innocence:

> "Wholeheartedly and eagerly, I send greetings and wishes for a full recovery to you and your family. May it be God's will that the Divine Presence support all your deeds, and may the founts of your knowledge trickle out to the world. May your name be revealed in every land, and may you merit to live until the days of the Messiah. Amen!"

Just before Pesach, Rav Kook returned to Jerusalem, and on the festival itself, he made a point of going out to welcome the many guests who had come to see him. Seven weeks later, on Shavuot, he was able to attend synagogue as usual, even leading the public recitation of the special *Akdamut* prayer – but by then he was unable to welcome guests. His condition continued to decline, and the doctors ordered that he be transferred to a convalescent home in the Kiryat Moshe neighborhood of Jerusalem. Before leaving his home, the Rav paid a last visit to each room of Merkaz HaRav, and also asked to be driven the length and breadth of Jerusalem. It was as if he had a premonition that he would never again set eyes on his Yeshiva or the holy city.

In the subsequent summer month of Tammuz, when his pupil Rabbi Yaakov Moshe Charlap (1882–1951) came to visit, Rav Kook asked him to pray for him. Rabbi Charlap published a leaflet encouraging people to pray for the Rav's recovery, thereby drawing the attention of the public to the gravity of the Rav's condition. Crowds of people flocked to the Western Wall to pray for his health. As part of the prayer schedule organized by the Rav's pupils, Rabbi Charlap travelled with the *Nazir* and young Shear Yashuv to the Machpelah Cave in Hebron, where they prayed for the Rav's recovery.

In his diary, the *Nazir* describes how, in the midst of his prayers, he placed his head on the outer wall of the Cave: "I heard a voice roaring from the depths, but I did not know how to interpret this, and I trembled, utterly frightened." On the bitter morning of 3rd Elul (1st September) 1935, the *Nazir* and his son visited the convalescent home in Kiryat Moshe to see the Rav for the very last time. These were the last moments of the Rav's life, and the Rav was aware of this. He therefore motioned with his hand to the *Nazir* and the boy to leave the room, on account of their priestly status, which forbade them from coming into contact with death. Even today, decades later, Rabbi Cohen clearly remembers the very last time that he, as a young boy, looked on the face of Rav Kook:

> "We went outside and suddenly an earsplitting sound was heard. It was the voice of Rabbi Yehiel Michel Tukachinsky [1872–1955], Dean of Yeshiva Etz Chaim. At the very moment of the Rav's death, Rabbi Tukachinsky recited the *Shema* prayer: '*Hear o Israel, the Lord is our God, the Lord is One*.' My father and I burst out crying. Suddenly, a wondrous sound could be heard, as if not of this world. All the people who were gathered around the Rav's bed were inspired in the midst of their tears to recite the words of the biblical *Song of Songs*. Whoever has heard and seen a thing like this once in his life – cannot forget it."

Rabbi Cohen added: "The Rav was quite simply like a grandfather to me, because I actually grew up in his house. His death was most difficult for me." From Kiryat Moshe, father and son walked to Rav Kook's home, where the eulogies were given. Rabbi Cohen recalls:

> "The first to give a eulogy was the great Rabbi Isser Zalman Meltzer [1870–1953], who commenced by saying: 'More traumatic is the death of a righteous man than the burning down of God's house.' He added: 'The backbone of *Klal Yisrael* – the entire Jewish people – has been broken today.' And at his words the entire congregation broke down and wept."

Moshe Neuhaus from Hadera relates the following:

> "On the Shavuot festival nearly a year after the Rav's death, in 1936, I was renting a room in the *Nazir's* house. I remember his son, Shear Yashuv, then around nine years old, singing in rhyme to the melody of the *Akdamut* prayer: 'The Chief Rabbi of *Eretz Yisrael* may be lying in the ground (*admata*), but he is totally aware of everything that is going on right now.' These words demonstrate how much the young boy missed the saintly Rav, who had played such a significant role in his early upbringing."

Harry and Mrs. Fischel with their grandchildren. The youngest grandchild, Naomi Goldstein – future wife of Rav Shear Yashuv – stands in front of Mrs. Fischel.

⇒   WITH HARRY FISCHEL

At ten and a half years of age, Shear Yashuv had hoped and expected to continue on the educational path marked out for him, by seeking entrance to Yeshivat Merkaz HaRav. However, he was not even Bar Mitzvah age, and considered too young.

Instead, the young Shear Yashuv began to study in the synagogue in the Harry Fischel Institute for Talmudic Research, popularly known by its Hebrew name, Machon Harry Fischel, or just "Harry Fischel." Shear Yashuv formed a *chevruta*, study partnership, with Rabbi Mordechai Zaks, son-in-law of Rabbi Charlap, head of the Institute and rabbi of the Zichron Moshe neighborhood. Rabbi Shear Yashuv later wrote that in studying with Rabbi Zaks, he acquired the traditional Jerusalem-yeshivot study method. Rabbi Zaks also utilized the more critical research methods that he acquired as head of Machon Harry Fischel.

Harry Fischel (1868–1945) was a well-known American philanthropist who used to stay in the apartment he built for himself in the Institute building whenever he visited Israel. He enjoyed chatting in Torah with the young boy studying in the synagogue, unaware that in years to come the young man would marry one of his own granddaughters.

⇒   THE BOY WITH THE LONG HAIR

As the boy grew up and matured in contemporary Jerusalem, he was nicknamed "the boy with the long hair," since he followed his father's *Nazirite* custom of not having his hair cut. In this context, Rabbi Cohen recalled years later an instance of the famous *Shirat HaYam* event on the seventh night of Pesach in Rabbi Charlap's home:

> "After reciting the Song of the Sea (Exodus 15:1–18), Rabbi Charlap would dance most wondrously among the assembly, singing the refrain: "*Melekh Rachaman*, Merciful King, have mercy upon us; good and beneficent One, care for us." I was standing in the circle of people around him as he danced in the center, when suddenly he stretched out his hand to mine and grasped it. I threw myself into dancing with him in the center of the circle. I had long hair because of my *Nezirut,* and tourists and other visitors thought that Rabbi Charlap was dancing with a woman, until they learned that I was the son of the *Nazir*. This was a dance of pure love. He put his hand on my shoulder and danced with me until the end of the *Melekh Rachaman* prayer. I will never forget it."

When Shear Yashuv was twelve years and one day old, a halakhic question arose: If he did not declare on that day – the first day of his 13th year – that his *Nezirut* was merely a "practice" and not an "oath," he would remain a *Nazir* in every sense of the word. He would therefore find himself liable for biblical punishments if he cut his hair in error or drank wine. In addition, he would not find it easy to end his *Nezirut* status. It must be emphasized that the *Nazir*'s commitment to *Nezirut* was not a binding vow, but rather a custom that he, and later his son, voluntarily took upon themselves in order to raise their spiritual level.

Therefore, on the advice of the foremost Torah scholars in Jerusalem, headed by the great Rabbi Meltzer, a gathering of rabbis was organized in the home of the *Nazir*. Those present included the two Chief Rabbis of the Holy Land, Rabbi Isaac HaLevi Herzog (1888–1959) and Rabbi Ben Zion Meir Chai Uziel (1880–1953). Two other famous rabbis who attended the gathering were Rabbi Moshe Haskin (1872–1950) and Rabbi Mordechai Sender HaLevi Kopstein (who had been the Rabbi of Radin and was also the *Nazir*'s brother-in-law). In the presence of all these rabbis the boy announced publicly that he was voluntarily taking upon himself, and not in the form of a vow or oath, the custom of *Nezirut*.

⇒   BAR MITZVAH

Well before reaching the age of 13, young Shear Yashuv began preparing to take on the yoke of Torah and its mitzvot (commandments), as well as to think about his *drashah*, the address that he would give on that occasion under the watchful eye of his father. Many years later, he described the procedure of writing his special Bar Mitzvah *tefillin*:

> "He who did not see this holy event, never saw a holy experience in his life. Father and the scribe went to the *mikveh* together, then returned and seated themselves on opposite sides of the table, wrapped in his prayer shawl and *tefillin*. They then set about writing my Bar Mitzvah *tefillin*. Every time they reached the ineffable Hebrew name of God, they would return to the *mikveh* and immerse themselves in it, reciting all the *kavanot* (prayers of entreaty). It took 19 hours to complete the writing of the *tefillin* passages – one day for the hand *tefillin*, and the next day for the head *tefillin*. When Father handed me the *tefillin*, he said: 'These are very special *tefillin* imbued with the spirit of the Divine Presence and possessed of unique qualities.'"

Later on in this work, we shall find out what happened to these *tefillin* during the 1948 War of Liberation

For the Bar Mitzvah itself, the boy had prepared two *drashot* (Torah speeches). One was on the subject of *tefillin*, and was given on Shabbat Lekh Lekha (Genesis 12–17), when he was called up to the Torah in Merkaz HaRav. The second *drashah* concerned the halakhic concept of *hazmana milta*, concerning whether one's intention can effect a change in the status of an object, in this case the preparation of the *tefillin*. This address was given on the very day of his Bar Mitzvah, during the special vegetarian festive meal prepared in his parents' apartment on Amos St. in the Geulah neighborhood.

This Bar Mitzvah meal was one of a kind. Guests included many of the foremost rabbis of Jerusalem, representing every shade of Torah Judaism. The efforts made by the boy to master the subject matter for his Bar Mitzvah, both at the Yeshiva and with his father, had borne fruit. The *Nazir* himself records in his diary that the rabbis who heard his *drashah* that day felt as if a true Torah scholar had been speaking. Rabbi Eliyahu Mordechai HaLevi Walkovsky, a member of the High Rabbinical Court of the Jerusalem Chief Rabbinate, was filled with emotion when, during his own address in honor of the Bar Mitzvah boy, he reminded his fellow

ב"ה ירושלים

הננו מתכבדים להזמין את כב' לחגיגת

בר מצוה

של בננו

אליהו יוסף שאר ישוב

הכהן נ"י

שתתקיים, אי"ה, ביום א' פ' וירא, ט' מרחשון תש"א,
בדירתנו, כרם אברהם, רחוב עמוס 25,

עליה לתורה בש"ק פ' לך, בישיבת «מרכז הרב».

דוד כהן ורעיתו

Invitation to Shear Yashuv's Bar Mitzvah

Rabbi Shear Yashuv dancing at a Torah celebration

guests that the boy came from a distinguished line of 17 generations of rabbis, each following in turn in his father's footsteps.

After delivering his speech, the boy played some religious songs on the violin, which added yet a further boost to the proceedings. All in all, the spiritual high experienced by all at this very special Bar Mitzvah celebration was a fitting prelude to the boy's entry to Yeshivat Merkaz HaRav.

CHAPTER THREE

In the Tents of Torah

⇒ AT MERKAZ HARAV

After four years of study at Machon Harry Fischel, Shear Yashuv moved to Yeshivat Merkaz HaRav. Only 14 years old, he studied Gemara in a "*chavruta*-lesson," as he described it, for three or four hours every day with Rabbi Yehuda Gershuni (1908–2000). Known as the "genius from Grodno," Rabbi Gershuni followed the style of his own teachers: the Rosh Yeshiva of the Grodno Yeshiva, Rabbi Shimon Shkop (1860–1939), the Rosh Yeshiva of Kaminetz, Rabbi Boruch Ber Lebowitz (1864–1939), and the Rosh Yeshiva of Radin, Rabbi Naftali Trop (1871–1928). Rabbi Cohen describes his learning experience with Rabbi Gershuni:

> "I was lucky to be able to study every day for nearly five years at Merkaz HaRav, as well as at the home of Rabbi Gershuni – whose home was full of notebooks written by his teachers on issues raised in the Gemara and the Rambam [Maimonides, 1135–1204]. My father had asked Rabbi Gershuni to expand my awareness of the different methods of the foremost rabbinical minds so that I would experience 'greatness of Torah,' as he so wondrously phrased it."

Shear Yashuv studied Bible and the Hebrew language with teacher and writer Rabbi Yaakov ben Shlomo Zlotnik. He also studied with Rabbi Noach Zvuloni (1910–2004). Rabbi Cohen recalls:

> "Members of all the Underground groups that formed during the British Mandate period sat together on the Yeshiva benches. There were members of Etzel (the Irgun founded by Ze'ev Jabotinsky: [1880–1940], Lehi (the Stern Group), and the Haganah [which later

became the core of the Israeli Defense Forces]. Included among our ranks was David Raziel [1910–1941] of the Irgun. Many leaders of these groups studied at Merkaz HaRav, temporarily forgetting their different approaches to the British as they sat together to learn the words of Torah in harmony."

During his time at Merkaz HaRav, the young Shear Yashuv also became very close to the son of Rav Kook, Rabbi Tzvi Yehuda, who later became the Yeshiva's Dean. Rabbi Tzvi Yehuda was in many ways his role model, and they would spend long hours in conversation together. Shear Yashuv would then walk home with him, as the *Nazir* lived on Amos St., around the corner from Rav Tzvi Yehuda's home on Ovadia St. Rabbi Cohen later described their relationship:

> "After getting to know Rabbi Tzvi Yehuda for a number of years, I felt like one of the family. It was as if he were my own uncle. And I felt that he loved me as well, drawing me closer to him as if I were his own son. We deliberately prolonged these walks home as much as possible, in order to discuss every possible topic on the way. I have the feeling that of all his many students, I can claim the record of having spent the most 'Rav Tzvi Yehuda hours.'"

During this period, Shear Yashuv also got to know the *Menahel* (director) of the Yeshiva, Rabbi Shlomo Natan Raanan: "Rabbi Raanan was truly like a father and uncle to me. I learned a great deal of Torah from him, especially regarding character and ethics, and how to behave in the real world, which was for him a subject of the highest importance."

Rabbi Shear Yashuv also remembers Rabbi Yitzchak Arieli, the spiritual advisor of the Yeshiva, with whom he conducted "wide-ranging conversations on Jewish thought."

WITH THE ROSH YESHIVA, RABBI CHARLAP

We have already noted the assistance given by Rav Charlap, one of the leading teachers in Merkaz HaRav, to Shear Yashuv's father, in his editing of Chief Rabbi Kook's work, *Orot HaKodesh*. This, combined with Shear Yashuv's own studies at the Yeshiva, led to a deepening of the bond between the young man and Rabbi Charlap. Rabbi Cohen reminisces:

> "Rabbi Charlap used to teach Gemara in Yiddish, as had been customary at *Yeshivat Etz Chaim*. In contrast, my own studies at home with my father, the *Nazir*, were conducted only in Hebrew.

Rav Tzvi Yehuda Kook with his student Rav Shear Yashuv at a 1973 memorial for the Nazir, who had died a year earlier.

This meant that at first I wasn't able to understand Rabbi Charlap's classes. But he felt truly responsible for his flock, and the little lamb mattered as much as the fully grown sheep, and so Rabbi Charlap would invite a group of us into his room to hear the lesson again, this time in Hebrew. So we often ended up in his presence

*The verse "I place God before me always"
(Psalms 16) – Rabbi Shear Yashuv's
hand-written version that he always kept before him during his studies in Merkaz HaRav.*

on a Friday morning, when he would go over the same lesson again
in Hebrew just for us."

"On the other hand, Rabbi Charlap did use Hebrew to teach
his classes on Jewish thought. This was a most inspirational class,
which he gave every Sunday evening. It would always open with
the words, 'You've got to learn this! You've got to learn this!' The
classes dealt with the very complex contemporary topics that
occupied our thoughts, such as Faith and Science, Secular and
Religious Zionism, Aloneness versus Togetherness, Individual vs.
Community, and how we should relate to what the Haggadah calls
the Wicked Son.

"I once asked Rabbi Charlap why he started his classes with the
words 'You've got to learn this!' His answer was that everyone is
aware of the importance of studying the legal aspects of Judaism,
found in the Gemara and the Halakha (Jewish Law), but he wanted
everyone to realize that the non-legal *aggadic* texts are also essential learning. For if Halakha can be compared to the body of Torah
teaching, then *aggadah* must be compared to the soul of Torah,
and we must never give up on the soul.

"Rabbi Charlap lived in a modest home on the west side of
Jerusalem and was therefore affectionately known as 'the Light

of the West.' Every Friday he would stop writing at noon, in order
to immerse in the *mikveh*, don white garments, and get ready
for Shabbat. Although he was constantly involved in study, or in
writing original thoughts on the *Torah*, we students never stopped
going to see him at home with any question that happened to
come into our heads; we knew he would always welcome us with
open arms. It was during those very special times, just before the
onset of Shabbat that his face would really shine as a light from
heaven. At those times Rabbi Charlap was completely relaxed,
and it was then that we could chat with him straight from the
heart, opening up our innermost souls to him. We loved to visit at
these times, simply to imbibe the amazing ambience in which he
appeared to us as one of God's very angels. At these times, too, he
would answer our questions and assuage the various doubts that
had assailed us throughout the week.

"One particular conversation sticks in my memory. This was
after we had received news about what was going on during the
Shoah. At that time I was one of the younger students at the
Yeshiva, and was agonizing over the religious significance of this
unspeakable Holocaust, the dreadful annihilation of our fellow
Jews in Europe. The Shoah went far beyond the comprehension
of any normal man or woman, and certainly beyond the comprehension of a young Yeshiva student like me. I asked myself how
the Holy One, Blessed be He, could allow His children to suffer
so greatly at the hands of their enemies, slaughtering them at that
very moment in their hundreds of thousands. My father, of saintly
blessed memory, did not want to discuss these things with me, so
to whom could I turn, if not to Rabbi Charlap?

"Late one Friday afternoon, I plucked up my courage and
decided to ask Rabbi Charlap a question that, in retrospect, appears to me to be somewhat *chutzpadik*, but which came from
the depths of my grieving heart. 'Perhaps,' I asked him, 'God has
made up His mind that we are no longer His people? Maybe our
sins and transgressions are so great that our covenant with God
has actually been annulled? How otherwise can we explain that
millions of Jews, including foremost Torah scholars, 'Cedars of
Lebanon,' mighty advocates of the Torah, are going up in flames
before our very eyes? How can this holy people have become the
most afflicted people on earth?'

"I will never forget the change that came over Rabbi Charlap's
face, as the blood drained from his face. Closing his eyes in a
gesture of love, he tenderly placed his hand on my shoulders and

replied: 'Listen, Shear Yashuv (for he always addressed me by my first name), it is clear that the Shoah is an extreme example of God's *hester panim,* hiding His face from us. But this in no way implies that He is no longer with us, Heaven forbid. It is the very gravest of sins to believe, or even consider, that God is not in our midst. The truth is that the Shoah that we are currently experiencing signals the birth-pangs of the redemption which precede the Days of the Messiah, through which we are living now. When God decides to end this *hester panim*, we shall receive great salvations and great missions. Just as the Shoah has brought inconceivable catastrophe and agony, in times to come we will witness unprecedentedly great salvations in its wake."

Rabbi Cohen added that after the establishment of *Medinat Yisrael* in 1948, Rabbi Charlap would often repeat this idea in his classes, adding: "The establishment of *Medinat Yisrael* was the natural continuation of the pangs of Messiah which began with the Shoah; *Medinat Yisrael* is simply the prelude to the Redemption."

Rabbi Cohen has many more anecdotes about his time in Merkaz HaRav under his great teacher Rabbi Charlap:

"Whenever I want to get into the right framework to recite the *Shema*, all I have to do is close my eyes and instantly I hear the unique voice of my Rosh Yeshiva, Rabbi Yaakov Moshe Charlap. His trembling voice would erupt into a roar once he started reciting the *Shema*. After his weekly class on Jewish thought, the Rabbi would recite the Evening Prayer together with us in the Yeshiva. He would sit on the eastern side of the Bet Midrash and recite the *Shema*. The contrast between this recitation and the deep silence which traditionally preceded it was utterly extraordinary. We could actually sense the *kavanot* – the power of his holy concentration. Never in my entire life have I experienced anyone anywhere recite the *Shema* with such intensity. The very walls shook. This was not just a powerful voice, but an inner voice. Countless students would sit in the Bet HaMidrash and experience the sound of his voice penetrating to the very depths of their being. Rabbi Charlap's recitation of the *Shema* taught us how to pray. Not only did his voice pierce our hearts, but surely rose straight up to the Heavens.

"The same thing happened during *Sefirat HaOmer*, when he would 'count the Omer' between Pesach and Shavuot. Again, Rabbi Charlap's voice would reverberate off the Yeshiva walls. It was a unique voice, embracing both enthusiastic joy and resonant awe.

You could see that he truly lived the unique prayer for each day of the *Sefirah* period. I remember that he drew out the preliminary blessing alone for at least five minutes. To this very day, whenever I myself make the blessing over the counting of the *Omer*, I simply close my eyes and picture the voice of my Rosh Yeshiva."

IN THE HOME OF RABBI ISSER ZALMAN MELTZER

At this time, through the good offices of Rabbi Tzvi Yehuda Kook, Shear Yashuv was also put in touch with some of the other leading Jerusalem rabbis who had been close to Rav Kook. One of these was Rabbi Isser Zalman Meltzer, Dean of the famed *Etz Chaim* Yeshiva, where Rav Kook had served as President.

Every Thursday, the young Shear Yashuv visited the home of Rabbi Meltzer, in order to be examined on his Talmud studies. Years later he would recall how, in those very special moments before the examination began, Rabbi Meltzer would sing the praises of Rav Kook and of the Rav's outstanding student, the *Nazir*, his own father. He would then add the following: "When I stated in my eulogy for Rav Kook that he was 'the backbone of the entire Jewish people,' I was not exaggerating."

From that very special period, Rabbi Cohen recalls an interesting episode which demonstrates Rabbi Meltzer's great desire for truth, no matter who pointed it out to him. Rabbi Meltzer used to test Shear Yashuv on his Talmud studies by having him read a relevant section from his own work, *Even HaEzel,* a commentary on the *Mishne Torah* of the Rambam. The Rabbi would ask him to repeat over the passage by heart, and then to compare and contrast it with the commentaries of Rashi (Rabbi Shlomo Yitzchaki, 1040–1105), the Tosafot (glosses on the Talmud), and the other Rishonim (ca. 12th-15th centuries). What was unique about this method was that it tested not only one's expertise in the subject, but also, and more importantly, one's depth of understanding. Rav Shear Yashuv relates:

> "Once, referring to a particular halakhic ruling in the Rambam's Laws of Monetary Damages, Rabbi Meltzer asked me, as was his habit, to review the passage and then explain it to him. However, I noticed a contradiction of Rabbi Meltzer's analysis from a particular Gemara passage. When I pointed this out to Rabbi Meltzer, he was overcome with joy, and shouted to his wife in colorful Yiddish: 'Beila Hende, Beila Hende, isn't it great! The boy is right! Bring him something special to eat, he deserves it!'

Brothers-in-law
Rav Goren
and Rav Cohen

"To be honest, I'm not entirely sure that I was right; however, *post facto*, I am certain that what my great teacher was trying to teach me was a lesson about the love of truth from whatever source. As he never ceased to remind us in Yiddish: 'It is forbidden to deceive oneself; truth is above all else.'"

AT THE *LOMZHE* YESHIVA

After five years at Merkaz HaRav, young Shear Yashuv transferred to the Lomzhe Yeshiva in Petach Tikvah. "Moving to Lomzhe was my 'youthful rebellion,'" recalls Rabbi Cohen with a smile. His enormous mass of hair attracted a great deal of attention in Petach Tikvah, where he was completely unknown. There he became acquainted with its Dean, Rabbi Reuven Katz (1880–1963), author of *Degel Reuven*, a three-volume commentary on the Talmud. Rabbi Katz was the Chief Rabbi of Petach Tikvah, as well as Head of its Rabbinical Court.

Every Friday, Rabbi Katz would invite the young Shear Yashuv to his room, to review his studies and the general lesson he had given in the Yeshiva. Although Rav Katz delivered the public *shiur* in Yiddish, as was the norm, the young man would review it in Hebrew, and enter into a discussion with him on fine points of Halakha. Rabbi Katz loved listening to his student, and often gave him money so that he could treat himself to some special vegetarian food which would remind him of home cooking.

When Shear Yashuv asked Rabbi Katz why he did this, he answered that it was not a gift, but rather a "way of giving back what I received from your own grandfather and uncle. When I lived in Radin, I ate regularly at the home of your great-grandfather, Rabbi Zechariah Mendel Katz (1830–1897) and then, after his death, at the home of your great-uncle, Rabbi Mordechai Kopstein, who replaced him as Rabbi of Radin. Now it is my turn to give back to his grandson a tiny bit of what I received from them."

One memory etched on Shear Yashuv's heart from his visits to Rabbi Katz's home concerned the case of an *agunah* – a woman whose husband would not, or was not available to, give her a Jewish divorce. A *dayan* (religious court judge) had come to discuss the case with Rabbi Katz, but was apparently of the opinion that there was no way to be lenient. Young Shear Yashuv overheard Rabbi Katz sternly reprimanding the *dayan*: "If you want to be a *tzaddik*, don't do so at her expense! A legal way must be found to unchain her!"

From that day, when Rabbi Cohen gave his own lectures to future *Dayanim* who studied at his *Kollel*, he would impress upon them the moral of this story: The importance of releasing a woman from her status as an *agunah*, if there is any halakhic way to do so; he must not seek to be stringent at her expense.

⇛   WITH THE CHAZON ISH

One day, a fellow student in Lomzhe suggested a visit to the Bnei Brak home of Rabbi Avrohom Yeshaya Karelitz, the renowned Chazon Ish (1878–1953). The Chazon Ish had not yet attained the great fame he was later to achieve. According to Rabbi Cohen:

> "We arrived at the home of the Chazon Ish, which stood on a hill in Bnei Brak. His wife was very keen on protecting her husband from being disturbed, and therefore refused to open the door to us Yeshiva boys. We circled the house and saw the Chazon Ish sitting and studying in his room. We knocked on his window, and he gestured us to enter via the window. We jumped in and sat ourselves down in a circle around him. I remember that we asked him: 'What do we have to do to become great *Torah* scholars?' His answer was: 'Make a pact with the *Yetzer HaRa* (the Evil Inclination) that he allow you to devote twelve hours a day to Torah study – for just a week. Afterwards, God will do the rest!'"

This was the first of Rav Shear Yashuv's many visits to the Chazon Ish, who "sang the praises of Rav Kook every time I came," he said. The last visit was when he invited the Chazon Ish to his wedding. However, when the latter learned that the bride hailed from the United States, he was concerned that the young couple might make their home abroad, and therefore asked Rav Shear Yashuv, "Does someone as great as your father, the *Nazir*, really countenance the possibility of your leaving Israel to live abroad?" To which Rabbi Cohen replied that his future bride had expressly moved to Israel to live there permanently, and wouldn't leave, even if he, her future husband, ever wished to do so.

⇒   THE ESTABLISHMENT OF THE PONEVEZH YESHIVA

One day during Rabbi Cohen's time at the Lomzhe Yeshiva, Rabbi Yosef Shlomo Kahaneman (1886–1969) paid a visit. He was interested in persuading a number of rabbinical students to continue their studies in a brand new Yeshiva that he hoped to establish. When Rabbi Kahaneman heard that one of the Lomzhe students was the son of the *Nazir*, he could not contain his joy. He told the young student about the profound friendship between the *Nazir* and himself, and especially about the time they were both "told off" by the Chofetz Chaim (Rabbi Israel Meir Kagan, 1838–1933) as follows:

In 1904, the *Nazir* was a student at the Chofetz Chaim Yeshiva in Radin, together with Rabbi Kahaneman and Rabbi Petahia Menkin. All three of these outstanding students were invited to take turns on consecutive Sabbaths to give a *drashah* in the town's Tiferet Bahurim Synagogue. They based their sermons on the relevant weekly Haftarah (the non-Pentateuchal reading) together with *aggadot* taken from *Ein Yaakov* (a 16th century compilation of the non-legal passages in the Talmud). Their sermons went on for hours, drawing throngs of Radin Jews who filled not only the main room of the synagogue, but also the side rooms and the entrance. The three young rabbinical students were not sure that the Rosh Yeshiva, the Chofetz Chaim, was pleased with their practice, but they concluded that he accepted it since he chose not to say anything to them.

Just before Sukkot, a large fire broke out in Radin, and all its buildings went up in smoke. The young Yeshiva students were farmed out to neighboring villages, and the *Nazir* was one of ten students sent to the village of Naca. On Shavuot, he was asked to preach in the local synagogue. He spoke for three hours, firing up the congregation with emotion and bringing many to tears. The Chofetz Chaim heard of this and called in the three young preachers: "Up to now, I haven't commented on your sermons, and I was even pleased. But I have now heard that you are causing Jews to cry on a festive day! Return to your studies!"

When the *Nazir* and Rabbi Kahaneman were both settled in Israel, they kept up their deep friendship, and the latter visited the *Nazir's* Sukkah every year.

It was this same Rabbi Kahaneman who led the young rabbinical students from the Lomzhe Yeshiva in Petach Tikvah to a barren hill in the neighboring town of Bnei Brak, with the words: "Here we will build a new Ponevezh Yeshiva, to replace the original which was destroyed in Lithuania."

Rabbi Shear Yashuv: "It was a wonderful sight to see Rabbi Kahaneman standing on the hill with his *tzitzit* (fringed garments) fluttering in the wind while he talked about the Yeshiva he was going to build there. He even had plans for a swimming pool for the use of the students." The young Shear Yashuv considered joining the founding nucleus of the new Yeshiva, but his father wanted him to stay at Merkaz HaRav. In obedience to his father, he returned to Jerusalem and immersed himself there totally in Torah study.

THE *NAZIRITE* HAIRCUT

As young Shear Yashuv grew up, the long tresses crowning his head constantly attracted attention from all and sundry, and in fact became his trademark. As mentioned above, at the age of 12 the young man made a public announcement that his *Nezirut* was voluntary and not an oath-like commitment. But now, after many internal struggles, he decided to tell his parents that he no longer wished to adhere to this specific aspect of his *Nazirite* life-style, namely the custom of growing his hair. Many years later he recounted his motivations for this decision:

> "Even as a small boy, I was aware that my father led a way of life that was holy and special. My parents explained to me that I, too, was being brought up in this way. So, within the protective four walls of my home, I grew up as a *Nazir*. I genuinely saw myself continuing in the path of my holy father, and this made me feel superior to everyone around me. Only after I left home did I experience it differently. When I mixed with other people I wanted to be like them. Attending Yeshiva was the turning-point in my decision to release myself from this particular custom, when I was no longer within the four walls of the home in which I was adored and protected."

Just before his first haircut

Although the *Nazir* found it difficult to accept his son's decision, he respected it, and asked only that he wait until his 16th birthday. During the ensuing months, the *Nazir* studied Tractate *Nazir* and the early commentaries with his son. These discussions of the relevant purity laws, including issues surrounding the shaving of hair, were designed to impress upon the young Shear Yashuv just how special it was to be a *Nazir*. The *Nazir* also sent letters to a number of rabbis in Jerusalem, including to Chief Rabbi Herzog, proposing a contemporary *Order of Nazirite Purification*, requesting their considered opinions and affirmation.

The *Nazir* Haircutting Ceremony, once a familiar one when *Nezirut* was more common, was set for 9th Heshvan (7th November) 1943, the evening of Shear Yashuv's 16th birthday. As the special event drew near, silver scissors were made ready for the cutting ceremony. Despite the *Nazir's* best efforts, news of the event made waves throughout Jerusalem. The fact that this was probably the first such haircutting since the destruction of the Temple caused many of the foremost scholars in Jerusalem to make their way to the *Nazir's* door. These included Rabbi Charlap, Rabbi Tzvi Yehuda Kook, Rabbi Shlomo Yosef Zevin (1888–1978), Rabbi Aryeh Levin (1885–1969) and Rabbi Natan Raanan. News of the special ceremony was even featured in many newspapers inside and outside the Holy Land.

The ceremony took place in the evening, but many rabbis arrived early. They joined with the *Nazir* and his son in reading the Biblical section (Numbers 6:1–21) that lists the sacrifices brought by a *Nazir* – for the Sages taught (*Menachot*, 110a) that those who study the relevant Torah passages on a sacrifice are regarded as having actually brought the sacrifice themselves.

When evening arrived, and the house was overflowing with visitors, the *Nazir* recited the entire Biblical section pertaining to the *Nazir*, as well as relevant commentaries on *Nazirite* Purity from the Mishna, Talmud, and Rambam. During the modest meal that followed, a letter of blessing arrived from Chief Rabbi Herzog. Other rabbis spoke in honor of the occasion, and young Shear Yashuv himself expounded on the laws of *Nezirut*. He explained that he was renouncing the external manifestation of *Nezirut*, but would continue to carry on the inner-spiritual life of a *Nazir*, expressed in abstention from wine.

Then, in the presence of all, the young man was presented with a basket of two kinds of unleavened loaves, ten of each kind – reminiscent of the two kinds of unleavened offerings brought to the Temple by the *Nazir*, as recorded in Numbers 6:15.

Then came the haircutting itself. This consisted of each guest taking hold of the special scissors, thus becoming a symbolic "partner" in the cutting of the hair. They appointed the actual barber as their "emissary" in the actual haircutting (which took place in an adjoining room).

ON BEING A SPIRITUAL *NAZIRITE*

While this ceremony marked the end of Shear Yashuv's external adherence to the customs of a *Nazir*, it did not stop the young man from continuing to observe the other customs which he had followed in his father's house. To this day, for example, Rabbi Cohen will not touch meat (though it is not forbidden to a Biblical *Nazir*) or wine. He recites the Friday night Kiddush over challah-bread, and for morning Kiddush he uses *chamar medinah* – literally, a "popular local beverage" – one that people generally purchase in a store, such as apple juice.

For the Pesach Seder, in place of wine, Rabbi Cohen drinks the Four Cups of apple wine. This custom follows the legal ruling handed down to the *Nazir* by some of the foremost rabbis in Jerusalem, including Rav Kook and Rabbi Meltzer. When Rabbi Cohen conducts a wedding ceremony, he recites the blessing over wine, which is drunk only by the bride and groom.

Rabbi Cohen continued another custom of his father's: wearing only non-leather shoes (though this is not a Nazirite obligation), until he was badly wounded in his leg during the 1948 War of Liberation and was taken prisoner by the Jordanians. From then on, he was unable to continue this custom for health reasons. Rabbi Cohen thus keeps the *Nazirite* food practices and takes periodic haircuts – "for we have also found a type of *Nazirite* custom where the *Nazir* has his hair cut every so often," he hastens to point out.

THE "RAV KOOK STUDY CIRCLE" AND *SEMICHA* STUDIES

While continuing his studies at Merkaz HaRav, the young man also became part of a unique study circle, which had been set up by Rav Kook's pupils after their teacher's death. In 1940, on the fifth anniversary of the Rav's passing, the study group was formed in *Bet HaRav*, the Rav's home, to study his teachings on a weekly basis.

This study circle met regularly until the establishment of *Medinat Yisrael* in 1948. It was initiated by Professor Chaim Lifshitz, one of the Rav's students. The *Nazir* and Rabbi Tzvi Yehudah would normally take turns leading the study. Sometimes one of the participants would take over, and outside speakers were occasionally invited, including foremost Zionist rabbis such as Chief Rabbis Herzog and Uziel. In the course of the lecture, discussions often developed concerning the ideas of the Rav. Thus, every Monday evening, the late Rav's best students would be gathered around his table. These included his son Rabbi Tzvi Yehudah, the *Nazir,* and Rabbi Raanan. From time to time, Rabbi Charlap would join in, as well as other rabbis and academics, such as Rabbi Eliezer Meir Lifshitz and Dr. Moshe Zeidel.

Although Shear Yashuv was one of the youngest members of this group, this did not prevent him from taking an active part in the discussions. The group studied works such as *Orot HaKodesh* (*Lights of Holiness*), *Resh Milin* (a Kabbalistic explanation of the meaning of the Hebrew letters, grammar and punctuation), and *Orot HaTorah* (*Lights of the Torah*).

Rabbi Cohen later recalled:

> "When the study session had formally concluded, which tended to be in the small hours of the morning, we found that our thirst for the Rav's teachings had not been quenched. And so, an essential part of the study meeting was when we accompanied Rabbi Tzvi Yehuda and the *Nazir* to their homes. On these walks, we discovered a whole treasure-trove of memories and stories that simply poured out of these two sages. The journey home would

Rav Shear Yashuv as a young man of 19, wearing a suit, with his fellow students from Yeshivat Merkaz HaRav, on the day of the Bar Mitzvah of Rav Kook's grandson Rabbi Eliyahu Shlomo Raanan (later murdered by Palestinian terrorists in 1998 in Hebron) on 12th Tishrei 1947.

sometimes last several hours, and would occasionally prove more interesting for the students than the class itself."

While still continuing his Yeshiva studies, the young man now embarked on his study for *semicha* (rabbinic ordination). Not only did Rav Shear Yashuv come from a long line of rabbis, but his father had also greatly encouraged him to follow in their footsteps. Both these factors spurred him on to continue his rabbinical studies. In the spring of 1945, after his sister Tsefyia married Rabbi Shlomo Goren (1917–94), he studied Jewish Law with his new brother-in-law. He also prepared for his rabbinical exams with Rabbi Goren's father, Rabbi Abraham Goronchik. Many of Rabbi Cohen's original thoughts on Torah from that time have been preserved, as well as halakhic discussions with a number of leading Torah scholars, including Rabbi Tzvi Pesach Frank (1873–1960).

But these were not usual times. Who could have predicted that the ensuing events, such as the bloody Arab riots and the War of Liberation, culminating in the establishment of *Medinat Yisrael*, would change and give a new direction to the plans and aspirations of the young man?

Brit HaHashmona'im (The Hasmonean Covenant)

Once again this year we will sit, reclining at the table on this holy night of Pesach, drinking the four cups of wine, remembering and reminiscing. Would that our voices ascend and pierce the heavens, our thunderous song and cries of suffering rise up to the highest firmament as we recite, "We were slaves to Pharaoh in Egypt . . ."

We will sit here in Zion, reclining at our tables with the shutters closed tight, while the pounding of waves of foreign occupiers engulfs our song, merging with it. Some of us will sit in prison camps in far-off lands . . . Others will recline on the sullied soil of Europe, from where so much blood cries out to us . . . We will recline as we await our death yet dream of redemption and vengeance for our unbearable anguish, as we recite the prophet's words: "And I will pass over thee and I will see thee writhing around in thy blood." *(Ezekiel 16:6)*

The blood will then boil and the tears will burst out, and our question will pierce all buffers: "Why, O God, dost Thou stand far off, concealing Thyself in these times of affliction?" *(Psalms 10:1)*

And this is the response – honed through the stakes of generations, refined in the agonizing flames of the tortures we have endured, yet "as pure as the likeness of sapphire" *(Exodus 24:10). The response will bring us comfort in the darkness of our anguish, will encourage in the very midst of our agonies:* "I say unto thee, through thy blood you shall live; through thy blood, live!" *(Ezekiel 16:6)*

And the downtrodden soil of thy homeland raises her head that very night and pays great heed. For, behold, the voice of her children cries out, a rumbling roar throughout the Exile: "Next year in Jerusalem." And in response, Zion answers, with tears rolling down her cheeks and her prayer soaring heavenward: "In Jerusalem, in Jerusalem the rebuilt."

Passover Eve 1947,
Shear Yashuv Cohen

Brit HaHashmona'im (The Hasmonean Covenant)

➥ DAYS OF BLOOD AND GORE

While the young Shear Yashuv advanced in his understanding of Torah, the dangers surrounding the age-old Jewish community in Israel, known as the *Yishuv*, threatened its very existence. The Arab riots and hostile British policy had led to horrific bloodshed against the Jewish populace. From the start of the official British Mandate in 1923 (British civil administration had actually commenced in 1920), the Yishuv had felt uneasy. Ferment and agitation increased as relations with the British Mandate Authority deteriorated on account of its discriminatory policy towards the Yishuv in the face of Arab riots. The last straw was the 1939 MacDonald "White Paper," which slammed the door on Jewish refugees fleeing to Israel from the Nazi sword of World War II.

Great anger rose within the Yishuv. As a result, as mentioned above, three Underground organizations were established within the Yishuv: the Haganah, the Irgun and Lehi (The Stern Group). The last two organizations advocated activism against the British occupation, while the first preferred a policy of "*havlagah*" (restraint). But all three organizations shared a passion for defending the Yishuv and eliminating British occupation, while at the same time constructing a new political alternative.

The repercussions of the Arab riots and news of the establishment of the Underground defense organizations did not pass over the benches of Yeshivat Merkaz HaRav. Most rabbis and Yeshiva heads tried to keep their students well away from these Underground organizations and their individual members. In fact, students who came from traditional backgrounds were forced to choose between staying at the Yeshiva, or joining the Underground. Merkaz HaRav had the opposite approach. The *Rosh*, Rabbi Charlap, together with his close colleagues and friends, Rabbi Tzvi Yehuda and the *Nazir*, encouraged their students to do both: to fight in the Underground while continuing their Yeshiva studies.

In fact, one of the most famous alumni of the Yeshiva was David Raziel, who later became Commander-in-Chief of the Irgun. Most students at Merkaz HaRav had come from the *Etz Chaim* Yeshiva, which was generally considered as belonging to the "Old Yishuv." This was the "strictly Orthodox" Jewish community that had lived in the Old City of Jerusalem up to the time of the "First Aliyah" of 1882. Raziel, on the other hand, had studied at the more modern and progressive Tachkemoni School which belonged to the "New Yishuv."

Later, Rabbi Cohen would comment that:

> "At the Yeshiva, Hillel Kook [1915–2001], a nephew of Rav Kook and better known as Peter Bergson, studied in a *chavruta* study partnership with David Raziel. One day, Raziel didn't turn up at Yeshiva. Hillel went looking for him in his room. He found him lying unconscious with a high temperature. On his table were prophetic poems about Israel, Jerusalem and the Redemption. At the bottom of the page were the words: 'I wrote all this down after coming back from a shiur given by the great *Nazir*.' Hillel Kook said to himself: 'This young man is definitely worth knowing!' He took Raziel to a hospital, and from that time on the two became firm friends, eventually setting up the Irgun Underground movement together."

Subsequently, one of the reasons Rabbi Cohen gave for naming his own daughter Eliraz was to memorialize David Raziel, whom he had gotten to know during their Yeshiva days together.

> "After Hillel Kook left the Merkaz HaRav, I replaced him and even 'inherited' his lectern (*shtender*). Later, when I was taken prisoner, my dear father, the *Nazir* of blessed memory, asked the administrators for the lectern which I had used at the Yeshiva and which had also belonged to Hillel Kook until he had finished his studies. And from that moment, my father used the lectern until the day of his death. He said: 'This lectern was used by Hillel Kook and Shear Yashuv Cohen, who were both instrumental in the establishment of *Medinat Yisrael*.' Many years later, when Hillel Kook came to console me upon the death of my father and heard the tale of

the lectern, he looked at it and began to cry, and said, 'When I returned from the USA after operations on behalf of the Irgun, I experienced a great deal of abuse from the Yishuv. The only person who appreciated what I had done was the *Nazir*, who told me that I had helped accelerate the redemption of *Medinat Yisrael*.'"

Not only did the *Nazir* give words of encouragement to the members of the Underground organizations, but also offered them practical assistance. For many years, he provided his own home as a shelter and refuge for combatants from all the different "streams" of the Underground. These included the Commanders of Irgun, as well as the leaders of the Haganah. The home of the *Nazir* was a haven and hideout, a place of safety and succor, of peace and quiet, where the combatants could gain rest and respite under the watchful and benevolent eye of his wife, the Rabbanit, who always made everyone feel welcome. In addition, the youth group, *Brit HaHashmona'im*, would meet every single Shabbat in the house, which was also a synagogue, where they attended the *Nazir*'s weekly *shiur* and the Afternoon Prayer Service. The history of this particular youth group takes up much of the present chapter.

Rabbi Cohen also provides an illuminating eye-witness report of the relationship between Rabbi Tzvi Yehuda and those members of the Underground who were captured by the British occupying force.

"Under the British occupation, members of the Underground Lehi (Stern) movement were captured and held in the Central Prison in Jerusalem known as the 'Russian Compound', formerly a hostel for Christian pilgrims, but later nicknamed 'Bevingrad' under the British occupation. These prisoners were held there pending trial for the crime of belonging to a 'terrorist organization', which incurred the death penalty. One of the accused, Anshel Spielman of blessed memory, a Lehi commander, managed to escape and made for the home of Rabbi Goren, brother-in-law of Rabbi Cohen, and subsequently Ashkenazi Chief Rabbi of Israel. At the time, Rabbi Goren had close links with Lehi and even stashed away a cache of arms for them. The plan was for the fugitive to remain in Jerusalem until he had grown a beard, and then make for the *Shefela*, the coastal plain, and hide out there. But it happened that while Anshel was hiding at Rabbi Goren's, the British Mandate police were conducting a man-hunt for him in the very same vicinity. The decision was taken, therefore, to move Anshel immediately to Rabbi Tzvi Yehuda's home."

Shear Yashuv was given the mission of accompanying Anshel *en route* from Rabbi Goren's home on the edge of the Rehavia neighborhood of Jerusalem to Rabbi Tzvi Yehuda's home in Geula – through the city streets. This is how Rabbi Cohen described the adventure in his own words:

> "The mission wasn't easy. It took some ingenuity to slip unnoticed through the city streets and alleys from one hideout to another. When we finally made it to Rabbi Tzvi Yehuda's home, he welcomed us with open arms, accompanied us from the hall to the sitting room, and invited us to sit down. This gave him time to ponder on a fitting personal gesture of 'making guests feel welcome,' which he now had the pleasant, if unexpected, opportunity of fulfilling, in line with the Jewish precept of hospitality.
>
> "After taking a seat, Anshel asked me to bring him a *kippa*, the head-covering for a Jewish male who fulfills the religious precepts, as he was bare-headed. When Rabbi Tzvi Yehuda heard the request, he immediately stood up with the words: 'If you do not usually cover your head in your own home, since you had no choice but to choose the house of a rabbi for your hiding-place, please assure me that you won't change your habits just for me, but will behave in my house as you would at your own home!' We were astounded that the Rabbi was making such a big issue of the *kippa* question, as there were a whole range of behaviors that shocked us, and that offended not only against *halakha*, but against the normal courtesies.
>
> "Anshel, the tough combatant, felt extremely ill-at-ease, but pursued his request, nevertheless. 'Explain to the rabbi that I feel uncomfortable without a *kippa*.' At this, I took my life in my hands, and ventured to suggest to Rabbi Tzvi Yehuda that in my opinion not only did we have to give him a *kippa*, but to make it a large one. For if a stranger were to drop in unexpectedly and noticed someone pottering around the house 'kippa-less,' that person would immediately be suspected of Underground activities, and would most likely be handed over to the British police. This argument the Rabbi definitely understood, and finally handed a *kippa* to Anshel"

This is a story that Rabbi Cohen never tires of repeating as an illustration of the relationship between Rabbi Tzvi Yehuda and Jews who do not observe the religious precepts. He recalls that after the establishment of *Medinat Yisrael*, Rabbi Tzvi Yehuda joined "The League Against Religious Coercion." However, he parted company with the League soon after, when they started fighting against religious marriage *per se* and essentially became "The League for Anti-Religious Coercion." Rabbi Cohen continues by guiding his listeners on the right path if they wish to attract people who are far away from religious practice.

> "If there is genuine love, people can feel it in their hearts. Love draws people near. It is very important that a Jewish person who does not carry out the religious precepts experiences no sense of superiority in you. Preachy people are basically those who feel that they are 'the bee's knees.' But where love is, superiority is not. A non-practicing Jew who comes to Shul has to be treated with love and affection. Bear in mind constantly the possibility that this same non-practicing Jew is actually on a higher level than you. For all we know, he or she may actually be carrying out the religious precepts, or may have done so in the past, whether wittingly, or unwittingly. And the Holy One Blessed be He regards this person as on a higher level than the person who appears outwardly to be nearer to Him. We do not know the thoughts of the Holy One Blessed be He, nor how He assesses a fellow human being."

THE "HOSTS" OF THE MESSIAH

Most members of the Underground movements did not adhere to Jewish precepts, and were sometimes quite blatant in their "secularity." Therefore, the Merkaz HaRav students decided to establish a new Underground movement whose members would adhere to the precepts of Judaism. In addition, however, they would follow the original nationalist ideology of Rav Kook (the Chief Rabbi until his death in 1935), as well as the Revisionist political theories of Zeev Jabotinsky. The declared aim of this new Underground movement was to remove British occupation and establish a *Jewish* State based on *Jewish* teachings and *Jewish* law and justice. In this they emulated their spiritual forefathers, the Hasmoneans, who had fought in their own era (166–37 BCE) against the Syrian Greek occupation. Not only had the original Hasmoneans fought to annul the decrees introduced by the Syrian Greeks against fulfilling the Torah, but also succeeded in removing their foreign occupation of *Eretz Yisrael* altogether.

In contrast to most contemporary Zionist movements, this new Movement's own aim was clear: they wished not only to establish *Medinat Yisrael*, but also to "repair the world," and sanctify God's name by living a life which followed the Torah. Full of youthful fervor, the young

Shear Yashuv formulated the conceptual foundations upon which the new movement would be based. The following extract is taken from the diary in which he describes his own participation as a combatant in the Underground, starting in 1946, on the tenth anniversary of the founding of *Brit HaHashmona'im*. It should be added that, from the outset, *Brit HaHashmona'im* welcomed girls into its fold, in keeping with the custom for groups in those days. These girls played a significant role in every aspect of the group's existence and underwent combat training together with their male counterparts.

"*Brit HaHashmona'im* is not a political Movement . . . . Its combatants have always come from different backgrounds. They have never had to betray their own ideologies or political stances through belonging to our Movement. *Brit HaHashmona'im* sees itself as the direct intellectual descendant of the original Hasmoneans. Our spiritual ancestors learned to rise above all momentary problems. They plumbed the depths of the Torah we were privileged to receive at Sinai, and in so doing, extracted the secret of heroism. The '*dry bones*' of the people are in need of a '*new spirit*' (see Ezekiel 37). But this spirit will not be found among those who have hewn their path from foreign sources. . . . The fruits of their teachings, all their hidden benefits, come from one source only, the one that we sanctify. Forget about 'national-religious' and 'Torah plus service.' These will not save us. Artificial constructs are no use at all if our goal is to be the redemption of Israel. No – if our goal is the resurrection of our people – then only a wholehearted return to the source will suffice. Only through a complete change of heart will the great War of Liberation be effective. Purified and refined of all foreign dross, the holy hosts of Israel will be able to conquer anyone and anything. Just like our original heroes of Israel, we are the few against the many, the pure against the impure. And if we fail to purify ourselves in our every-day lives, let us at least learn how to preserve the purity of our ideas, and to walk a path that is both very new and very old, but which has been forsaken for so many centuries. If repentance is wholehearted, all the forced exiles and defeatism will be seen merely as products of assimilation and exile . . . .'

"The approach of most religious Zionist leaders to the problems faced by the Yishuv, and the Jewish people in general, is purely intellectual, and not related to trust in God. For example, their approach to the problem of Partition has not in the past accorded with the core principles of Judaism, which teach us to rise above the moment and internalize our own understanding of history. By contrast, a number of *Mizrachi* religious-Zionist leaders, and especially their President, Rabbi Meir Bar-Ilan [1880–1949], opposed the 1937 Partition Plan and the 1939 MacDonald White Paper. They advocated civil disobedience and non-cooperation with the British occupation administration, and are therefore a good example of the kind of core nationalist approach which I am proposing.

"Be that as it may, there is no movement within the Yishuv, or within Zionism generally, for which the Torah is the sole foundation and light in every single deed and action. For example, the non-Zionist ultra-Orthodox sect, *Agudat-Israel*, makes out that it is flying the flag for the people of the Torah. However, this sect deliberately distorts and disregards some of the major fundamentals of Jewish teaching. *Brit HaHashmona'im*, on the other hand, sees itself (whether others recognize this or not) as a Movement without comparison. This Movement dedicates itself root and branch to a holistic approach, in which nationalistic, educational, and political elements combine to form a complete and rounded Jewish education. . . . The Movement educates us to be enthusiastic in our love of *Eretz Yisrael*, to always be ready and prepared for war, and finally, to abhor slavery and oppression."

⇒   ESTABLISHMENT OF THE MOVEMENT

Let us go back a few years. During the spring month of Nissan 1936, three friends had met in Jerusalem. They were Menachem Amittai, Chaim Brandwein and Baruch Duvdavani. The three were all students at Merkaz HaRav, and it was there that they decided to establish a national religious youth organization: *Brit HaHashmona'im*. Later, Rabbi Moshe Tzvi Segal (1904–86) and Meir Medan (1915–89) joined the leadership team.

The Movement attracted members, and one year later, upon the conclusion of the Pesach holiday, on the evening of 21st Nissan (2nd April 1937), a group of two hundred people gathered to formally confirm the establishment of the Movement. Their slogan was: *"Salvation is the Lord's!"* The membership decided that the Movement would have a military character, and that its members would wear a uniform. So, about six weeks later, when Shavuot had arrived, an official parade had been organized with dozens of recruits. The parade culminated in a march through the streets of Jerusalem to the *Kotel*, the Western Wall of the Temple.

From this time on, demonstrations and protests took place against the policy of the British Mandate, leading to arrests at the hands of the British and a struggle against the members of the Movement. The Movement flourished and attracted hundreds of members, divided into "nests," or "branches." One of young Shear Yashuv's closest friends was the Commandant of one of these "nests." He was the well-known Kabbalist, Rabbi Naim Eliyahu, later to become the Rabbi of the Bukharian neighborhood of Jerusalem. His brother was Rabbi Mordechai Eliyahu (1929–2010: Sephardi Chief Rabbi of Israel 1983–93).

The Movement introduced many reforms which emphasized its distinctive approach to Jewish teaching. In winter they organized Chanukah parties for the general community in commemoration of the original Hasmoneans. In spring they organized a nation-wide conference on Pesach. In addition, during the month of Elul, which falls either in August or September, they marked the anniversary of Rav Kook's death.

Their other activities were not only aimed against British occupation. They also demonstrated against the desecration of Shabbat and the sale of non-kosher meat. Trips were also organized throughout Israel in order to get to know the country better. Later, many members of the Movement went on to join the "Hish" – the main surface armored corps founded by the Haganah in 1939. Others joined the Irgun or Lehi, Underground groups which shared their outlook.

⫸   THE YOUNG "HASMONEAN"

Young Shear Yashuv absorbed the fighting spirit of *Brit HaHashmona'im* from his *chavruta* partner at Merkaz HaRav, Baruch Duvdavani, who was ten years older than he was, and had encouraged him to join the Movement. Shimon Barmatz (1922–2009) was a member of both Lehi and *Brit HaHashmona'im*. These are his words:

> "When the future Rabbi Shear Yashuv Cohen joined the Movement, he still followed *Nazirite* practices. Therefore, because of his exceptional appearance, which made him stand out, it wasn't possible at first to let him join in the clandestine Underground activities. So we assigned him the educational role of setting up branches and committing the philosophy of the Movement to writing. This meant that if a member of the British secret police came to find out exactly what the younger members of the Movement were up to, they would come up against the young Shear Yashuv. He would inform the police that he was, as they could see, not only vegetarian, but a peace-lover to boot. So it was

under this guise that the younger generation was educated in the values of the Movement."

In this manner, the young Shear Yashuv coordinated a number of branches, trained many young members, and instilled the spirit of the Movement into the young cadets. Despite his own youth, he quickly stood out among his peers, and this is what they said about him:

> "Shear Yashuv is a rising star! Only yesterday he was 'one of the youngsters,' but today he is quickly ascending the highest echelons of the Movement. He is a young man with literary talents, one of Baruch Duvdavani's students. He has left the ranks of youth, but has not quite yet made it as an adult.
> Among the 'youngsters' he is old, but among the 'oldsters' he is still young. His youthful ability, however, promises great things. If the Movement looks after him and treats him well, the 'veterans' will come to see in him and in his comrades the future of the Movement. He has flair, and has already made his mark, which doesn't sit well with his peers. But learn to digest the wisdom of great minds from him. Shear Yashuv: onwards and upwards!"

In its day the Movement had many difficulties to contend with. Some of these difficulties were financial, for the Movement lacked funds. There were also many fierce disagreements over its spiritual direction. Should it follow the *havlagah* policy of restraint toward the British occupation, or actively fight against them. In his diary, the young Shear Yashuv describes one of the Movement's conventions in which he took part, and in which this question was raised. Here he describes the difficulties which arose, and which accompanied the Movement throughout its existence. He also describes the special spirit which never left the individual members of the Movement.

> "Whenever the wheels of the bus are turning on the road going downhill from Jerusalem to Tel Aviv, you can tell by my face that I'm really scared. Members of this convention, it's you I'm driving at. I have thought about it long and hard, and decided that my own destiny is inextricably linked to that of the Movement. The gamut of problems engaging the cosmos is larger than ever. And many new difficulties are laid in the path of our young combatants, even though they remain firm in their faith. But we need to face this general confusion head on, and stop burying our heads in the sand. We have to gird ourselves with courage, and hone our

awareness. We must see things as they really are, warts and all. Are we really up for it? We have all experienced, year-round, the conclusion of Shabbat, when Jews putter around their own home, their own little 'nest'. But here it is different. Here, we are made up of many units of young men, all from different worlds and of different outlooks, who meet by chance in the same lodging place – the lodging place of the *Brit HaHashmona'im*. Here we have sat ourselves down at our table, to listen, all ears, to the discourse.

"Moshe Segal, our leader, spoke first and raised a principle that was both new and old. 'Our Movement,' he said, 'must adopt the concept of 'love for Israel' as the core pillar of our faith. This is the goal we must set for ourselves in everything we do. This is what is new about our Movement.' A bitter dispute ensued. Many argued that what Moshe said simply wasn't the whole truth. Certainly, love for Israel was an important part of original Hasmonean teaching. But surely there were also additional principles. There was contempt for servitude, love for God, for *Am Yisrael* (the Jewish people) and for *Eretz Yisrael*. There was yearning for the Messiah, pining for the Kingdom. Were these equally important principles really to be found within the other Movements . . . ?

"Moshe answered the people who argued against him: 'You may well say all this. But I want to emphasize the important core value of 'love for Israel' of which I just spoke. I certainly didn't intend to ignore the importance of the other core values. Get back to what you were doing, my friends. Argue all you want. Get all worked up about it. What do I care?' We reached an amicable agreement, and any remaining difficulties were ironed out.

"While this was going on, the writer of these lines took it upon himself to stand apart from the majority and express his own views. He started by saying 'Just look at how these young people argue about the basic laws of the Torah, how anxious and meticulous they are over every dot and tittle in their spiritual study, so that there shouldn't be the slightest blemish, God forbid! But, as far as our work is concerned, merely telling the community what to think and doling out punishments is not good enough. For we have already imbibed and internalized the teachings of the Torah and the Mishnah at the *Bet HaMidrash*. Our comrades simply don't need to go over this type of learning yet again!

"I felt greatly encouraged inasmuch as the more deeply we delved, the more passionate we became, and the more scathing the arguments for and against. For is it not true that if we are able to argue about these 'non-practical' subjects, the sacrifice is even more worthwhile in the case of the 'practical,' which brings its own reward?

"One of the Movement's leaders now rose to speak at the dais. By this time the Shabbat lights had gone out and the hall was growing dim. The only light now came from the moon which softly illuminated the faces of those seated, engrossed in their thoughts. The young man spoke. His subject was activism, a concept which touched the hearts and minds of the young people present. Passions ran high. Words were bandied about in thin air. There was heckling, followed by questions and answers. Nevertheless, things were becoming clearer. Each word was like a spark.

"At long last, the session came to an end and we departed, each to our own home. Some of us slept on mattresses, others on the floor itself, covered with a sheet. In two and threes, we slept in the houses of our friends. But even here the night session did not cease. Down-to-earth conversations were continued, discussions went on, and then the final words: 'Let's see tomorrow: the day is still before us!'

"When morning broke, it was the turn of all those who had restrained themselves up until that point . . . . However, you could easily tell the difference between those disputants who remained calm, and whose being was rooted in the Movement, and those who criticized for criticism's own sake. But even this was for the best. Better to have criticism than nothing at all. Because criticism can lead to something more profound. However, for every point made by the critic, came the obligatory rejoinder. Why didn't those who were 'winning' realize this?

"Shabbat had concluded and the time for Meleva Malkha arrived. Time for a third and final meeting to discuss those 'practical' matters which are not suitable subjects for Shabbat . . . . We could see from the clock on the wall that midnight was approaching. But still the arguments continued. Deep sleep hovered over the faces of the young men and women, but they stubbornly resisted. They kept banging on the table to drive home their points before they simply vanished into thin air. And you, my friend . . . have you too thought of dozing off? Today is a *'night of watchfulness,'* as we say on Seder night. *'Thy destiny is to be decided today,'* as it says on Yom Kippur.

"One hour after midnight we finally concluded. We finally elected a leader. In his quiet voice, he expressed the emotions of responsibility which he felt most deeply, as he asked us, the *madrichim*, for our loyal assistance in the cause. We *madrichim*, the trainers and educators of the Movement, linked hands in unity, as together we sang the *HaTikvah*, our anthem of hope. Almost imperceptibly, so as not to disturb the repose of the local residents, the sounds of *HaTikvah* reverberated throughout the hall. There was a tremor in our throats, and a tear in our eyes. 'Salvation is the Lord's.' For now, at long last, the wheels of the bus really *are* making their way toward Jerusalem! Our hair stands on end as a still small voice enters the depths of our soul and gently encourages us: 'Don't worry; everything will be OK; we *will* overcome!'"

Although Shear Yashuv was fully occupied in his educational role within the *Brit HaHashmona'im*, this did not mean that he stopped studying at the Yeshiva. In the surviving pages of his diary, we find, together with his contemporary notes on the subject, summaries of *Hilkhot Melicha*, the rabbinic Laws of Salting, which he was studying as part of his rabbinic curriculum for *semicha*.

In 1946, the young Hasmonean became the editor of the official newspaper of the Movement, known as "*The Hasmonean.*" Young Shear Yashuv edited the paper for only about half a year, until its publication was halted temporarily. The Jewish Agency had supported the paper financially, but put an end to their support after the paper published articles critical of their cautious approach toward the British occupation.

⇒ ON BEING A MOVEMENT LEADER

At the beginning of 1947, the Joint Jewish Resistance Movement was dismantled. This was the result of the blowing up of the Headquarters of the British Mandate Authority, principally the Secretariat of the British Mandate Government, and the Headquarters of the British Forces in *Eretz Yisrael* and Transjordan. Young Shear Yashuv took part in establishing a new resistance movement which was identified with *Brit HaHashmona'im*. The aim of this new Movement was to maintain the unity of all the combatant organizations in their shared goal of continuing the struggle against the British occupation. One of Shear Yashuv's new assignments was to set the membership to work plastering posters on city buildings, which called for unity among all the combatant organizations. He was even "on loan" to the intelligence service of the Haganah (known as *ShY* for short), who used him in surveillance operations which they were too timid to carry out themselves. Over the course of time, he gave many lectures to the Movement's leadership and membership, and even led the training of *madrichim* at a nation-wide convention for the leaders of *Brit HaHashmona'im*.

One day, representatives of the British Secret Police arrived at Merkaz HaRav. They held a top-secret meeting with the Dean of the Yeshiva (who was now Rabbi Tzvi Yehuda), complaining that a section of the student body was "in cahoots with a suspicious character." Shear Yashuv Cohen was one of the names mentioned. The Rabbi answered that "it is not our job to help our students make decisions of a political nature." However, the young Shear Yashuv was "privileged" to experience the inside of a British jail for the first time at the conclusion of the Fast of 9th Av (6th August) 1946. The Fast itself commemorates the destruction of the Temple.

What led to this draconian punishment for such a young man? After the Fast, Shear Yashuv had joined his comrades from *Brit HaHashmonai'im* and made for the *Kotel* of the Western Wall. On arrival, the young man had committed the grievous "crime" of singing *HaTikva*. He was arrested on the spot by the British police, but was released shortly after, on account of his youth.

On 17th Shevat (19th January 1946), members of the Irgun and Lehi had tried to break into the Central Prison in Jerusalem, better known as the "Russian Compound," or "Bevingrad," as mentioned above. Their attempt failed, and one of the combatants, Yosef Vitelson (1926–2012), was caught by the British. Throughout his interrogation, Yosef stuck to his version of events: namely that on returning from praying at the Kotel, he had found himself caught in crossfire. Vitelson's home was searched, and a list of members of *Brit HaHashmona'im* was found by the British police. These were merely names of *potential recruits* to the Irgun. But the British thought they had secured the list of members of the Irgun itself. They therefore made for the addresses of the people whose names were listed, in order to arrest them.

This is how members of the British Secret Police happened to arrive at the home of the *Nazir*. When young Shear Yashuv heard them knocking at the door, he escaped from his own balcony to the one next door. However, the next time he was not so lucky. On that occasion he was arrested and thrown into the Latrun Detention Camp. Sticking to his vegetarian principles, he hardly touched his food while in jail. This is how he tells it:

> "After being held at the British Police Station, I was transferred to Latrun. During that time I hardly ate a thing on account of keeping *kosher* and also sticking to my vegetarian diet. On arrival at the camp, I immediately recognized Yosef Vitelson, who had already been arraigned there. He noticed that I looked extremely pale, and realized that due to my vegetarian diet and adherence to the laws

of *kashrut*, I had not had a bite to eat for a very long time. I had just finished one of my many interrogations, when suddenly the door opened, and there was Yosef with a tray of vegetables and a cup of milk. He had managed to sort this out thanks to his excellent links with the cook. When I saw the tray, I said: 'I see that even here I find myself among friends.' To this very day I still remember how good that special meal tasted!"

Shear Yashuv was released from prison after one week. This was due to interventions on his behalf from two opposite poles of the Zionist spectrum with ties to his father, the *Nazir* of Jerusalem, and to his brother-in-law, Rabbi Goren. Yehuda Golan was an aide to the left-leaning Moshe Sharett (1894–1965), Head of the Political Section of the Jewish Agency, and subsequently the second Prime Minister of *Medinat Yisrael* (1954–55). Dr. Aryeh Altman (1902–82), on the other hand, was one of the leaders of the Revisionist Movement in *Eretz Yisrael*.

The British Secret Police were completely taken aback when two such important personalities from opposing ends of the political spectrum both appealed for the release of young Shear Yashuv. They interrogated the young "warrior" and asked him which group he himself belonged to, to the Haganah, or to the Irgun, as both factions were asking for his release.

Some years later, Rabbi Cohen described how he answered his interrogators:

> "I told them that judging from what they told me, it appeared that I didn't actually belong to any specific group, and that I should be released immediately. And it was in fact the case that the *Brit HaHashmona'im* did not belong to any specific Underground group, as our dream was to bring all the different Underground factions together and work as one."

On 2nd Nissan (23rd March) 1947, Shear Yashuv was elected as one of the five leaders of the Movement. Moshe Rusnack was also elected (and later became Commander of the Haganah in the Old City of Jerusalem). Chaim Kovarsky (Nachshon) was elected as the overall leader of the Movement.

THE UNITED NATIONS PARTITION PLAN: A TIME TO REJOICE, OR A TIME TO WEEP?

The combined efforts of the Underground and the political work of the Yishuv bore fruit. On the night of 29th November, in the village of Lake Success (just outside New York and, from 1946–51 the temporary home of the United Nations), the U.N. General Assembly voted to partition the British Mandate of *Eretz Yisrael* and establish a Jewish State. It is almost impossible to describe the rejoicing that exploded onto the streets of Jerusalem. Tens of thousands of people merged onto the streets, dancing and praising the establishment of a Jewish State. These included students from Merkaz HaRav, who joined in the festivities with the myriads of people who packed the streets that night. At *Kikar Zion* Square and around the Jewish Agency Headquarters, Golda Meir (1898–1978: Prime Minister 1969–74) and other political leaders addressed the many thousands who were waiting to hear them speak. This is how Rabbi Cohen described it:

> "There is absolutely no doubt that we regarded the very fact of the declaration of the establishment of a Jewish State in *Eretz Yisrael* as a miracle from heaven. But for some reason or another, we all overlooked the negative implications of the decision. These included the internationalization of Jerusalem, and the establishment of an extra Arab State across the Jordan built on large chunks of land belonging to *Eretz Yisrael*. The enthusiastic dancing in the street went on until the small hours of the morning. And we could hear the words of Psalm 28:9: '*Save Thy people and bless Thy inheritance: Be their Shepherd and exalt them forever*,' as hundreds of thousands of dancers came together in song.

A TIME TO WEEP

> "When dawn rose, and there was a lull in the activity, one of my Yeshiva friends approached me and whispered emotionally: 'I have heard that the Rosh Yeshiva, Rabbi Yaakov Moshe Charlap, has been seen walking with his son and son-in-law across to Bet HaRav Kook.' Shortly after, another Yeshiva friend came and told me that a few moments earlier, colleagues had seen our own rabbi, Rabbi Tzvi Yehuda, walking along in the dead of night to the Yeshiva housed in Bet HaRav Kook.
> "This friend proposed that we should go along to find out what

was going on there. When we reached Bet HaRav Kook, the building was entirely shrouded in the faint flickers of dawn which just precedes sunrise. Only on the second floor, did light burst forth from the 'little room' in which the Rav had studied during his life. This was a small room with a table, chair, lamp, and small bookcase. We immediately climbed up the steps of the courtyard to Bet HaRav Kook and proceeded towards the holy room. We found it locked, or at least, closed. Naturally, we young students did not dare to open the door. We merely came nearer to listen, and what we heard completely overwhelmed us. For the sound of dreadful weeping entered our ears. The voice of our Rabbi Tzvi Yehuda, crying out: 'Where is our Hebron? Where is our Shechem?' And Rabbi Charlap continued: 'Where is our Jerusalem?' First came the sobbing and weeping, and then total silence. But this was then followed by a sudden outpouring of the refrain of Isaiah 8:10: '*Take counsel together and it will come to nought. Speak a word and it shall not stand, for God is with us*.'

"It is almost impossible to describe how shocking this experience was for us. The streets still reverberated to the sound of the thousands of joyful dancers, punctuated by cries of 'A Jewish State! *Aliyah* for all! Long live the Jewish State!' And what is more everyone danced together. The '*chofshi'im*', the 'free-thinkers' as they were then called, linked arms with observant Jews, and even with the 'ultra-Orthodox', non-Zionist Haredim. Some danced in long garments, and others wore khaki shirts and pants. Members of Irgun and Lehi danced together with members of the Haganah and with left-wing kibbutzniks who had poured into Jerusalem from all sides.

"In our own holy sanctuary, by contrast, in which the great contemporary prophet of the Redemption had lived and worked, there erupted – at the height of the festivities – the sound of uncontrollable weeping. Not only was there a veritable ocean of tears, however, but also the sound of prayer and entreaty, as the three rabbis intoned their continued loyalty to the holy cities of Jerusalem, Hebron and Shechem, pledging allegiance to a faith that would never falter, come what may. For the last words we heard from behind the closed door were Psalm 118: 23: '*This is the Lord's doing. He is wonderful in our eyes*.'

"We fled from the place – out of awe and respect for our teachers and rabbis. And when later I repeated what had happened to my revered father, the *Nazir*, who was famous for being a man of few words, and who weighed every word carefully before speaking, his reaction was to cite Psalm 2:11, '*One eye laughing, the other eye weeping. But we still wait expectantly for salvation.*' And that was it!"

IN THE RANKS OF THE HAGANAH

After a few months in which he served as part of the leadership of the *Brit HaHashmona'im*, the young Shear Yashuv was recruited to the Haganah, and served in the *Moriah* (61st) Battalion, part of the Haganah *Etzioni* Brigade. At Gush Etzion the Haganah taught him combat fighting in built-up areas, as well as the use of machine guns and mortars. He fought as a member of this Battalion from the outbreak of the anti-Jewish riots (which increased after 29th of November, the date of the implementation of the Partition Plan), up until the final battles for the Old City of Jerusalem, which will be described in the following chapter.

After the War of Liberation the leadership of the *Brit HaHashmona'im* decided to disband the Movement. As far as they were concerned, the establishment of *Medinat Yisrael* meant that their mission was now completed. Young Shear Yashuv was one of those who opposed this decision. He claimed that not all their aims had yet been realized, for the character of *Medinat Yisrael* was not religious, as had been one of their stated aims. Nevertheless, on 17th Adar (27th February) 1949, the vote was taken to disband the Movement.

Much later, in 1966, the Government of Israel fully recognized the part played by *Brit HaHashmona'im* as one of the combatant Underground organizations which had joined the struggle to establish *Medinat Yisrael*. In recognition of all their hard work, Rabbi Cohen and his colleagues were awarded the "*Al-Heh* Crown." *Aleph, lamed* and *heh* are the first Hebrew letters of the three words: '*Itur lochmai hamachtarot*, "The Crown of the Underground Fighters." This Crown is awarded to any individual who fought in the Underground against British occupation, in order to establish *Medinat Yisrael*.

Under Siege

The following chapters are mostly extracts from a diary written by Rabbi Shear Yashuv Cohen during the siege of the Old City of Jerusalem, the War of Liberation, and his imprisonment by the Jordanians.

Under Siege

Jerusalem holds the record for having suffered far more pogroms and violent attacks than any other city, whether in peace-time or in war. The reason for this is that Jerusalem is situated on a mountain *"with mountains surrounding it"* (Psalms 125:2). Water is a luxury, so the residents of Jerusalem rely on the *Shefela* coastal plain in order to quench their thirst. This water is pumped from the *Shefela* via a network of pumps and pipes lining the route between the two areas. Jerusalem's children have been awarded the accolade of residing in the holiest city in the world. But the pogroms and violent attacks which have accompanied the holy and elevated side of life have also roughened their edges. Jerusalemites are proud of this apparent contradiction and enjoy pointing it out to others, saying: "Look at our furrowed brow, the result of both holiness and humiliation."

Furthermore, more than any other city, Jerusalem is a huge melting-pot of different Jewish communities; she is home to all manner of sects and the only thing these different sects have in common is that they all hate each other and are continually at each other's throats. But there are some who, in their heart of hearts, are true 'children of the covenant'. Their main motivation is love of fellow Jews. When danger arises, these Jews manage to rise above all the strife and contention. At these critical times they come together and unite as a 'fortified wall', in order to defend themselves against that very 'stiffneckedness' which otherwise is the hallmark of Jerusalemites.

By contrast, there are those who are not 'children of the covenant'. They include the various groups within Edom-Christianity and Ishmael-Islam, who hate each other simply for the sake of hating. But the only thing these two groups have in common is their profound hatred for Israel. Around this banner they rise up and unite: their ultimate goal being the eradication of Jews and Judaism from Jerusalem.

Both outside and inside the walls, the city is divided into several quarters according to ethnic-national-religious communities. There are four quarters in the Old City: the Jewish, Armenian, Arab-Muslim, and Christian. The Jewish Quarter runs from south to north and abuts onto Zion Gate, just outside the Arab and Armenian Quarters. Its alleys are narrow and its buildings ancient. It was built layer upon layer. Many of the original houses now lie below the ground, but there are also traces of the days when kings reigned here in all their resplendent majesty, the days when Jerusalem was Jewish and the capital of an independent Jewish state.

Every resident of the Jewish Quarter has a tale to tell; each individual has their own unique story and, whether they know it or not, an aura of sanctity hovers over each and every one of them. Hardship and suffering are etched on their brow, and there appears to be little dignity in their hesitant, yet pedantic, movements. These Jews of the Old City have known nothing but persecution and bloodshed. They have always been prone to bitterness and anger, grumbling and strife, self-abnegation and disappointment. Nevertheless, despite rumors and claims of misappropriations of charity funds, one thing outweighs all these faults. All Jerusalemites, whether good or bad, love Jerusalem with a sanctity and devotion so powerful that it is inscribed in trembling behind the heavenly Throne of Glory.

Whoever loves Jerusalem must assuredly love Israel. And whoever loves Israel must assuredly love Israel's Torah. And whoever devotes his whole being to Jerusalem must assuredly devote his entire being to sanctifying the Name of the Lord and the Name of Heaven in the eyes of the whole of creation. Whoever loves the Old City of Jerusalem – Zion within the Walls, the holy stones of the *Kotel*, our very own *Kotel*, the Western Wall – must assuredly cleave to the *Shekhina*. This Divine Presence has never has departed from, and never will depart from, the site of the *Mikdash* [the Holy Temple], even in its ruins, as it states in *Midrash Exodus Rabba* 2:2.

There are some who were spared those terrible days of trial and tribulation between Pesach and Shavuot of the Jewish year five thousand seven hundred and eight since the creation of the world [1948]. These include a number of our own people whose defeatism might have affected the minds of the brave combatants risking their lives during that dreadful siege, thereby aiding and abetting the enemy. But even they did what they did out of love for Jerusalem. It was love of Jerusalem that drove them to their actions. And whoever has Jerusalem in their heart will be forgiven.

During the siege of Jerusalem and the first period of my imprisonment by the enemy, I wrote the following lines in blood *(dam)* and tears *(dim'a)* with trembling pen and a tear in the eye. In a tent whose canvas sheets flapped about in the wind, on the back of a wooden bed, I took notes in a diary. These lines have been taken from these notes. Sand from the Khom Desert flew into my eyes as I wrote by the dim light of a paraffin lamp.

We were saved by the Underground fighters, who brought us back to freedom into the newly created *Medinat Yisrael*. What they did for us at that time is still as fresh in our minds today as it was then. You will see this for yourselves on reading the following lines, which present an authentic eye-witness account by someone who lived through those historic events. We have to tell our side of the story while we wait in anticipation for our Messiah and Liberator to come through the City Walls and consecrate them as the Kingdom of Israel, when the Redeemer shall come to Zion and our eternal capital city, Jerusalem, is once more united – may it be speedily in our own day, Amen!

In the following account I have done my best to preserve precise chronology. If the style is a little rough around the edges, circumstances are to blame, and for this I apologize to you, the reader. May I just add that in my account I have not altered one iota from my original impressions. I am well aware that I did not always have all the information at hand, and may not have seen the entire picture. But this account is not a legal testimony, but simply a personal impression. Nor is it a literary elaboration of that glorious and holy chapter of our history (albeit tinged with anguish and menace) when Jerusalem fell into the hands of a wretched foe. The following lines express the innermost thoughts and emotions of one of many prisoners who were privileged to play their part in the struggle, and who will never ever forget those decisive long weeks of that heroic campaign.

The story begins with the siege of Jerusalem and concludes with its fall and the capture of her combatants.

Shear Yashuv Cohen

5708 (1948)

The final year of servitude

and the first of freedom and redemption

⇛   UNDER SIEGE: THE ORDER IS GIVEN

Rosh Hodesh Nissan 5708 (April 1948)

It is the fifth month of the campaign for the city of Jerusalem. It is the fifth month since that unforgettable night when the United Nations General Assembly declared the establishment of our country, *Medinat Yisrael*, in a relatively small section of *Eretz Yisrael*. On that other night we sat glued to the radio, listening to the debate as it was broadcast from New York, capital of a far-away world. A wave of joy swept over us

*Rabbi Cohen with friends during Haganah training in preparation for
the entry into Jerusalem.*

and, like drunken crazies, we made for the city walls. If you have never
experienced that sort of joy, you have never experienced joy at all: the joy
of Jerusalem celebrating, Jerusalem, the normally sedate, quiet, serious,
and *'adagio'* city, now burst all barriers, swept away all impediments,
threw off her yoke, and went out to dance!

We were part of a group who knew each other well from serving
together both in defense and in combat. That entire night our minds
were as if in a trance. We rejoiced. We sensed a rebirth, the rebirth of the
world, albeit in pain and affliction, in sorrow and agony. But although
our entire bodies were reborn in truth and hope, something also stuck
in our throats. We *did* dance that night. But when morning came to us
outside the National Institutions Building, as dawn broke over Mount
Zion, interrupting our song of hope, our true destiny also dawned on
us. Imperceptibly, our joy was diluted by the fear that now assailed us as
we waited, consciously or unconsciously, for the imminent call to arms.

We didn't have long to wait: the call-up came that very same morning.
That was the day we were called up to defend, to be on the alert and to
fight. And now, as I write these words, five months have gone by: each
day the battle has grown fiercer, and many lives have been sacrificed. Our
own group had sung with particular joy, but many of them have fallen in
the intervening months and are no more. In every part of the country the
campaign has become worse. But the worst of all has been the campaign
against our own city, the battle for Jerusalem.

Last night I returned home on a short period of leave. I have left
my comrades in the firing line. They are at military positions scattered

Rabbi Cohen in the Moriah Battalion of Jerusalem, just before the onset of the War of Liberation.

from north to west, from west to south, and from south to east of the modern section of Jerusalem, at Sheikh Jarrah, Pagi, Tel-Ezra, Romema, Bet-HaKerem, Katamon, Yemin-Moshe, the Commercial Center, Notre Dame, Mea Shearim, Batei Ungarn, and back again. This chain of positions is being held by the local Jerusalem defense corps. Here, men have been crouching during cold wet nights and frosty days, holding on to their weapons with hands as cold as ice. Their eyes are filled with fear of the enemy, whose numbers are far greater than theirs and who keep attacking them with murderous 'gnashing of teeth.'

This is all taking place under the very nose of the foreign 'peace-making authority,' whose envoys have brought death in their wake. It is the British who are responsible for outrages such as the blowing up of the offices of the *Palestine Post* and the Jewish Agency, the explosions in Ben Yehuda Street, and the massacre of the passengers on the Sheikh Jarrah-Hadassah Hospital convoy. At every post, and in every part of the city, childhood friends have fallen who once shared memories and dreams together, while now all we share are wars and combat. Every single nook and cranny of the city has been drenched in blood. And if the streets aren't red enough, they seem to lie there, mouths agape, pleading "Enough is enough!"

⇛   THE COMBAT YESHIVA

On arriving back home, I found a yellowed certificate waiting for me on my table. This was my draft exemption on the grounds of my being a Yeshiva student, involved in 'the study of *Torah*.' The exemption had come from the *Mercaz Lemifkad Sherut HaAm* ('Home Guard Center') on the recommendation of the *Mif'al Hatorah* ('Torah Enterprises') and the *Va'ad HaYeshivot* (Yeshiva Committee).

I was engulfed by a sea of emotions. Tears welled up inside of me and stuck in my throat, as I struggled with myself. What was my primary duty? To rescue the inhabitants of the Jerusalem I loved, or to carry on studying the Torah which had been part of me, both at home and at Yeshiva, for the entire twenty years of my life.

I climbed on top of the roof, from which you could see modern Jerusalem and Mount Scopus to the north, while to the east lay the Walls of the Old City. It was a bright, fresh night, a typical tranquil Jerusalem night, sad and terribly beautiful. From time to time, a single shot could be heard in the distance, with a volley of gun-fire in response. Occasionally, fireworks would appear, lighting up the neighborhood, followed by a period of silence. I surveyed the north of the city, then the east over Mount Scopus rising up in the gloom, and finally the walls of the Old City, concealed among castle turrets and domes of mosques and churches – '*orphaned and lamenting, in alien hands*' (as it says of Jerusalem in Lamentations 5: 2–3).

At that moment the idea was born. I dreamed a dream. And in my dream I envisioned a group of Torah scholars and Yeshiva students living the words of verse 7 of the wonderful Psalm 149 of David. I dreamed of the majestic crown of the Kingdom: '*Let the high praises of God be in their mouths, and a two-edged sword in their hand – to execute vengeance among the nations and punishment upon the peoples*.'

A group of us had served together over a year earlier in the Moriah Battalion of one of the Jerusalem field corps. We had all been studying at the Yeshivot Merkaz HaRav and Hebron. The majority were clear-think-ing, serious students, devoted to *Torah Lishmah* – Torah study for its own sake. But there also raged within us a holy sea of emotions, a dream of the liberation of Zion and her complete redemption. It occurred to me to try and enlist these young men just as they finished their regular defense service, and were returning to their student lodgings in the Yeshiva. This was surely just the right time for Torah and sword to come together under one roof. What an attractive idea!

In my dream I envisioned a new type of synagogue in the Old City – shrouded in mystery, terribly beautiful, and as old as the hills – spreading her wings and embracing this combat division of Talmud scholars. '*By day sitting and learning Torah, and by night stretching out their hands and seizing their weapons*' (as it says in Nehemiah 4:11). The idea '*became covered with skin and laid with sinews*' (Ezekiel 37: 6–8). In other words,

Members of the Brit HaHashmona'im in training.
Rabbi Cohen at left, bottom.

it really 'took off' in a flurry of meetings. During one of these meetings, a former Commander of the Old City happened to turn up. He had been betrayed by what the Talmud in Tractate *Gittin* 6:2 calls *'achilat-kurtza'* – a secret informer, and had just been thrown out, but was keen to return and help his men who were still there.

But after the dream – disappointment. Only very few students agreed to take part in the first 'Combat Yeshiva,' and to enter the Jewish Quarter of the Old City through such 'unchartered waters.' The idea was simply too audacious, and my precious friends too conventional, to overcome their dread of innovation and out-of-the-box thinking.

To add to this confusion, a 'manifesto war' had broken out between the different rabbis, all of them basing their reasoning on one towering authority, none other than our teacher and master, the Light and Sanctity of Israel, Rav Abraham Isaac Hacohen Kook (may his memory be for a blessing). The rabbis insisted on fighting over a passage in his *Sherut Milkhama*, which deals with the relevance of the draft and military service for Yeshiva students. The rabbis maintained their heated discussions because they were afraid of taking the plunge and actually making a decision. They seemed to prefer to sit and wait with folded hands for a final decision.

This was not enough for me. The dream was not being fulfilled. I thought that if I myself made the first move, then others would follow me. I no longer allowed false modesty to hold me back. My place was there among the combatants: fighting and engaging in Torah – two sides of the same coin – theory buttressed by practice. I also said to myself: 'How can

*Rabbi Cohen, bottom right, in Haganah training
in preparation for the entry into Jerusalem.*

I look the mothers of my fallen comrades in the eye? How will I be able
to hold my peace when everything inside me is clamoring? How will I
manage to stand by the sidelines and watch, when death sends its darts
into the heart of my people, while I find myself a safe little corner of Torah
away from the world, studying the discussions of the early Sages such
as Abaye and Rava.' In truth, I didn't believe it was feasible to serenely
study Torah amid firestorms of shells detonating all around us, with our
comrades dying by the dozen. I did not want to see scrolls on fire with
letters flying up (see Tractate *Gittin*, p. 18a); I wanted to see letters of life.
I did not believe in a heavenly Jerusalem if there was no earthly Jerusalem
here below.

⇜ IT'S A FRAUD!

My plans met with the approval of my teacher, Rabbi Tzvi Yehuda Kook
(the son of Rav Kook) and my father, the *Nazir*. However, the Dean,
Rabbi Charlap, refused to get involved. Rabbi Charlap's sons and many of
his students argued that they should continue to study Torah. They based
their views on the following Talmudic passage: '*How do we succeed in
war? By means of the gates of Jerusalem: the place where students engage
in the study of Torah*' (Tractate *Makkot* 10a).

But although Rabbi Charlap and some of his close associates followed
this dictum, Rabbi Tzvi Yehuda and the *Nazir* supported *our* approach.
Father only made me promise to wait until after the Pesach Seder before

leaving. In any case, I would never have volunteered to fight in the most dangerous part of Jerusalem without father's agreement and blessing. The idea was to establish a new military framework, combining Torah study with combat and defense. Within this framework we would have eight hours of study, eight hours of reserve duty, and eight hours of food and rest.

Imagine my devastation when two of the founder members of our initiative were killed in battle. These were the saintly Rabbi Yosef El Nadav (may the Lord avenge his blood), scion of the famous Yemenite rabbinical Al'nadav family, and Rabbi Yaakov Rosenberg (may the Lord avenge his blood), my *chavruta* study partner during our *semicha* days.

Some members of our initial group belonged to the Irgun and Lehi, while others belonged to the Haganah *Hish* field corps. The Jewish Quarter of the Old City of Jerusalem was chosen as the site for our combat service, given the already-existent joint combat unity among these three Underground organizations, who were there under a shared command. The Commander-in-Chief of the joint unit was a member of the Haganah; his deputy was a member of the Irgun; and many of the combatants were members of Lehi. This joint command was in fact a continuation of the original Jewish Resistance Movement, which had itself been a fusion of the three Underground groups.

On 22nd July 1946, the understanding between the three Underground groups was jeopardized, when the Irgun bombed the King David Hotel. Nevertheless, although the Haganah regarded this attack as a step too far, the three groups continued to talk to each other. This dialogue now made it possible to establish a joint command in the very heart of Jerusalem – the Jewish Quarter of the Old City!

The winter of 1947 saw the opening in Jerusalem of a *Misrad Kishur* (Liaison Bureau) to serve all the combatant units in the Old City. The bureau was headed by Chanoch Tempelhof, leader of the younger generation of *HaPoel HaMizrahi*, the Religious Socialist Zionist Party in Jerusalem. I was encouraged by Tempelhof to start organizing a group of young Yeshiva students willing to enter the Old City and join its local combat and defense force. I received Rabbi Tzvi Yehudah's personal consent to this plan in a most unusual way, as follows:

Some students of Rabbi Charlap joined together with several other Yeshiva Deans who opposed the idea of the draft, stating that young Yeshiva students should devote their time to Torah rather than to army service. A flyer was produced for distribution in the streets of Jerusalem, with the headline: 'Our great rabbi, Rav Kook (of blessed memory), was against the draft for Yeshiva students.' The flyer cited a letter written by the Rav, containing some very sharp words on the subject. Citing Tractate

Sotah 10a, the Rav had stated that it is forbidden to impose 'forced labor' on Talmud students. It was shocking, however, that the opponents of the present draft had quoted Rav Kook without explaining the context in which the original letter had been written.

One winter's day in 1947, when I was very active in the 'defense of Jerusalem,' I was just leaving the Yeshiva when I was astounded to encounter one of these huge flyers hanging in the entrance to the Bet HaMidrash. It just didn't make sense. I knew that Rav Kook [the first Chief Rabbi of *Eretz Yisrael*] had supported his own son, Rabbi Tzvi Yehuda, in everything he did. In addition, the Yeshiva's administrator, Rabbi Raanan [Rav Kook's own son-in-law], was also in favor of the draft. Moreover, Rabbi Raanan's son-in-law, Rabbi Mordechai Frum [1928–1972], was actually the coordinator of the Jerusalem 'draft office.' Was it really the case, therefore, that we, the Rav's own students, were actually acting against his will? Surely, if that were the case, it was unlikely that the Rav's foremost students, his son Rabbi Tzvi Yehudah, and my father, the *Nazir*, would be actively supporting and encouraging the draft. As for me, the son of one of these foremost students, I was completely distraught and bewildered.

Leaving the Yeshiva, I made my way down the road towards *Kikar Zion* (Zion Square). And who should I see walking up towards me, but Rabbi Tzvi Yehuda, who was limping as usual. I stopped to say '*Shalom Aleichem*,' in respectful greeting to the rabbi. But when he saw my face which had gone a deathly pale, and knowing me very well, he immediately said: "What's wrong, Shear Yashuv?" When I didn't answer, he wouldn't let me go until I told him about the flyer which had cited his father, the Rav, forbidding Yeshiva students to be drafted.

At these words, and to my great surprise, Rabbi Tzvi Yehudah stood rooted to the spot, and then began to shout: 'This is a complete fraud – a distortion and utter falsehood' over and over again. I was totally dumbfounded. After calming down, he explained that the letter I had quoted was a letter written by his father, the Rav, to Dr. Josef Hertz [1872–1946], the then-Chief Rabbi of Great Britain. The original letter referred to the draft of Yeshiva students who had arrived in Britain as refugees from Poland and Lithuania during the First World War, and who had been expected to join the British army. The British exempted trainee priests and ordinands from the draft, and had therefore also exempted the Yeshiva students as 'trainee rabbis.' This is why their names had been omitted from the lists presented to the British government by Chief Rabbi Hertz.

Rav Kook's original objection to the draft situation facing Rabbi Hertz was totally different from the present case, whose context was the war for Jerusalem. This is why his son, Rabbi Tzvi Yehuda, was so vehemently angry over such a comparison. In the present case we were fighting to hold our own country, *Eretz Yisrael*, and its ancient capital, the holy city of Jerusalem, whereas in England they were fighting in a foreign army.

The present case was a prime example of a *milhemet-mitzva*. This is a compulsory war which is fought to safeguard *Eretz Yisrael* from foreign occupation, in the sense of '*coming to the aid of Israel to remove her from the clutches of the foreign oppressor who has assailed her*.' The source for this important ruling is Rambam's *Hilkhot Melakhim* 5:1, known in English as '*The Laws of Kings and their Wars*.' [These Laws come right at the end of Rambam's monumental work and *magnum opus*, the *Mishne Torah*, written between 1170 and 1180].

On hearing this, I immediately suggested that Rabbi Tzvi Yehuda write a clarification, which I promised to have published, although at the time there was no working printing press in the whole of Jerusalem. Because of the siege there was no fuel, and all the printing presses were shut except for the *Roland* printing press (nowadays situated inside the *Klal* Tower Block building), which worked for the Haganah. I turned to Dr. Yitzhak Rafael [1914–1999], Head of *HaPoel HaMizrakhi*. At that time Dr. Rafael also chaired the *Vaadat-HaMatzav* (the Jerusalem Emergency Committee), and I told him the whole story.

Dr. Rafael took care of everything and, to cut a long story short, a pamphlet was printed with the title, *Le-Mitzvat Haaretz* ('*Regarding our Obligation toward Eretz Yisrael*'). In this pamphlet, Rabbi Tzvi Yehuda made it clear that to participate in active combat and defense of Israel is a clear *halakhic* obligation. I myself was not privileged to see the pamphlet immediately, but only some months later, as my services were required in combat and defense activity for the Old City of Jerusalem.

Rabbi Tzvi Yehuda not only 'preached,' he also practiced what he preached. Although he was fifty-seven years old at the time, he joined the *Mishmar-HaAm* (the Home Guard). These were voluntary units which included people who were too old to be drafted into the regular forces. Their job was to maintain law and order in areas of Jewish residence, and assist the besieged civilian population. At the entrance to Jerusalem, in the vicinity of the Central Bus Station, next to a Home for the Elderly and situated on the border between the Jewish and Arab neighborhoods, a post had been set up to check for car bombs.

One day, as I was approaching the checkpoint, I couldn't believe my eyes! There stood a Jew with a black beard and wisps of hoary grey hair. On top of his head perched a black cap, and his long coat sported a ribbon with the words '*Mishmar-HaAm*.' The old man was inspecting every car that approached the checkpoint. Yes, there right in front of me was Rabbi Tzvi Yehuda! I was stunned that the rabbi had been assigned to this role.

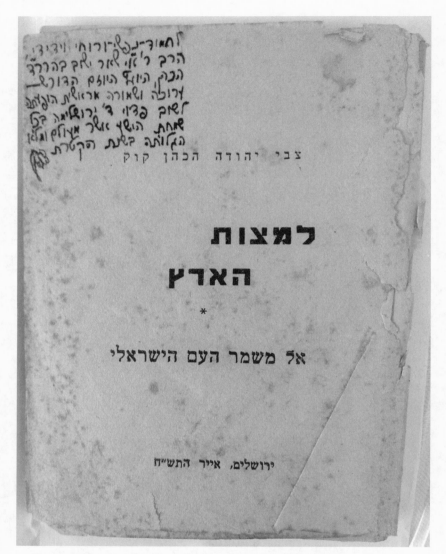

The pamphlet that Rav Shear Yashuv received from Rav Tzvi Yehuda, with a personal inscription by the latter.

But calmly he told me that he had volunteered and was carrying out his assignment of his own free will.

We, his students, decided to appeal to the Home Guard and let them know that it was wrong to exploit such an important Talmudic scholar. We learned that there had been some sort of a mix-up. The official who had assigned Rabbi Tzvi Yehuda to checkpoint duty clearly had not realized who he was. Nevertheless, at a later date, on a Shabbat, when

Rabbi Cohen training to use arms in preparation for the entry into Jerusalem. Behind him is an armored vehicle that traveled in the convoys to besieged Jerusalem.

it was announced that a convoy of the armed corps of the Arab Legion was advancing on Jerusalem, Rabbi Tzvi Yehuda left what he was doing, in order to start digging trenches to prevent the convoy from entering the city. In doing this, Rabbi Tzvi Yehuda was acting in accordance with a *heter* (a *halakhic* permission) which had just been published by Chief Rabbi Herzog.

INSIDE THE CITY WALLS

The day I had been anticipating for weeks (while continuing my studies at *Merkaz HaRav*) had now arrived. At long last I received my 'permit to go inside the city walls as 'Commissioner for Cultural Affairs,' on behalf of the defense forces in the Old City of Jerusalem.' I was to get up early and make my way to the gate of the British security sector, where I was to wait for a convoy. To tell the truth, I would have preferred to have gone in as one of the combatants, without any pretenses, and not as the 'Commissioner for Cultural Affairs.'

At that time I was unaware that inside the walls everyone was liable for duty. It was terribly sad that I was the sole surviving Yeshiva student from the group which had originally been organized under the auspices of the Haganah defense force. The other students had eventually given way to the entreaties of their families and the opinions of some of their rabbis that they were exempt from the obligation of war for the very important reason that they had taken upon themselves the 'yoke of the Torah.' In my humble opinion, however, this was a time of *milhemet-mitzva*, a compulsory war from which no one was exempt. In this I was encouraged by my teachers at Merkaz HaRav, Rabbi Tzvi Yehuda and my father, the *Nazir*.

I rose and left my father's house full of yearnings, visions and great thoughts. I left my mother's house, full of love and consideration for others. I rose and, as one of a group, quietly joined the ranks of those who were closest to my heart, those living within the eternal heart of Jerusalem, the residents inside the City of David.

The walls of the Old City were closed. No one came out and no one came in. Meanwhile, the jackboots of alien invaders stamped up and down the stones of the outer city walls, as if they were saying: 'So far and no further!' Yes, Edom-Christianity and Ishmael-Islam were conspiring together on the city walls, and were fighting together as one. Their formidable union was sending out an unmistakable message to each other and to the whole world that: 'Never will there be within these walls freedom or liberation, rebellion or revival, the rebirth that precedes redemption.'

The Jewish residents of the Old City went about their business as if nothing had changed. Young and old alike they sat, dressed in all types of clothes, hunched reverently over their books, engrossed in their studies, as if they did not have a care in the world. The streets were filled with the hustle and bustle of the populace, carrying on with their everyday business.

Devastation and destruction might be piling up at the edge of the Old City, but nobody paid any attention. Nor did anyone heed the shots ringing out from snipers at their firing positions. Blindness reigned supreme. It was as if Jerusalem wanted to forget – erase from her consciousness – the imminent danger that was at hand. But darkness was descending. Tops of the trees swayed to and fro, as if waiting to be chopped down, and stones cried out over the bloodshed of past, present and future.

Young combatants would occasionally appear in the streets of the Old City, managing to smile and look serious at the same time. They would be dressed in their uniforms, bearing arms. Sometimes they would be accompanying their fallen comrades to their eternal resting place, while at other times –when they were on leave – they would simply stroll around without apparent rhyme or reason. Their rhythm alternated loud and soft, while the ominous in-between silences seemed to carry a threat. 'This is only the start. What you see fluttering in the wind is only the prelude, before the first chapter appears and the real bloodshed begins.' For in the days to come, all would be blood, and all would be splendor. For the days to come would also bring us, signed, sealed and delivered, *Yom Yerushalayim*, our very own 'Jerusalem Day.'

The road wound its way along the City Wall, whose stones cried out, crushed and oppressed. 'Nests' of armed men hid within the wall, also waiting for day break. Here and there a shot rang out. But all was still, waiting for the dawn, as if anticipating the imminent command. I went up to the residents inside the walls, to those who were waiting, either consciously or unconsciously, to be (in the words of Job 30:5) '*driven forth from behind men*', towards '*that terrible and awesome Day*' (Malachi 4:5).

And what is '*that terrible . . . Day*'? It is the day on which, according to our Rosh HaShanah and Yom Kippur liturgy, the Almighty chooses who will live and who will die. It is also the day on which, according to the penultimate words of our last biblical prophet, Malachi, we can also look forward with hope in our hearts to the redemptive era of the days of the Messiah. And this is what we were fighting for.

⇒   *GALUT* – OUR LIFE AS EXILES IN OUR OWN LAND

The Old City remained bottled and barred. No one came out and no one came in, except under the control of the British guards and with the consent of the Arab guards, who never took their eyes off the weekly convoy, so concerned were they lest combatants or weapons might somehow find their way into the besieged City. For this reason, the way down from modern Jerusalem to the Old City within the walls was not at all easy, and necessitated a great deal of ingenuity and skill.

The British secret police kept a very strong grip on anyone hitching a lift in the food convoys travelling to the Old City. And if not for the Jewish trait of compliancy, which foreign occupiers have always taken for granted, it would have been impossible to smuggle in either combatants or weapons. Eventually, I received the final detailed and precise instructions on how to enter the Old City.

One of those unforgettable spring mornings of the month of Nissan 1948, a month etched forever in the psyche of all those who played a part in the Battle for Jerusalem – a month of convoys, breaches, and bloody massacres – I was sent to the Rehavia neighborhood of Jerusalem. From there I walked down to the gate of the British Security Sector which, in those days, encompassed a large complex adjacent to the offices of the former Jewish Agency and The National Council of Jews under the Mandate. A convoy of trucks loaded with food and medical supplies was about to leave for the Old City.

On arrival, I encountered a huge number of Jewish residents from the Old City, who had earlier left their place of residence and attempted a mad dash over the barbed-wire fences of the Security Sector, so that they could smuggle themselves onto a food convoy in order to return to their homes. These 'refugees' were standing there, waiting for a British police officer to announce the exact moment that the gate would be opened.

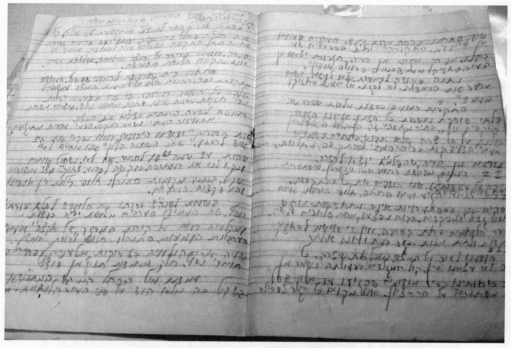

Rabbi Cohen's diary detailing the siege and the POW camp, written in pencil.

And, although, to all appearances, the spectacle was both depressing and degrading, there were also some positive signs.

Scores of Jewish men and women of every age and background were packed like sardines, right next to the barbed wire, and all of them were doing their very best to squeeze themselves onto the convoy. Most of them were residents of the Old City who had left for some reason or another, and were now cut off from their families. Others were residents who had, at the onset of the siege, fled to the 'modern city of Jerusalem outside the wall.' But now they had all become terribly homesick and were trying their best to get back to their homes in the Old City.

Members of the Haganah and Jewish public officials intermingled with teachers and nurses so as to enter the Old City and carry out the tasks which were awaiting them. I tried to slip onto the convoy of teachers, nurses and food, which had 'official permission' to enter the Old City, in the guise of a teacher. And to be honest, this was not far from the truth. For had I not genuinely been assigned, as it were, the role of 'Commissioner for Cultural Affairs' to the residents within the walls, who were increasingly suffering from the inertia, due to the months-long siege?

But that day, the convoy did not make it to the Old City. No senior member of the British police materialized as expected, and the junior officer who arrived at the gate in his stead declared that the convoy had been cancelled as a 'collective punishment'. For it turned out that two rifles and two pistols had been stolen from the police station in the Old City! Until these were returned, food convoys into the Old City would be cancelled. The extent of this perfidious and criminal reaction on the part of the British can be judged by the fact that, on the very same day, dozens of British and Arab policeman had deserted with their weapons, in order to join roaming bands of lawless Arab criminals – with no one fluttering even an eyelid. Yet two rifles and two pistols aroused the full wrath of the British and such grave punishment.

Every day without fail I joined the long queue which trailed along to the barbed wire gates of the British Sector, inside the City of Jerusalem, but to no avail. Our convoy was held up for a whole week, while we idled away the time, hanging around the gates each morning, and being constantly let down! Meanwhile, painstaking negotiations were being held on the subject of the two rifles and the two pistols, until at last a 'compromise' was reached.

The Jewish security forces outside the Old City agreed to replace the two rifles and the two pistols, handing them over to the British police, in exchange for the lifting of the blockade. The compromise included the delivery to the Old City of a number of weapons at double their normal price, which had the added bonus that the pompous British were able to 'save face'. Oh, the joys of *Galut*!

UNDER SIEGE

We were thoroughly searched, and then transferred through the British Sector to a spot near the American Consulate, where we found 'our' vehicles waiting for us. Our luggage underwent magnetic clearance, and then we ourselves were thoroughly searched once more and declared 'clean'. With the assistance of several bottles of wine, we managed to get the guards 'tipsy'. This encouraged them to turn a blind eye to a shipment of weapons, including one machine-gun, which we smuggled onto our convoy *en route* to the Old City. This machine-gun was a big 'catch' for Jerusalem in those days!

Then we hoisted our luggage onto the vehicles. But as soon as it was all safely on board, we ourselves were told to wait outside the American Consulate for the vehicle to turn round and set off. It occurred to us then that the so-called British 'law-enforcement agency' had exploited the short space of time during which the vehicle was out of our sight to perpetrate the mass theft of all our possessions! Eventually, however, we were also hoisted up onto the vehicles.

There were twenty of us in all in the convoy. These included teachers, clandestine members of the army and Eliyahu HaCarmeli, né Lulu [1891–1952], representing the *Vaad HaMatzav le-Kehilat-Yerushalayim* (The Emergency Committee for the Jewish Community in Jerusalem). Travelling with us were also some residents of the Old City, including women who were returning to their families whom they had left at the onset of the Arab riots. 'From far off I blew you a kiss, Mother, as you waved me your hand in farewell.' The atmosphere was fraught in anticipation of the looming catastrophe: *Shalom*, Mother, Goodbye, We'll see each other again – some time.

Getting to know these people, I encountered for the first time the inner secret of the residents of the Old City. For, I discovered within them the most profound love of Jerusalem, the most profound desire to return despite all the dangers, to their city. I turned to one old woman, who was curled up and withdrawn in a corner of the British lead vehicle, muttering verses of Psalms to herself as a kind of therapy.

This is what I asked her: 'Tell me, Grandma, do you think it is actually safe in the city, now that you are returning inside?' [By 'city', all understood this to mean: 'inside the walls of the Old City']. 'Wouldn't it be safer to stay outside the walls with your grandchildren?'

'Young man, young man,' she responded, her voice full of pity and scorn: 'What do you think 'love of family' really means? This is where I grew up, got married, and experienced both good and evil. This is where you will find real holiness, true Judaism. This is where I live, and this is – God willing – where I will die. There is no way I can exist outside. I simply must go home.'

Her face was creased and her back was bowed, as if two thousand years of Jewish suffering rested on her shoulders. Her voice trembled from fatigue. But what trust and faith pervaded everything she said! And what unequivocal love she possessed – love of truth, the maternal love of a mother for her daughter, and most of all, love of Jerusalem.

This was my response: 'More power to you, Mother! If only you knew how much we needed these words of consolation that you have so generously showered upon us just now which will assuredly encourage and enable us in the days to come.'

In an operation of the utmost and most deliberate cruelty, we were made to squeeze into four vehicles, lying packed in on top of each other, like tins of sardines, all up-tight, our nerves on edge. How easy it would have been for the British to add one more truck to the convoy. But, after careful consideration, and with malice aforethought, they refused:

"We'll make it so hard for those cursed Yids that they'll get tired of go-ing to Jerusalem." We gritted our teeth and kept our mouths shut. At the street corner, soldiers were treated to some liquor, for the descendants of Esau can't do without their drink. Cheers!

As tarpaulin covers were lowered onto the vehicles, the convoy started to move toward the walls. To the front and rear, our convoy was escorted by armored tanks full of soldiers – rifles at the ready. With a heavy heart we silently listened for the final order to get going. The convoy set off. Through slits in the canvas, we managed to catch a glimpse of the Arab streets all around us; here too, it seemed, life was going on as normal.

INSIDE THE WALLS

We reached the Arab Quarter. Near the checkpoint at the ancient Jaffa Gate, the convoy was halted by members of the 'Arab People's Guard.' Green ribbons were pinned to their shoulders, and their pistols were snugly ensconced in sparkling holsters. The Arabs approached the British officer in charge of our convoy, and commenced negotiations. The Arab officer's language was so foul-mouthed and obscene that we could feel our hearts pounding with fear. At that moment one of our comrades reminded us of the story of four Jews who had been handed over by the British to the Arabs and had subsequently been found dead by The Lions' Gate. We shut him up.

Facing us stood the Tower of David in all its tall majesty with the flag of the 'Arab Liberation Army' fluttering away at its very top. In front of us stood a concrete checkpoint, manned by ten Arab guards. Machine-gun muzzles and other firearms protruded through slits in the walls which had originally been built by the Ottoman Turks. An ominous silence reigned. The British officer got off the truck and exchanged a few words with his Arab counterpart. After another moment's silence, the check-point was opened.

We turned to the right at Mount Zion, heading towards Zion Gate, originally built by Jews. This gate faces south and provides the entry to the Jewish Quarter of the City, Mount Zion, and the original Temple Mount, where the First and Second Temples once stood. Zion Gate – synonymous both with Jerusalem itself and with *Eretz Yisrael.*

The convoy halted opposite the Gate. The British officer ordered us off the vehicles. His soldiers arranged themselves into a semi-circle to separate us from a large group of armed Arabs who had congregated at the 'Mount Zion School' on the other side of the street. The heavy bolt of the large iron door, which was firmly fastened on every side by a stop bar, clunked open. Inside the gate, packed in like sardines, a great assembly of Jews was there to welcome us – the newcomers. The entire Jewish population of the Old City – old and young, women and children – was represented there before us in all their glory with cries of '*Shalom*, welcome!'

All of us who entered the Old City that day were moved to tears. But the 'welcome party' looked puzzled. This is how one of the old women expressed it: 'They are so young. What's the point of such idiocy – what's the point of bringing healthy young people to a sick bed?' The old woman certainly didn't mince her words, which really hit us where it hurt. We reacted with a mixture of disdain and apprehension, producing an uneasy sensation which is hard to define – maybe a sort of stiff-necked obstinacy of the condescending variety: 'Now now, Grandma, don't worry your head about such matters!'

Members of our defense forces mingled with the residents, concealing their weapons under their clothes, stealing us sideways glances of encouragement. Abraham Mordechai Weingarten [1895–1964], known as the '*Mukhtar*' of the Jewish community in the Old City, struggled through the hurly-burly, and was busy pressing the flesh of anyone who managed to get close. His daughter, who was dressed in the white attire of a nurse, took down all our names. I met up again with several acquaintances for the first time since they had been shut in behind the walls. They made their way to me, slapped me on the back, reintroduced me into their circle, and accompanied me to their 'base.'

What would your reaction have been in 1948 if you had arrived for the first time from a free and autonomous modern Jerusalem to the other Jerusalem which lies within the walls? I can only compare how you would have felt to the way our Sages describe it in Talmud *Chagiga* 5b, commenting on Lamentations 2:1. There they describe the feeling as akin to '*falling from a roof so high to a pit so low.*' It is no exaggeration to say that on entering the Old City you would also have entered your very own black hole, your individual 'Slough of Despond.' For at that time the Old City was under a 'double siege' – from both the British and the Arabs.

Let me explain what life was like for people in the Old City of Jerusalem. From time to time the British military would appear out of the blue on one of their unexpected sorties. These generally consisted of conducting savage on-the-spot searches, when they would round up the usual young 'suspects' (for the most part commanders of our defense forces), and haul them back into the modern part of Jerusalem. This was all done deliberately. Their express intent was to sabotage any attempt whatsoever by the weak and defenseless Jewish Yishuv to defend itself.

The atmosphere in modern Jerusalem was also tense, but this was the tension of freedom, new-found dignity and military alertness. The buds of Jewish independence had been blossoming for some time, and were now in full and glorious flower. Armed Jewish troops could be seen marching in the streets of a 'new' Jerusalem, governed by its own autonomous Jewish administration.

But in the Old City, it was a case of 'the calm before the storm.' The so-called *Vaad-Ir* ('Council for the Old City'), headed by the *Mukhtar*, had no authority whatsoever, being under total British jurisdiction. For this reason, an unofficial 'Council' was set up, which operated clandestinely to defend the Yishuv on behalf of all the Underground forces. Irgun staff members worked in coordination with the Haganah, which was in control of the fighting. These combined forces were constantly on the look-out for the British police and military, whose idea of 'keeping the peace' was to set up a network of key strategic points, which they kept heavily manned, in order to separate the Jewish Quarter from all the others.

The Underground defense forces were composed principally of the people who had arrived to take up this role in November 1947. They had already been at it without a break for six months. So, by the time we arrived, it is not surprising that they were worn out – at the end of their tether– and their cynicism knew no bounds. For example, our report about a newly-established Jewish (or rather, *Israeli* army), whose uniformed and well-armed troops – proudly wearing full insignia – were marching right now outside the wall in the streets of modern Jerusalem, was greeted as though it were a far-fetched fairy tale – a gripping and marvelous yarn and a figment of our overactive imaginations, their eyes popping out of their heads.

When we eventually reached a secure environment, we set to work inspecting the baggage we had brought with us on the convoy, and discovered that a very large part of our possessions had been stolen by the British Military. I didn't mind so much being 'ripped off' by such determined and disciplined thieves. What really upset me, however, was that they had also taken my precious *tefillin*, which had been written with such care and attention by Rabbi Nachman, a Hasidic scribe, in the presence of my dear father, the *Nazir*. The moment I realized that the *tefillin* were gone, my heart was filled with a terrible foreboding. All my best efforts to find them were in vain. And I therefore had to draw the painful conclusion that the motive for this particular theft was nothing but pure, unadulterated anti-Semitism. For what other motive might a British soldier have had for stealing a pair of *tefillin*?

➥   THE SWORD AND THE BOOK

Otherwise, provisions inside the Old City walls were not bad. Large convoys of food arrived at regular intervals, and there was even a rumor that further supplies (together with more weapons) were being smuggled in across the lines. Life was well organized. The British military were in complete control, and had certainly done their homework on all aspects of life in the Old City. For their task was not easy! The Commander-in-Chief had his work cut out for him, and found this aspect of government his largest headache. Not only did the 'natives' come in all shapes and sizes, but, in addition, they were unused to discipline of any kind. The mood was tense. It was a case of '*the sword without, and terror within*' (Deuteronomy 32:25). From time to time violence would break out for no apparent reason, even ending in bloodshed occasionally. A siege mentality reigned over all.

The arms supply in the Old City was so deficient as to make any observer weep. The people who were responsible were fully aware that although a show-down was imminent, their hands were tied. Anxiety gnawed at their heart, as their alarm grew daily. You could see the dread on people's faces. It was etched on the heavily-lined brows of those young people who had suddenly aged overnight.

To start with I sorely neglected my assigned role of implementing the study of Torah. But in spite of this, I was able to get something going before long. People thirsted for Torah. In spite of their nerves, all it needed was a small push to get them back on track once again. Thus it was that, all huddled together, packed in tight, we found ourselves in the quarters of the *Hish* reservists, who had found a temporary home in the courtyard of the *Shaar-HaShamayim* ('Gate of Heaven') Yeshiva, which was well known for being dedicated to the study of Kabbalah. Here we awaited our orders.

While we were engaged in regular study of the Talmud Tractate *Sanhedrin*, the company of combatants would assemble inside the building. There was a general consensus among the 'students' that if not for the battle raging on all sides, these classes would have reached a new high, since at that time nothing comparable was being offered anywhere else in Jerusalem.

For us religiously observant young Torah students, halakhic questions would occasionally crop up in the course of our patrol duties. For instance, were we allowed to carry arms on Shabbat? We were not sure whom to ask. We had no relationship with the elderly rabbis of the Jewish Quarter, and it did not even occur to us to turn to Rabbi Zev Velvel Mintzberg (1872–1962), a prolific Torah author who belonged to the haredi-religious

Old Yishuv. Similarly, we were at first hesitant to ask Rabbi Ben-Tzion Hazzan (1880–1952), Dean of Yeshivat Porat Yosef.

We decided instead to approach Rabbi Shlomo Min-HaHar (1911–2000, né Bergman, lit., man of the mountain). At that time, Rabbi Min-HaHar was only 37 years old, and a member of the Citizens Committee that worked in cooperation with the Haganah. In Rabbi Min-HaHar we discovered a man after our own hearts. And the way he answered all our halakhic questions went down very well indeed.

⇒   THE JEWISH *"MUKHTAR"*

During the crucial 5-week period between Pesach and Lag B'Omer, we remained under siege inside the City walls, surrounded by waves of hatred from the enemy. Those were days of pogroms and bloodshed, followed by dark nights eaten up with suspicion and dread. During those fateful days, when we didn't know what might happen next, we were divided on how to relate to the Jewish *Mukhtar* of the Old City, a Jerusalemite of many generations, Abraham Mordechai Weingarten, who has been mentioned above.

During the fighting, some of us recognized the *Mukhtar* as our official representative in negotiations with Arab and British representatives. But others deeply resented any negotiations whatsoever with the enemy, as these took place without our consent, and sometimes even without our prior knowledge.

Throughout this period, Reb Avraham carried on the only way he knew how, devoting himself tirelessly to working together and saving the love of his life – Jerusalem within the walls. He never once flinched from his noble mission. Many people did not understand him, and for this reason many people hated him. At times he even endangered the lives of his own family by exposing them to our national enemies, and he even became a potential target of the National Underground Movement, which regarded him with the utmost suspicion and mistrust.[1]

But the *Mukhtar* kept on believing with perfect faith that his was the only way to save the Old City within the walls. It was faith alone that drove him to preserve the old ways during that critical time in the annals of Jerusalem's history. It was for the sake of his faith that he was prepared to sacrifice himself completely, risking not only his position in society, but also his spiritual standing – his entire reputation in fact.

---

1. He attempted to avoid war in the Old City even at the cost of making a deal with the murderous Arab gangs. See below for a description of how R. Avraham and his daughter saved Rabbi Shear Yashuv's life.

In an audacious, yet naïve, attempt to prevent the Jewish Quarter of the Old City from being sucked into the whirlpool of bloodshed which threatened to wipe out *Eretz Yisrael* altogether, the Jewish *Mukhtar* was ready to make the ultimate sacrifice. And yet, ironically, we now know that it was this very same whirlpool which gave birth to *Medinat Yisrael – 'the beginning of the flowering of our Redemption'.* Reb Weingarten's brave attempt to stem this tide did not succeed, but during the war he earned his share in the World to Come by saving many lives.

⇒   PREPARATIONS FOR BATTLE

So this was what life was like for us as 15th May approached – the date when the British Mandate would end and the British occupiers would leave. A showdown was imminent. Rumors abounded as to the *precise* date on which the British army would leave the Old City. Our liaison with the British sweated, running around to find out the exact date and time of their departure. In the meantime, we made ready to take over the British positions as soon as the British left, to preempt any Arab takeover.

When the Arab mobs broke through into our area, all the positions were in Jewish hands. We had decided to defend the Old City only with our own forces. We would have succeeded, if not for the militarily 'neutral' intervention policy of the British, who managed to wrest the most important positions from us. From that moment, these positions were the focus of constant provocation against the Jewish residents. The following locations were the sites of the key military positions: Yeshivat Porat Yosef, the Medan Checkpoint, behind Bet Turjeman, the Karaim post, Rabinowitz, Batei Varsha, and Lubinski. These were a chain of positions that divided off Rechov HaYehudim (The Street of the Jews) from the Shalshelet Market and the Arab Quarter.

The most important southern positions were on Chabad Street, Bet Weingarten, HaKimor, HaTzlav (The Armenian Church of the Crucifixion) overlooking Zion Gate, and the Ashkenazi Hakurah. It was clear to us that if we did not occupy these positions in time, they would end up in the hands of the Arabs. Everything depended on speed and an element of surprise. Our men were specially trained for this sort of operation and were therefore all set for their difficult mission, code-named Operation Shefifon ('Viper'). Our Commander-in-Chief was a former colleague from *Brit HaHashmona'im*, Moshe Rosnack, and his Deputy was Irgun member Issar Natanson.

The Battle for Jerusalem

"A storm is raging, and the bone-racking cold has seeped in. Night, tense and indifferent, plots evil in the murk and gloom. A man, flesh and blood, wordlessly takes his cold iron weapons, instruments of slaughter made of material not meant for the altar, and waits. His eyes are focused on the enemy – the savage battle to come. With his entire being he listens for the rhythmic step of the approaching enemy. He aims the muzzle of death at the darkness, and will aim his fire at some unknown point.

"The enemy approaches his position, and he begins to run amok. Here he wounds the dark figure who rises in the field before him and has begun to run toward him, and there he hurls a grenade at a black figure opposite him. He is all fighting, all fire, all iron wall; no one will pass through. Screams are heard in the field in front of him. They are getting louder. The frightened and wounded plead for their lives, others flee from the battle, never to return.

"The enjoyment of victory overwhelms him, driving him battle-crazy. Nothing will now hold him back from slaying his foes and finishing them off completely. Like 'the plentiful corn after the sheaf' (see Jeremiah 9:22), he sets about mowing down bodies. The enemy retreats, but he runs after him. With wild screams from his throat, with

weapon at hand, he rushes madly to destroy everything in his path.

"The commanding officer orders him to abandon his chase and return to his position with his comrades. Thick with sweat, his heart beats fast and his eyelids tremble. A bitter taste fills his mouth; it sticks in his throat and won't go away.

"He lifts his hand and reflects. He examines his fingers, pale in the moonlight, and thinks: 'These hands have shed blood.' It is not a matter of logic; it is that his heart rises up, the humanity in him demands its due. With head bowed, he falls to the ground and shudders like a sinner. He seeks out refuge. He is all regret – all man.

"His lips utter a silent prayer, giving thanks to the Creator for keeping his humanity alive, for the fact that he does not rejoice at killing during battle. For each battle, he recites a prayer, a blessing and supplication: 'O God, watch over us so that we may preserve our humanity, our image of God, during battle; strengthen us, so that we may overcome the savage enemy, and avenge the spilt blood of our brothers, and defend our stronghold. Give us courage, dear God, Amen.'"

Shear Yashuv Cohen,
"Adam BaK'rav" (*"Man in Battle"*),
Jerusalem 1948

The Battle for Jerusalem

Thursday, 4th Iyyar 5708 (13th May 1948)
Operation *Shefifon* ("Horned Viper")

The preparations were completed. We were given instructions and assigned our duties. The order was given to 'stand by.' The operation was called 'Horned Viper' (see Genesis 49:17), and we were given the password: 'the *shefifon* has risen.' The operation included seizing the military positions held by the British, who were scheduled to leave *Eretz Yisrael* on 15th May precisely. The whole operation had to be over in fifteen minutes. The time was now 12:45.

The British were acting suspiciously. Soldiers were running about, completing outstanding negotiations, and taking their leave of neighbors whom they had befriended during the long siege. A "ready for action" status was declared. Maps were scattered all over the table; people in battle gear sat around and waited. We were assigned to our units and informed of our duties. A feeling of listlessness hung in the void, a feeling that the long period of respite was over and battle was imminent.

Suddenly, the strained atmosphere was broken by the wireless broadcasting *The Voice of the Haganah*: 'Heavy attack on Gush Etzion! The Arab Legion is charging with a great many tanks and artillery. The situation is serious!' The faces of those around me went white out of concern for their comrades who were engaged in the fierce battle for the defense of Jerusalem. Our hearts became heavy. Everyone looked into the face of his neighbor. Someone put a disk on the phonograph, to distract us from our worries. We had our own impending battle to contend with, so our instinctive response was: 'Comrades in the Gush, God is with you.'

It was 17:45 when we received information that the British army would evacuate their positions in fifteen minutes. The men were ready for action. At 18.00 the British army, having stashed away every weapon in the city, evacuated the positions separating the Jewish Quarter from the others. At the same time, combatants from the Haganah, Irgun and Lehi Underground groups clandestinely stole past these positions. I crossed the street and found myself face to face with a most interesting scenario.

The British legionaries were marching proudly and rhythmically through the reverberating streets, in full military dress and arms, adorned with steel helmets. Unknown to them, however, our own comrades were simultaneously taking over the British positions, dressed in 'civvies,' armed with any weapon that they had managed to lay their hands on. The regional reserves, our top military force in the area, broke into the Batei Varsha position, and a battle broke out. The orders for our side had included the careful preservation of a truce, but in this location they were unable to withstand Arab fire, and so they returned fire.

It fell to me to work as the liaison officer between headquarters and the periphery. The internal phone never stopped ringing, with messages coming and going all the time. On the whole, the situation wasn't too bad, except for grenade and sniper fire at some of the positions. Two of the only machine guns in our possession were passed from one position to another. This gave the impression that we possessed far more ammunition than was actually the case. The Arabs over-estimated our machine gun strength and halted their offensive after being taken by surprise when we seized the military positions.

THE ABANDONMENT OF THE *"HATZLAV"* POSITION

Night fell, a night typical of any cool Jerusalem night. The Old City of Jerusalem between the walls was submerged in the calm before the storm. At 21:30 when things became relatively quiet, a number of us officers, doctors and nurses entered the operation room based in the Misgav Ladach Hospital. For all it was worth, we savored the joyful feeling of having survived unscathed in the course of the battle, with our hospital team temporarily having 'time on their hands.' But, deep down, we knew that this happy situation would not last.

On the diplomatic scene, negotiations had started which contributed to the eventual fate of the Old City. At 22:10 two men knocked at the Zion Gate, announcing that they were representatives of the 'Consular Committee.' We asked them to come around through the Jaffa Gate via the road to the *Kotel* and meet us at Zion Gate. These men, a Jew and an Arab, were officials sent by the French Consulate, who had been assigned by the United Nations to pin down precisely who had broken the truce. The positions had been ordered to stick to the 'cease fire.' The two representatives surveyed the entire area, and then sat down for a cup of tea with the district officer.

At 1.00 AM some fifteen Armenians appeared at the border between the Jewish and Armenian Quarters, led by the Deputy to the Armenian Patriarch. They asked us to preserve the neutrality of the Armenian Quarter and abandon the position situated at the Armenian Church, otherwise known as the Church of the Crucifixion. This position was situated inside the large Armenian Church which commanded the approach from the City Walls to HaYehudim Street (The Street of the Jews).

The Armenian delegation assured us that, in return, they would preserve the neutrality of the Armenian Quarter. We did not trust them, and rejected the proposal. So, after an hour, the Armenian Patriarch himself went to see the Jewish *Mukhtar*, Abraham Weingarten, in his own home. The French consular representatives were also invited, but the Armenians refused to allow them to participate in the negotiations.

There, it was agreed that we would abandon the critical church position, while the Armenians promised not to hand over any of "their" territory to the Arabs. They later blatantly violated this promise, handing over critical locations – the Armenian School and the former HaTzlav position itself – to Arab gangs and the Arab Legion. This act of bad faith on the part of the Armenians was one of the main contributory factors to our eventual retreat from the Zion Gate.

During that entire night, our preparations continued for passages of various types from house to house, and for retreat routes from the dangerous front-line positions, just in case. To complete one of the critical passages, we had no choice but to detonate a bomb, at 4:30 AM, near the gate of an Armenian structure known as the "house with the green shutters." The explosion could be heard throughout the city, and we immediately received telegrams from our government institutions in the new city asking, "What are those explosions at your end?" They demanded, consistent with their approach, that we adhere carefully to the United Nations ceasefire order.

Friday, 5th Iyyar 5708 (14th May 1948)
Our First Fatality

This day – which became Israel's Independence Day – passed quietly, more or less. The Arabs were concentrating their forces and appeared to be preparing a heavy offensive against us. We requested military equipment from west Jerusalem but were turned down because they themselves had just begun an assault on the Arab neighborhoods in their own part of the city. In the meantime, on our side, what we called the

"Hell on Earth." Rav Shear Yashuv, with hat, facing away from the camera, in the Misgav Ladach Hospital in the Jewish Quarter of the Old City.

'Battle of Warsaw' continued inside a group of houses belonging to the complex belonging to the Kollel Batei Varsha (Warsaw).

These houses were in a unique strategic position. Our side was stationed in a complex which adjoined an Arab-owned building containing a machine gun. The distance between our two positions was only about three or four metres in some places, so we tip-toed around. The slightest sound would result in our being hit by an Arab grenade. It was a terrible shock to see our men firing at the enemy while lying on top of a great pile of scrolls and holy books. Some of these books were very ancient, and filled an entire room in the Batei Varsha complex. But the men had no choice. The 'Battle of Warsaw' was a serious affair and lasted the whole day.

At this time, we also suffered our first fatal casualty. Our firing party was attacked while moving toward the city wall. One of our comrades was very badly wounded. A young messenger brought me the news of the injury. I made my way to the Misgav Ladach hospital and told them about the injured man's hopeless condition. We were distraught but little did we know that in another two days our streets would be piled high with the bodies of slain and injured with nowhere to bury them.

It became evident that the Arabs were preparing a heavy assault. We noticed concentrations of military reinforcements, with new positions being constructed right under our noses. The order was given to obstruct this building program. Small skirmishes took place, especially around the Arab positions in the Armenian Quarter.

The Arabs paid a very heavy price for their illegal assault, whereas we had no casualties. By now, however, our men were worn out, having managed only a couple of hours sleep. As for the officers, they did not sleep at all. There was a severe shortage of manpower, so we had to draft in teachers and girls to fill the positions. This extra draft eased the situation to some extent, but it was only a makeshift solution. Despite our fatigue, we had to find a way to fortify our position.

Our fighters were a mixed bag of people assembled from all over the world. These included 'Anglos,' Yemenites and ultra-Orthodox Haredim from the Old Yishuv, who joined forces together. Individual acts of heroism became a symbol of unity, removing all barriers between the various Jewish traditions. Sephardim from Morocco and Ashkenazi Hasidim from eastern Europe [many in their traditional dress of kaftans, and some even with their trade-mark sidelocks, known as '*peyot*'] manned the positions against the common enemy. Women and children also volunteered to take part. Together with the 'organized' combatants, all these different groups formed one large field corps which was quickly moved to any weak spot. This whole operation was carried out as a critical emergency measure to protect the Holy City from total destruction.

⇒   WE DECLARE THE ESTABLISHMENT OF *MEDINAT YISRAEL*

At about 4:00, I was part of a small unit operating a most primitive mortar in the 'German Courtyard' of the Batei Machse complex, facing Bet Rothschild. That very moment, a special session of the Emergency People's Council had been hastily convened in the auditorium of the Tel Aviv Museum. David Ben Gurion (1886–1973), his recognizable voice thundering with emotion, was reading out the declaration of the establishment of *Medinat Israel* (The State of Israel). Courtesy of the defense forces, we were able to hear this live historic broadcast on the radio. It was completely quiet in the Jewish Quarter except for the sounds we could make out of the shots being fired by Arab marksmen, which were blending in with the dramatic words of Ben Gurion:

"*Eretz Yisrael* was the birthplace of the Jewish people. Here their spiritual, religious and national identity was formed. Here they achieved independence and created a culture of national and universal significance. Here they wrote and gave the Bible to the world."

Ben Gurion continued reading the entire text with great solemnity. Then, when he reached the words: "By virtue of the natural and historic right of *Am Yisrael*, the Jewish people . . . we hereby proclaim the establishment of the Jewish State in *Eretz Yisrael* (the Land of Israel), to be called *Medinat Israel* (the State of Israel)," tears of joy streamed down our cheeks.

This joy was contagious and spread to every corner of the Jewish Quarter, affecting everyone – men, women and children. There was something very special about our rejoicing, which embraced the entire Jewish community. Under one umbrella came the Haredim, the modern Orthodox and the completely non-observant; the political left and the political right. As for the Underground, the Haganah, the Irgun and Lehi were now also united in joy as well as in the united fight for their freedom.

Yet in the midst of our rejoicing, our hearts were filled with fear. Would we really be able to stand up to our enemy at this critical juncture in the history of our people? Could our very own Jerusalem, both inside and outside the Wall, really defend herself against this wave of adversaries, armed to the teeth?

The Jewish population in the Holy Land – the Yishuv – had no illusions about the inadequacy of its own armory. The fate of Jerusalem within the walls lay in the balance, the City of Holiness and the Sanctuary, the heart and strength of the nation, including its dozens of synagogues, yeshivot and Torah study halls, and its thousands of residents, children and mystics. Our military strength was negligible. We were only 200 Jewish combatants with barely any weapons, facing 30,000 armed Arabs, several thousand of whom were experienced and disciplined soldiers.

With all this, however, our spirit was steadfast and our resolve firm. To save our Jerusalem, we were determined to fight until the bitter end.

As soon as the battle started, a proclamation was issued by the senior rabbis of the Jewish Quarter. These included Rabbi Zev Mintzberg (the leader of the Haredi community) and Rabbi Ben Zion Hazzan (Dean of Porat Yosef), who were mentioned above. These two ultra-Orthodox rabbis worked together at this seminal moment with our commanding officers and the heads of the local residents of the Jewish Quarter.

Together, they summoned the community to join them at nightfall for a thanksgiving prayer service in the Yohanan ben Zakkai Synagogue. This site was like a natural shelter, as it was below street level. Moreover, according to ancient tradition, the shofar of Eliyahu the Prophet was thought to be buried here.

Friday night, 6th Iyyar 5708 (14th May 1948)
Hallel (Psalms 113–118)

When night fell, the battle abated. The Arabs, who were accustomed to fighting only during the day, temporarily halted their onslaught. I was therefore able to enter the underground Ben Zakkai Synagogues complex for a short time, in full battle gear. The candelabra were all lit with oil, shining a special light throughout. In all four synagogues of the complex could be heard emotional and joyous prayers and songs for the occasion. Among them we sang of the great scholar Bar Yochai girding himself with strength and fighting the battle of Torah. Psalms were also recited for the victory of our fighters and the salvation of the besieged city.

The prayers and songs intensified my belief and faith, as well as my will for victory. The possibility that Jerusalem, our courageous stronghold, might fall, did not enter my head. I was sure we would be able to hold our own, or even win outright.

The climax came after we recited the *Amidah* (the 'Standing Prayer', also known as the *Shemonei Esrei*), when one of the rabbis – I think it was Rabbi Hazzan – banged on the table. At this point, at the behest of the senior rabbis present, the *chazzan* (cantor) started to recite the *Hallel* prayer together with the blessings as is the practice on the first night of Pesach. On this all the rabbis were of one mind. Everyone joined in reciting the *Hallel* prayer, praising the great miracle of the re-establishment of *Medinat Yisrael* as a sovereign country after two thousand years of *Galut*. We gave thanks to the Holy One, Blessed be He, for this great miracle which He had performed for *Am Yisrael*, his very own people. For we were confident (in the words of Psalm 94:14) *'that the Lord will never abandon His people, nor will He ever forsake His inheritance.'*

ATTEMPTS TO BREACH THE OLD CITY

We were ordered to save ammunition by holding fire at night. We only had enough to last us for two days of sustained fighting. Late on Friday night, just before dawn, the phone rang. The Arabs had started bombarding the Weingarten position with cans filled with explosives. They had set up a position by the public toilet between the *'Kishla'* barracks and prison and the Old City. They were gradually advancing armed with these explosives. Our own positions responded with fire and hand grenades. We subsequently learned that the Armenians had betrayed us by allowing the Arabs to fire on us from their buildings.

The Arabs also started a 'war of words' against us. 'Chaim, you are a bastard!' 'Shlomo, come and get some bread!' 'You'll all be dead soon!' This is how they now addressed their next-door neighbors with whom they had been on first name terms since childhood. Our exchanges of fire continued throughout the day, becoming more severe in the evening. We succeeded in preventing any further advance by the Arabs, but suffered casualties. We learned from west Jerusalem that immediately after the announcement of the establishment of *Medinat Yisrael*, the Arabs had launched a joint attack, and had taken Gush Etzion. After we asked for more details, we were eventually told that America and Russia had recognized our new State.

Our situation was getting worse. There was a serious shortage of hand grenades, our main weapon in built-up areas. The regional bomb disposal expert from west Jerusalem worked all night laying mines around the key positions on the border between the Jewish and Arab areas.

At the same time, a severe battle was raging in west Jerusalem – we could hear the sound of machine gun fire and explosions. In response to our queries, west Jerusalem informed us that 'the gun fire and explosions are coming from our advancing forces,' which made us very happy indeed. As soon as we communicated this very good news to our positions, their mood improved and singing could be heard from the various bases.

Saturday night, 7th Iyyar 5708 (15th May 1948)
The Battle of Batei Varsha

During the evening, after Shabbat ended, the Arabs tried to bomb our position adjacent to the Varsha complex. One wall fell, and we therefore had to destroy the Arab position in order to prevent the Arabs from storming in through the breach. We waited six hours for the go-ahead from west Jerusalem, until it finally came: "If it is necessary, do it." It was clear that the west Jerusalem leadership still thought that the Arabs would behave reasonably in respect of the Holy Places in the Old City. Our operation was successful, although two of the officers involved were nearly caught under the rubble. In the event, the only serious casualty was the loss of a gun belonging to one of the officers. After this operation the Arabs fell silent and we enjoyed a night of peace and quiet.

Sunday, 7th Iyyar 5708 (16th May 1948)
The Jewish Quarter is shelled

When morning broke we could hear the sound of bugles from the Arab Quarter while Arab flags fluttered in front of our positions. Then the enemy began to shell the Jewish Quarter with incendiary devices which caused fires and panic throughout. We evacuated the residents from the top floors of their homes and transferred them to cellars and basements which caused us a great deal of trouble.

The residents were out of control. They ran amok in the burnt-out streets screaming with fear. We often had to threaten them with our weapons in order to persuade them to go back inside. It was difficult to control the situation. Luckily, we managed to extinguish most of the fires and others simply went out of their own accord.

The shelling, however, continued, and the commander of our own mortar base was hit. I was told to take over from him at the communication center, between the mortar base and headquarters. I therefore handed over my previous communications responsibilities to one of our young women. I should emphasize that the sum total of our own mortar stock came to precisely two 2-inch mortars, plus a small number of shells.

The mortar shelling continued throughout the afternoon, and revealed our helplessness. The residents began to gather *en masse* in the synagogues. Young and old prayed together. Rabbis, wrapped in *tallitot* and wearing *tefillin*, sent up their entreaties to the Almighty, interspersed with the blowing of the *shofar*. Blending in with the echo of battle and the incessant din of shelling, the cry of the *Yishuv* rose to heaven: "May God above spare His poor and needy people; may He have mercy upon us!"

We were hit hard that morning when the Armenians handed over the HaTzlav position to the Arabs. It was therefore not really feasible for us to keep hold of our position by the city wall. The Arabs now controlled access from the Armenian Church to the Zion Gate, as well as the city wall. We therefore retreated to positions nearer to the Jewish Quarter. The Arabs set up their standard in the areas gained by them, to the beating of drums and wild cries of jubilation.

We accepted this blow in silence, while preparing our own 'warm welcome' with which to greet the imminent charge expected from across the new lines. During the afternoon we were assailed from all directions. The situation was grim. Scores of Arabs attacked all our positions simultaneously hurling incendiary devices inside our lines. Their Fiat shells demolished one position after another without respite. Under heavy machine gun cover the enemy launched a three-pronged attack on our defenses: from the city wall, the Armenian Church and the Armenian School.

At Batei Varsha and Porat Yosef, we managed to fend off the Arab assaults. However, in the vicinity of the Armenian Quarter, the enemy managed to breach a number of our buildings while we responded in kind in order to block their passage to the Jewish Quarter.

About one hour after the heavy attack on our positions, we organized a counter attack on Medan Street. We started by occupying a position sporting an Arab flag, and managed to seize a small number of their weapons. Arab fatalities were scattered throughout the vicinity but this did not deter them from continuing their assault on us. We withdrew from several positions in order to prepare an adequate line of defense. Towards the city wall we still held the Hakurah position, which was strategically placed at the entrance to the Jewish Quarter.

The Arabs responded by renewing their assault. They managed to break through our new lines and enter the Jewish Quarter. A dreadful skirmish took place in the streets, during which our men behaved with great heroism. We launched an attack on the 'no-man's land' between our positions and theirs as well as on their front line, which halted their assault for about half an hour.

Meanwhile we had used up our entire stock of shells and ammunition, and our headquarters were beginning to seriously consider surrender. We had suffered a large number of dead and injured. The doctors had their hands full. The small room that we had put aside for the dead was over-flowing with corpses. At that dreadful juncture, we decided to withdraw and take stock. Many of us recited our last '*Shema*' prayer, after which many of us resolved to prepare ourselves for a '*Masada*' type of war, in which we would defend the Jewish Quarter to the bitter end. With this resolve we engaged in a counter assault which drove the Arabs out of the Jewish Quarter.

Once again the Hakurah position and the Sephardi religious schools were back in our hands and we had also regained control of access from the city wall. A telegraph arrived from west Jerusalem: 'Surrender spells utter destruction. Reinforcements on their way from town. Hold your positions.' We accordingly sent word to the positions: "Don't leave, at all costs. No retreat, no despair. Reinforcements are on the way."

The heavy grenade attacks continued throughout. We organized a defense around the Batei Machseh complex, which we had designated as our last stronghold if all else failed. Meanwhile we could hear the deafening roar of *Davidka* mortars. These heralded the attempt from west Jerusalem to break through and weaken the Arabs. We received news that the *Palmach*, the striking force of the Haganah, were coming to our assistance.

The enemy blew up the steps to the 'house with the green shutters' which dominated the Armenian section. However, our own regional demolition expert from west Jerusalem immediately blew up the position itself, to prevent the Arabs from firing from it. Although our men had to retreat from the area, it was now impossible for the Arabs to carry out their operations from the building.

Meanwhile, a building collapsed in the street next to the Weingarten position, and a new strong offensive had begun against us. We managed to fend off all the attacks, and dozens of Arabs were dead. Our shelling of the Armenian Church had caused a great deal of damage. The Arab positions were silenced and put out of action, unable to operate at least until evening. Things were now much easier for our own men at the front line in the Armenian section.

Nightfall arrived, and with it much-needed respite. The exchanges of fire continued but the shelling stopped. Our side experienced a great shortage of commanding officers, now that many of them were injured, some very badly. The number of ordinary soldiers had also decreased significantly. There were simply not enough people to maintain all our positions and counter-attack at the same time. We informed west Jerusalem of the situation and were promised assistance. We did not sleep a wink all night. We could hear the sound of MG-34 machine guns, which were nicknamed "Maglads," firing from west Jerusalem. Our troops over there told us that they were hitting buildings as far away as the Hotel Fast (near the Jaffa Gate), as well as leading an assault on Mount Zion. We expected them to break through to us at any moment.

Monday, 8th Iyyar 5708 (17th May 1948)
The Great Retreat

Dawn broke, but our much-anticipated reinforcements from west Jerusalem had not broken through. We were most despondent. The rising sun revealed the fighting city, the pale faces and the bodies in the streets. We cursed the night that had passed so swiftly, well aware that at sunrise the onslaught would begin all over again and then we would have to hold our positions till evening.

We informed west Jerusalem of our perilous situation and were assured of assistance. We therefore asked west Jerusalem to carry out a parachute drop. We also opened a factory for homemade grenades from empty food cans and similar materials. Our work progressed well, and these "rubbing" grenades saved the day. Their effect on the enemy was all the greater because they made a loud bang on explosion. In fact, these homemade bombs were found to be no less effective than the British Mills grenade, and we produced dozens of them by the hour.

A loudspeaker could be heard close by. Those who knew Arabic provided a translation. The tone of its message changed as it proceeded. "Beloved Jewish friends," it began, "let us extend our hands in mutual goodwill. We will give you a breather until 10:00 to surrender . . . If you don't, we will make mincemeat of you . . . We will take your daughters for ourselves . . . Please be so good as to surrender," signing off amid raucous, evil laughter. Most of our positions greeted this barrage of insults in complete silence, while others exchanged obscenities with the Arab commanders.

Just before 12:00 noon I took my Lewis machine gun and walked down to Porat Yosef. Utter devastation covered the silvery roofs of the Yeshiva, which faced the Temple Mount. Its Dean, Rabbi Hazzan, circulated among our troops. They drew comfort from his gray beard and aristocratic eyes. Most of all his soothing voice encouraged the men to carry on and hold their positions. Meanwhile, the Arabs set up many different kinds of machine guns and artillery on the walls of the Al Aksa Mosque. At the nearby Arab positions gun fire was exchanged for a good hour accompanied by the aiming of incendiary devices. Part of the Turjeman position was blown up.

We stood facing the *Kotel* [its plaza was then only a few metres wide], towering over the embattled Old City in glorious silence. From time to time we glanced in its direction, drawing encouragement. In our midst was a bearded Bratzlaver Hassid who lived in the Old City. He was my very close friend, Rabbi Moshe Burstein [1914–2011]. He would help us move our machine gun and magazines from one place to the next. We warned him of the danger involved in running from one location to another under artillery fire. But he refused to listen. For, how could he resist performing this great *mitzvah* which had landed in his lap?

The hours before noon passed in this manner. Bugles sounded from the Arab Quarter. West Jerusalem had started shelling the Arab Quarter with 3-inch mortars and Davidka rifles. From our vantage point at Turjeman we observed a large concentration of tanks and armored vehicles carrying 2-litre cannons. We also saw Browning machine guns on top of the turrets. From our positions we received news of sightings of red *keffiya* headdresses displaying Arab symbols. We concluded that the Arab Legion had now entered the fray, and duly informed west Jerusalem of this development. At the same time, we continued preparing for the assault that we expected during the afternoon.

Given the circumstances, we tried to keep up our spirits by exchanging tall stories and riddles that made us laugh. Even Headquarters were infected with our positive mood because immediately after the orders were given, we heard a *Gramushka* Yiddish melody being played in the command room. So, although we were all aware of the critical situation we managed to keep up our spirits.

At 14:00, the shelling of our positions began. The Jewish Quarter was shelled with 2- and 3-inch shells and cannons. The bombardment targeted Batei Machseh, Turjeman and Yeshivat Porat Yosef, apparently originating from the Temple Mount and the Arab village of Silwan.

The annals of the battle record that 'the first great retreat' took place at 15:00. The enemy increased its shelling and scores of armed Arab gangs attacked every one of our positions simultaneously. This took us by surprise and caused our rapid retreat but our men performed audacious acts of heroism. For instance, in the midst of the battle they managed to move the residents and especially old people to safer places away from their homes. It was that very special love of Jerusalem which exists between the walls that fortified their spirits and spurred them on.

The great Arab advance came mainly from the Armenian Quarter, but during our forced retreat we managed to inflict heavy losses on the enemy. Weingarten was the last position to be taken after the others were evacuated under cover of fire. Chabad Street saw heavy fighting, during which we took out the Arab machine gun position at the end of the street in order to prevent passage. In the meantime, we established a new line of positions in HaYehudim Street. We installed our Lewis machine gun in the police building to prevent transit between Chabad Street and the steps at HaYehudim Street. We managed to retain Lubinski-Rabinowitz, the Hurva Courtyard, the Police Station, Rabbi Hazzan's house and Hakurah.

It was imperative that we held on to the new line of positions come what may, because that day we had lost almost an entire section of our front line. We could not help experiencing moments of despair. We knew that if we abandoned our new line, the Jewish Quarter would be totally destroyed and lost to us.

Most of the civilian population were now concentrated in the complex of the Yohanan ben Zakkai synagogues. The stench was dreadful. Masses of men, women and children wallowed in mud and filth. Our combatants were not allowed to enter the locality. Their commanders did not want them to experience this dreadful spectacle of heart-rending suffering.

Once again we heard from west Jerusalem that 'reinforcements are breaking through to you from three directions: hold your positions.' This news raised our hopes. As far as we were concerned, reinforcements from even one direction would be a good start . . .

Nightfall was just about to descend once again on our City at war. This was the fifth night of battle. By this stage we were becoming weak at the knees; our eyes would not stay open, and every ounce of strength had been squeezed out of us. We were simply not able to carry on fighting. But somehow – I do not know how we did it – we managed to draw on hidden strengths of which we had been completely unaware. Men who had passed their breaking point were carrying on as if on automatic pilot.

We were losing more and more men. The hospital, itself under constant shelling, was overflowing with the wounded. The room put aside for dead bodies was also full. We were forced to take the drastic measure of moving the dead bodies to the Turjeman position. We laid these bodies on the ground and sometimes had to jump over or shift these bodies in order to be able to fire on the enemy. We were sick to our stomachs as the stench of putrid corpses permeated the entire Jewish Quarter. But somehow we managed to gather ourselves together and continue to fight, because we knew exactly what we were fighting for, and against which enemy.

The situation at Porat Yosef grew worse. I was sent there on behalf of our command, and found our combatants ensconced deep inside the building. They were surrounded by walls riddled with Schwartz machine-gun bullets fired from the Temple Mount.

A deathly fear was etched on the faces of our men. I gave them words of encouragement and we all returned together to our positions. Part of the position on the left had been blown up, leaving it completely exposed on that side. Under cover of fire I crawled into the rubble and managed to remove grenades and magazines which were buried underneath. The Arabs had installed a machine gun and covered the left hand position with fire.

I moved to another room and opened fire at the Arab position 20 metres away. I had to use a Baretta pistol, because the supply of Sten guns and Mausers stored at the position had been damaged during the fighting. The Arab machine gun, a Bren, fell silent. This whole situation summed up our situation in the Old City: a simple pistol versus a Bren machine gun.

The Arabs continued their bombardment from the Temple Mount. But we used Molotov cocktails to set afire the bushy areas around us, stopping the enemy in his tracks. We watched them fleeing for dear life across their positions, as the flames pursued them.

We eventually sat down to eat breakfast (!) at 17:00, but after half an hour the Arabs recommenced their attack. Our Stens and Mausers were unusable. In addition, by this time our ammunition had run out, so we had no choice but to use grenades to defend ourselves.

Many of our comrades sacrificed their lives. A particularly shocking disaster struck a young girl at our own position. A Mills grenade blew up in her hand, killing her on the spot. Two-inch shells and incendiary devices hit our position one after the other as the bombardment started afresh.

We telephoned the reserves for assistance. Luckily we received a Bren machine gun from a British officer (may he be remembered for good) who came over to our side and offered to help us. I handed over command of our Medan St. position to one of my comrades, after I was buried under an avalanche of sacks following an explosion. I was taken for hospital treatment, and two hours later I once again received the command of the position.

By the end of the day we had lost Section B, which was centered around Chabad Street. But Section A was still in our hands. The worst battle was fought around the Nissan Bak Synagogue (better known as Tiferet Yisrael), HaKaraim, Bet El Street, Porat Yosef, Medan Street, Turjeman and HaYehudim Street.

But throughout the night we could still hear firing outside the Jewish Quarter. It appeared that west Jerusalem was trying unsuccessfully to break through to us. In the Jewish Quarter itself we blew up an Arab house adjacent to our positions in Medan Street and Turjeman. We also found it necessary to remove the checkpost separating us from the Arab Quarter. This enabled us to break through to the Arab area and blow up the house from which the Arabs were firing incendiary devices at the Misgav Ladach Hospital, Porat Yosef and Turjeman.

Our operation was successful, but that evening tragedy struck Porat Yosef. The Arabs managed to advance under cover. Very late at night they managed to gain access underneath the left hand position into the Porat Yosef building, and set off an incendiary device. Two of our best combatants were killed and buried under the rubble. We felt compelled to clear the rubble and retrieve the bodies of our comrades who lay buried under the stones. We did this under cover of fire, while facing enemy machine guns. The second part of the night passed in silence and some of our men managed to get some rest. The promised reinforcements failed to arrive.

After the first two days of the campaign, it was obvious that we were at a distinct disadvantage. Chabad Street was by this time no longer fully under our control, and the enemy was also threatening HaYehudim Street. The civilian population was filled with fear. Worst of all, Abdullah el Tell's [1918–73] Arab Legion, commanded by former British policeman 'Brigadier' Norman Lash [1908–60], had joined forces with the enemy and also began to shell us.

This was not a good omen. Small fires broke out here and there all round the Jewish Quarter as a result of the incendiary devices which struck our most sensitive spots. Although water was also now running out, the battle continued. Our combatants clutched at every straw and left no stone unturned as they waited for salvation to arrive. Bloody battles raged every step of the way. We were attacked from all quarters. But the heroic deeds of our defenders is legendary.

Tuesday, 9th Iyyar 5708 (18th May 1948)
I am Wounded

The morning began with heavy artillery shelling and machine gun fire on our position. Before noon the Arabs made do with shelling, and refrained from a full assault. Our grenades liquidated the Arab position near Turjeman and they suffered many casualties.

At 13:00 the enemy began a full assault on our positions. Their method of advancement was to use a large variety of incendiary devices, which blew up one house after the other. This did not put us off, however. We simply moved quickly from one demolished house to another. We continued to fend off the attacks, taking hold of new positions, and setting up observation positions among the debris.

In the afternoon the Jewish Quarter was quiet. We sent the coordinates of all enemy positions to west Jerusalem so that they would know exactly where to bomb. Heavy shelling began from west Jerusalem, which apparently put off the expected enemy assault. But at 16:30 my own position at Medan Street was heavily shelled. I made sure that everyone stayed put, even though the enemy kept firing 2-inch mortar shells at us from a few metres away. During the shelling the Arabs tried to place an explosive device just behind Bet Turjeman. We stopped them by a rapid round of fire, and the explosives blew up in their hands. However, the Arabs retaliated with 3-inch mortars, which hit our position. This was when I was severely wounded and was transferred to Misgav Ladach Hospital.

HOSPITAL "TREATMENT"

From the 'city of slaughter' that was the Holy City, I was moved to 'hell on earth.' This description does not begin to describe the conditions in the hospital here at the front line. It was shelled incessantly. The flag depicting its international medical status was riddled with hundreds of enemy bullets, puncturing it like a sieve. First aid was applied under life-threatening conditions.

For 36 hours I was laid out on a hard floor, without even a mattress, and a sole threadbare blanket as cover. After that ordeal, I was promoted to one day's lie-in on top of a bed in a room for the seriously injured. However, that room also underwent nonstop heavy artillery shelling. I was therefore moved again, this time to a room where about twenty men lay on the ground in an unspeakable stench.

The hospital continued to undergo severe artillery shelling and its top floor was completely demolished. The doctors, nurses, female volunteers, and teachers from the Old City carried out their work with unimaginable devotion. These 'angels' were the only ray of light in the wave of horror that engulfed us. Every step of the way we witnessed one heroic act after the other. Youngsters who had just undergone complicated operations on their left hand, which rendered them almost immobile, would jump out of bed, as if nothing had happened. They would eagerly grab their rifle with their 'good hand', and carry on fighting as 'normal'.

⇛   BREAKTHROUGH AND DESPAIR

We received news from west Jerusalem that 'the breaching unit has left for the Old City: reinforcements will be with you in the evening, come what may.' We no longer believed this, but passwords were, nevertheless, distributed among the combat forces both inside and outside the city walls.

Shortly after midnight, we heard the sounds of the MG34 machine guns in action, as well as the roar of Davidkas. This time the 'breakthrough' was for real and the troops from west Jerusalem broke through Zion Gate and penetrated the Old City. The voice of Benny Marshak [1916–75], the Palmach '*politruk*' [political 'commissar' responsible for education], could be heard on the wireless, congratulating us on this great achievement.

The breaching unit had seized the strategic points along the road inside the city wall, preparing the ground for the *Hish* and Palmach troops armed with rifles and mortars – but not even one machine gun. They did not give us the impression of being genuine fighters. Most of them were aged 30–40, and some even older. This so-called 'force' would certainly not be capable of saving the day.

We waited for the *Hish* troops to arrive and seize the vantage points around the city wall. There was already great rejoicing in the Old City as we were sure that we had been saved from death and destruction. Members of the breaching unit were being hugged and kissed by all and sundry. The hospital staff and patients wept tears of joy. One of the commanders of this unit came into my room, pressed my hand and embraced me. Both of us had tears running down our faces. I was pleasantly surprised to hear from him that they had not suffered many casualties. Meanwhile preparations were being made to evacuate all the casualties and the civilian population from the Old City. We were filled with hope.

However, our joy turned into despondency and despair when we learned that the Palmach would be leaving at dawn. They claimed to be utterly exhausted after four days of fighting, and were simply incapable of carrying on, and would therefore be returning to their base in west Jerusalem. Our hearts were heavy on account of this breaching unit that had been sent in to storm the city walls, but which were now simply retracing their steps.

We asked west Jerusalem to send us *Hish* troops as replacements for the Palmach, but they turned us down. With tears in our eyes, we asked them at least to seize the vantage points around Zion Gate until we managed to evacuate the casualties and the civilian population. No response. We cried out desperately for help. Again, no response. Deep inside we feared that we had been fingered to absorb the dismal failures and the calamity of defeat.

Wednesday, 10th Iyyar 5798 (19th May 1948)
Despondency

Despondency fell on the combatant city. The Palmach were abandoning us and we could only look on as they left. The enemy recommenced their shelling and although other reinforcements arrived, this slight 'injection' was completely inadequate for our needs. I suppose it was just enough to prolong the agony of our death throes for another few days.

Once again we were forced to wait with bated breath for genuine re-inforcements worthy of the name. Zion Gate had been open until almost noon. Finally, in the heat of the day, two young men from the Yemin Moshe area of west Jerusalem appeared, bearing chickens for those under siege. The road had been clearly open the entire morning, but by 13:00 it was no longer possible for the men to return. By this time the Arab Legion had managed to capture all the vantage points.

All day long, the Jewish Quarter had to put up with increased shelling, which grew heavier by the hour: 2-litre and 6-litre mortars were strewn around the area. The dome of the famous Nissan Bak Synagogue was riddled with bullets. And this was just the introduction, for the onslaught intensified still further in the sector comprising Nissan Bak and the Karaim and Malkodet positions. After several hours the Arabs tried to access the synagogue building itself. It was the main vantage point in this area, and acted as a safeguard against infiltration into the areas held by our side. Nevertheless, in spite of the continued Arab onslaught, our men managed to hold this position.

The Arabs now tried a new tack. Until then they had not attempted to shell us at night, which had of course afforded us some respite. But now, as soon as darkness fell, those of us manning Porat Yosef were taken completely unawares by a very strong bout of shelling, unlike any we had experienced previously.

We responded by mobilizing our forces and answering fire with even stronger fire. At that point we had a reasonable supply of machine guns, Sten guns and rifles in our possession. Our view was that we had to curb any night assault from the outset, in case the enemy were deluded into thinking that they could get away with it. Thus, the enemy got more than they bargained for and were forced to retreat. But not before they had managed to blow up our positions and put them out of action. We returned to seize other positions that were higher up and protected the steps leading to Misgav Ladach. After the battle for Porat Yosef, the fighting died down in the Jewish Quarter for the night, except for sporadic firing here and there.

Thursday 11th Iyar 5708 (20th May 1948)
The Battle for the Nissan Bak Synagogue

As dawn broke, the Arabs started to bomb the Jewish Quarter with mortar fire, machine guns and the like, but we held our own. In the afternoon they began a serious attack on the Hakurah position. Our men retreated, and the Jordanian Legion took it over. But because of the position's critical strategic importance for the entire Quarter, it was decided to recapture it at all costs. This we did, and the enemy suffered many casualties. We also profited from a Bren machine gun, a case of bullet cartridges, three Thompson submachine guns, and ID cards.

The Arabs succeeded, briefly, in capturing the Nissan Bak Synagogue, and its beautiful dome was almost destroyed. Under the command of the regional commander, we waged a counter-offensive, and after a difficult, two-hour battle, we retook the synagogue. The area was cleansed of the enemy, who took up new positions.

From the "city" (west Jerusalem) came still more promises of reinforcements and a breakthrough that evening. We didn't believe them. Exchange of fire continued all night long. Our men took turns at their posts, enabling two hours sleep for each fighter. The reinforcements did not arrive.

Friday, 12th Iyyar 5708 (21st May 1948)
The Bombing of the Nissan Bak Synagogue

Our line of defense was decimated as the Arabs penetrated further, shelling and destroying one room after the other. We rushed from room to room, trying to hold on to our positions. By this time we were extremely short of ammunition and informed west Jerusalem, who always gave us the same answer: 'Hold position till evening!' These words were now treated with derision by our remaining men, who would repeat them mockingly.

Just before noon, the immediate vicinity of the Nissan Bak Synagogue

*The destruction
of the Nissan Bak
Synagogue*

was attacked. The Arabs occupied the neighborhood and blew up the synagogue itself with an enormous charge. Shock-waves reverberated throughout the entire Jewish Quarter over and above the din of cannon-fire and shooting.

Despite desperate efforts and diversionary tactics on our part, the Arabs destroyed the beautiful building. This splendid edifice had also been known as *Tiferet Israel*, The Beauty of Israel, in memory of Rabbi Israel Friedman of Ruzhin [1796–1850], the Hasidic Rebbe who had supported Rabbi Nissan Bak [1815–89] in its original construction.

The great dome of the synagogue disappeared, its walls collapsed, and the entire location was rendered entirely unfit for use, whether by us or by the Arabs. The enemy's aim was obvious: to fight an Islamic '*jihad*' which would eradicate any trace of Jews and Judaism from Jerusalem, in fulfilment of their own darkest desires.

We managed to take the positions overlooking the street in which the synagogue had stood, but the Arabs were now advancing through the Karaim position. The situation in the neighborhood was extremely serious. A battle was fought for five hours, during which positions passed from one side to the other. At 15:00, the Arabs retreated across the street and the battle abated somewhat. At 17:00 they took up positions at the Armenian Church ten meters away. We did not dare enter the street, as we were worried about being trapped inside. Instead, we occupied a commanding position over the synagogue from the new Bet El bloc.

Friday night, 13th Iyyar 5708 (21st May 1948)
The Arabs Observe Shabbat

That night we could hear the usual loudspeaker in the Arab area. But this time their message was aimed not at us, but at the Arabs. 'We will not surrender. Soon an Arab State will arise. Do not despair.' For some reason, the Arabs in the Old City were scared of us, so their mood was not as euphoric as might be expected. This was demonstrated by the fact that silence reigned supreme among the Arabs that entire Shabbat.

When Shabbat commenced on Friday night, our *Hish* ground troops attacked Jaffa Gate. We kept tabs on them with bated breath, but their attempted breach failed. The fortifications on Jaffa Gate were too strong for them and they had to withdraw. Within the walls, depression sank in. For this was not the first time that we had been let down. Would the breakthrough ever come? Shabbat passed quietly. Our men hung out together, joking that "the Arabs are observing Shabbat." Toward the end of Shabbat, in the evening, the firing intensified, but Saturday night passed without incident.

Sunday, 14th Iyyar 5708 (23rd May 1948)
The Parachute Drop

At noon the assault intensified in the Bet El neighborhood near the Orenstein position but stopped after an hour. We had run out of ammunition again and were promised a parachute drop by west Jerusalem. In the evening the Arabs attacked the Nissan Bak and Orenstein positions. The Arabs managed to break through and we counter attacked. The Arabs retreated to their positions. We continued exchanging fire, which halted only late in the evening. The long-awaited airplane from west Jerusalem circled around the location, trying to drop ammunition; however, for some reason it did not succeed. We informed west Jerusalem of their failure.

Monday, 15th Iyyar 5708 (24th May 1948)
We Lose All Trust and Faith in West Jerusalem

By this time we had reached the unhappy conclusion that west Jerusalem did not appreciate the gravity of our situation. They were always sending us radio messages of the 'don't panic' variety, but the promised reinforcements never seemed to turn up. It appears that some days earlier we had committed the cardinal sin of telling them that we would be unable to hold our positions for longer than one day, when in fact we did. Maybe west Jerusalem did not quite grasp the miracle that enabled us to hold our positions. It was not normal military prowess that had come to our aid, but the amazing heroism of our few men.

The electricity had been off for two weeks and was now back on again. So we were able to listen to the news on the battles in Ramat Rachel, and in the Old City. This news did not exactly cheer us up. The only glimmer of hope was the announcement that the United Nations had asked for a cease-fire throughout the entire country. The Haganah informed us that the cease-fire would begin at 20.00. During the afternoon, the gun fire decreased, but did not stop completely. Our comrades kept telling themselves that this time the cease-fire was for real. We clutched at straws like men drowning at sea, pinning our hopes on this latest intervention.

West Jerusalem showered 'Zionism' on us. All of them, including the two Chief Rabbis, Rabbi Herzog and Rabbi Uziel, Yitzhak ben Tzvi [later to be Israel's second President: 1952–63] and the District Commander had all been sending us the same message for two weeks now: 'Hold your positions. The whole world has been following our struggle with bated breath. Let us turn around the siege into a brilliant victory'. Day after day, reinforcements were promised us, but they never arrived. 'Hold your positions until evening', they cabled repeatedly, but real aid never materialized. We had lost all trust and faith in west Jerusalem and told them that, with or without their help, our remaining few men would fight to the end.

The heroism of our medical team surpassed all expectations. Our doctors and nurses worked around the clock without taking a break. The injured were tended at the Misgav Ladach Hospital, which was subject to constant shelling despite the flags indicating that the building was being used solely as a medical facility. The savagery of the enemy was there for everyone to see. Nevertheless, emergency surgery was carried out and many lives were saved. The operations were performed by dim flashlight, under extremely difficult and complex conditions. A makeshift 'operating chamber' had been cobbled together in a room on the ground floor. The operations took place under exploding shells from the constant bombardment, which caused the 'operating chamber' to shake throughout the surgery.

Would there be no end to the attacks? Would there be no end to the dead and injured? We began to move the injured men through the devastated streets of the Old City to one of the sturdy stone buildings in the Bet Machse sheltered housing complex. This was known as the 'Holland and Deutschland' Kollel (HOD). It was situated near the city walls at the crossroads to the steps of the *Kotel*.

The noose was tightening around us, with the Arab front line moving ever closer to the hospital. The only hope was to move the entire hospital as quickly as possible to Batei Machse. But that night fighting resumed in the Mount Zion area, thus preventing our planned attempt to transfer the wounded out of the Old City.

Tuesday, 16th Iyyar 5708 (25th May 1948)
Thoughts of Surrender

All through the following day the Arabs kept up their relentless shelling. We managed to hold our positions at the Jewish Defense Building, the Police Station, the Hurva Synagogue and the Bet El bloc. On the south side we also managed to retain the Hakura. A number of recent assaults from armored vehicles had nearly wiped it out. Nevertheless, with only one armored vehicle and a couple of men, we were able to hold our position against a multitude that would not give up. Hundreds of Arabs were killed or wounded, and the rumor spread among the enemy that we had thousands of men between the walls!

Reinforcements were promised for that night. And this time if they did not arrive, we really *did* intend to surrender. The very idea was like a mortal wound to us, but we could not allow the Old City to be totally destroyed. We told west Jerusalem that if they sent ammunition we would be able to hold our position for another day. They sent a plane that parachuted down two large crates of ammunition. However, these fell outside the area held by us, and therefore the drop failed.

We moved the entire Misgav Ladach hospital, including the makeshift operation chamber and first aid room, staff headquarters and radio station to Batei Machse. Skirmishes took place in the area around Porat Yosef, Turjeman and Medan Street. The new hospital building became a front line position. The number of men fit to fight was diminishing. We suffered about 20 casualties every day. In terms of manpower, we could hold out for two more days.

Wednesday, 17th Iyyar 5708 (26th May 1948)
Our Situation Gets Worse

The enemy attacked relentlessly, completely demolishing our front line with a combination of explosives, artillery shelling and 3-inch mortars. In HaYehudim Street, we did manage to hold the iron gate despite the Arab onslaught. However, the enemy advanced by blowing up one house after the other. In the Bet El bloc our situation was particularly grave. Porat Yosef was now in the hands of the Arabs. And our new positions barely prevented the enemy from erupting any moment into Medan Street and Batei Machse. Surrender was becoming more of a real option. Only a few experienced fighters were left.

Given our lack of young men, our positions were by this time manned mainly by members of the Home Guard. They had arrived one week earlier with reinforcements. They did their best, but could not be expected to fight like younger men. We abandoned the Lubinsky position and moved to an observation post at the iron gate. Once again fierce exchanges of fire could be heard throughout the night.

Those of us who were out of action through injury lay unattended in Batei Machse. We followed the course of the battles constantly. No one slept a wink the whole night. The sound of firing from west Jerusalem was like a balm to our wounds. The hours merged into one. The firing continued. The Arabs operated artillery even during their night skirmishes. We could hear the armored vehicles drawing near. Dawn broke. Once again, reinforcements failed to arrive.

Thursday (Lag B-Omer), 18th Iyyar 5708 (27th May 1948)
The Fall of the *Hurva* Synagogue

But we did not surrender. Instead, the civilian population of the Old City increased their pressure on the regional command. Their suffering was unimaginable – beyond words. We decided to try and hold our position for one more day. We spelled out to west Jerusalem that if they did not break through to us that day, 1400 local residents of the Old City would be slaughtered. The Arabs continued their attack. Although our men held on at several positions, staff headquarters were unable to do a thing. All the houses in the Bet El bloc had been demolished.

By now, most of the Old City was under Arab control. And now the Hurva Synagogue was in their hands too. This splendid synagogue which had been such a spiritual inspiration to Jews throughout the world had now been destroyed by the Arabs.

This was the very synagogue in which Rabbi Shmuel Salant [1816–1909] had sat and held 'court', handing out his decisions on all aspects of Jewish law. This synagogue had been the central hub for the entire Ashkenazi community, and now it had all gone up in flames.

We retreated from Bet El, from HaYehudim, and from our position at the Police Station. Instead, we decided to entrench ourselves in the Jewish Defense Building. This building overlooked the complex of the Yohanan Ben Zakkai Synagogues, in which the entire civilian population of the Old City had taken refuge. But the Jewish Defense Building itself was on its last legs, and was about to collapse at any minute. The campaign was over. From west Jerusalem, Benny Marshak sent us the message that 'we will be with you this evening', but when dawn broke the Palmach were nowhere to be seen. We were defeated.

Friday, 19th Iyyar 5708 (28th May 1948)
We Surrender

We now had only 36 men left – 36 versus thousands, who attacked us relentlessly every morning and evening. It was clear that we would not be able to hold position another day. If not for the many hundreds of civilians whose fate hung in the balance, the Jewish Quarter might have become a second *Masada*. But our commanding officers felt unable to assume the awesome responsibility of sacrificing the hundreds of families whose lives were now in mortal peril.

For had we not, but a few days earlier, witnessed before our very eyes the appalling fate of Kfar Etzion and its Kibbutz members, who had been slaughtered with unspeakable savagery? At Kfar Etzion they had chosen to defy death and risk everything for the sake of victory. But in our case, Rabbi Min-HaHar did not hesitate to make a very personal appeal to our men, pleading with them not to follow the *Masada* way. So it now fell to us to take the fateful decision to surrender.

A small group of men, bent double and waving white flags, walked very slowly toward the forces of the Arab Legion, who had acted under order of their Commander in Chief, Abdullah el Tell. Our group was headed by two rabbis of advanced aged, two of the most God-fearing and learned Torah scholars we possessed. These were Rabbi Mintzberg, who represented the Ashkenazi community and Rabbi Hazzan, Dean of Porat Yosef, who represented the Sephardi community. They walked with great difficulty and their hands were trembling, for the burden they bore was heavy indeed. Theirs was an impossible mission: to try and salvage what was left of the shipwreck. Because it was clear to all of us that there was, in fact, nothing left to salvage.

A short time later, one of the rabbis came back and told us that the Arabs were asking for '*Mukhtar*' Weingarten and a member of the Haganah to be present. So, accompanied by these two additions, they crossed back over to the Arab positions. Meanwhile a cease-fire had been declared. Arab Legion soldiers had managed to enter the Yohanan ben Zakkai complex. There they had installed a machine gun facing the residents. There was no way to prevent the surrender. The Arab Legion were courteous and even distributed cigarettes among the civilians. They tried to relieve us of our own weapons, but we refused to comply, stating that until an agreement had been signed, we would not hand over anything. So they desisted.

The surrender agreement was signed at 15.00. These were its terms and conditions: Those of our men who were still fit would be moved to Amman, Jordan. Our civilians and injured would be moved to west Jerusalem. Those who so wished could remain in the Old City.

A short time after the surrender agreement had been signed, Arab Legion officers entered our hospital building, accompanied by some of their men. They were courteous. Arab doctors did the rounds of the *mustashfa*, which was their term for 'hospital.' Our remaining weapons were handed over to the Arabs. Little did they know that we had already given them special 'treatment' to ensure that they would be rendered unfit for use. The other weapons were destroyed.

The terrible catastrophe represented by the Old City falling into the hands of foreigners was now a reality. The heroic war fought by the remnants of our men had come to its end. Hanging in the balance were the lives of many hundreds of civilians, men, women and children, as well as the lives of our thirty remaining men. Ranged against us were many thousands of foes.

We divided ourselves into two convoys: combatants and civilians. The combatant convoy was sent to the *Kishleh* (the local prison building dating from the time of the Ottoman Turks, and used by the British as well). The civilians were led through the Zion Gate. One by one, all those who were allowed to leave went through this gate. It was purely a question of luck. Age was not a factor: you could be taken into custody at 80, or at one year old. This is how the Arabs chose to interpret the agreement.

But, suddenly, a loud din could be heard – whoops of seemingly endless joy. One by one, a huge mass of Bratzlaver Hasidim emerged into the Jerusalem night air, dancing in circles and singing their hearts out. The voice of their Rebbe, Rabbi Dovid Shechter [1900–74] rang out: 'Fellow Jews, do not despair.'

The injured were placed under the guard of the Arab Legion in the makeshift hospital housed in one of the Batei Machse buildings of the Kollel of Holland and Deutschland (HOD) complex. These buildings were what remained of an enclave which had been staunchly defended by our men up until the very last moment before our surrender.

Several doctors and nurses volunteered to stay behind with us. Our comrades who were to be taken prisoner came to say goodbye. Before every attack of the past two weeks, the Arab Legion officers had appealed to us via loudspeaker to put down our arms and surrender with honor. These officers now kept their word. After the surrender was signed, they vigilantly protected us from the unrestrained fury of the armed Arab mob.

THE NIGHTMARE NIGHT, AND RESCUE

The sun set. Most of the residents had already begun their exodus through the Zion Gate toward the new city in west Jerusalem, while we were left on our own, with a much reduced team of doctors and nurses, waiting for salvation to come.

The nightmare began. The Arab mob, numbering thousands, burst into the Jewish Quarter, lusting for blood and bent on destruction. They sounded their victory bugles, accompanied by blood-curdling ululations.

Then they set to work completing the destruction of the area. First, they pillaged and ransacked the abandoned houses, helping themselves to anything of value. After this, the demolition work began in earnest. The houses were smashed to smithereens. Everything was set on fire. The flames spread. Entire streets were now aflame. We could hear the roar of the Arab mob, running amok and breaking through to the center of the abandoned Jewish Quarter, where they continued to ransack and burn.

Lying in bed, our ears were attuned to the sound of the mob shouting for joy; it was total depression for us. The smell of burning from the houses ablaze rose around us. We could tell that the rabble was storming Batei Machseh, and then we heard the din of firing close by; clashes broke out between the Arab Legion and their own Arab mobs.

Under our window, the wild cries of Arab men, women and children could be heard from the steps of the *Kotel*, seeking out Jews. One of the Arab Legion officers told them that this was a hospital, but the blood-thirsty mob was not placated. Even though the fire that had started in Batei Machse was now approaching the hospital, the Arab rabble tried to fight the Arab Legion soldiers and break through into our small enclave. It seemed that *"evil was set against us"* (see Esther 7:7).

While all this was going on I was lying with my comrades in our make-shift 'hospital' room as my leg was in plaster. There we were, silently watching out for any sign of salvation, hoping against hope, our lips moving in prayer, when suddenly several shots rang out, producing a metallic sound as they ricocheted against the heavy iron gate separating our building from the steps to the *Kotel*.

Then we heard the grating sound of iron doors opening. People were coming to try to rescue us and get us to the other side. Into the poorly-lit ward came a small contingent of Armenians and Arabs, headed by an officer of the Arab Legion, and accompanied by Masha, daughter of our "mayor" R. Mordechai Avraham Weingarten. A minute later, our doctors came in and announced: "Whoever can walk should go immediately to the Armenian School." Most of the injured, using their last ounce of strength, got up and fled.

But around 30 of us had leg wounds and could not walk. We were placed on stretchers and the transfer began. This rescue work vied with the progress of the fire surrounding the hospital. The rescue contingent feverishly began to transfer the injured from the devastated Jewish Quarter to a place of (relative) safety: the courtyard and apartments of the northern Armenian Monastery, inside the Old City, near Zion Gate.

SHA'ALI SERUFAH BAESH ('INQUIRE, O THOU WHO ART BURNED BY FIRE . . .')

The doctor in charge of us, Dr. Abraham Laufer, broke part of my cast, so that I could walk. Leaning on one of the nurses, I started to move. The pain was unbearable, but I had no choice. Then, officers from the Arab Legion brought over some members of the Arab mob and forced them to carry us on stretchers. These 'stretcher-bearers' had to tread carefully to avoid the flames.

On my right, the Old City was ablaze in the brilliant red of an utter holocaust. All her synagogues and *batei midrash,* including their valuable libraries, were caught in the inferno. On the left was Zion Gate, and next to it, angry Arab mobs menacing the civilians – remnants of the Old Yishuv waiting for the sun to come up so that they could begin their exodus to west Jerusalem. Practically naked, we limped with measured footsteps on our crippled legs. As we made our exodus, we witnessed before us the dreadful spectacle of the Old City being engulfed in the flames of annihilation.

Every single ancient synagogue of the Old City had been consumed by fire. Ancient centers of Torah learning had lost all their priceless libraries. The uncontrolled rage of a barbaric and savage enemy had destroyed everything. For as it says in the Book of Lamentations 2:1–2, '*the foe had no mercy in the day of his anger.*' The sight before our eyes was spectacularly terrifying, supernaturally breathtaking. For, that day, Jerusalem had been wiped out by tongues of fire, the first flames of the '*flowering of the light of our redemption.*'

As we dragged our feet up the hill between the Temple Mount and Mount Zion, the relics of a much older holocaust came into view and stirred our memories. For how could we ever forget the Destruction of the Second Temple which had taken place one thousand eight hundred years earlier in 70 CE? Within the flames engulfing the Jewish Quarter of the Old City of Jerusalem was something of the frightfulness of that much older conflagration – that earlier holocaust.

But, this time, there was one big difference. Deep within our hearts, we knew beyond the shadow of a doubt, with the intuitive knowledge that transcends all understanding, that this was not the end. The cycle that began with the flames of ancient Jerusalem had come full circle within the flames of the present-day Old City. For out of the conflagration and our deep physical and spiritual pain, we were also experiencing the birth of *Medinat Yisrael,* together with the rebirth of our people.

With my failing strength, I managed to whisper to one of my injured comrades: '*The day the Temple was destroyed, the Messiah was born*'

(Jerusalem Talmud Tractate *Berachot* 2:4). This was the sincere belief of all of us who were now prisoners of war, as we went that day into captivity and exile, to an unknown fate. We all sensed that despite the dreadful disaster that had befallen us, we were now in fact witnessing the birth of a new era, the very redemption of Israel. I promised myself at that moment that if the Israeli army were to take back Jerusalem, I would try with all my heart, with all my soul, and with all my might, to be one of the first to re-enter her gates.

My stretcher brought up the rear of the exiting convoy. I therefore felt that I was assuredly the last person to be forsaking the Old City. I looked around and could see that all was quiet – eerily quiet. The only sound came from the Armenian women gaping at us from their windows, performing a slow hand clap, a hand clap meant for outcasts.

The nurse who had been assigned to me noticed that the Arab mob were carrying one of my injured comrades through the fire in HaYehudim Street, instead of making for the Armenian School and Monastery by Zion Gate. She therefore made the tough decision to abandon me in order to save my colleague's life. I tried as best I could to continue on foot, leaning on two members of the Arab mob. We reached the vicinity of a *matzah* factory that had been destroyed by the Davidka shelling.

And this is where the Arabs 'got tired' and flung me to the ground. I found out the hard way what it felt like when uneven and jagged stones came into contact with my leg wrapped in plaster. Later we found out that quite a few of our men had been thrown to the ground by members of the Arab mob who were supposed to be looking after them.

Nevertheless, the desperate but heroic mission to rescue us eventually proved successful. We owe a deep debt of gratitude to the dedication and self-sacrifice of everyone involved in the rescue operation. It was one of those rare moments that is forever etched on the hearts of all of us who endured that dreadful period of our history.

I arrived at the Armenian School still just about in one piece and immediately fell asleep on the ground for about an hour guarded by the Arab Legion soldiers. When they found out that I had been wounded in Medan Street, they summoned everyone who had taken part in that battle. Despite the state I was in I had to endure a barrage of questions for a good hour.

A Greek member of the Military Red Crescent, whose name was Alex (may his name be remembered for good), devoted himself entirely to helping the injured. Eventually a stretcher arrived and we were then carried up to the Armenian Monastery. There, in very harsh, near-starvation conditions, we lay down side by side. Men died next to us, because there was no way to help them.

Friday night, 20th Iyyar 5708 (28th May 1948)
"From Out of the Turmoil"

We waited in the Armenian School for the Red Cross Committee to arrive. At 9:00 that Friday night, a delegation of "angels of destruction" appeared: Arab doctors, led by Dr. Canaan and Dr. Dajani, accompanied by a Red Cross official who simply obeyed their orders. The Arab doctors did exactly what they wanted with us, sending the seriously injured to Amman and releasing the lightly wounded to west Jerusalem – and there was nothing anyone could do about it. Even our own doctors were repeatedly duped by the Arab doctors.

Fifty-one of us had been earmarked for a prisoner of war camp, and were temporarily incarcerated in an isolation cell in solitary confinement. And then there were the constant interrogations and checkups as to whether some wounded man had escaped, or whether a person with broken legs hadn't by any chance managed to jump out of the fifth floor window!

That first Friday night of imprisonment in the walled Armenian Monastery of the Old City, we waited. And while we waited to find out what fate had in store for us, we intoned together the beautiful Kabbalistic prayer service which welcomes Shabbat into our midst: *Lecha Dodi* (*Come, my Love and meet the Bride*). And the message of one of its lines has not left us to this day: '*Royal Mikdash, Royal City, rise up and leave the midst of the turmoil.*' We prayed that our people should be strong, and that we would prove worthy of a great miracle, the miracle of our physical and spiritual redemption.

Then, after the conclusion of the prayer service, we burst into song once again. This time we sang patriotic songs and songs of war that had originally been sung in Yiddish by the Partisans in the Warsaw Ghetto: '*Wherever a spurt of our blood has fallen to the ground, there our might and our courage will sprout again.*'

From our window we could see the Old City and its burnt-out buildings which were now in ruins. We had fought for these buildings – buildings which now contained the remains of our comrades who had not been fortunate enough even to be taken captive. Our eyes were filled with tears as our voices soared from the upper windows of the ancient walled building. From these same windows we gazed at the site of the Temple, which at that very moment was wreathed in the pure gold of a Jerusalem sunset, and bathed in the calm that comes after the storm.

Our Arab Legion guards stood dumbfounded, feasting their eyes on the sight of injured, broken prisoners singing away as if they did not have a care in the world. If you did not understand the Jewish psyche, you would simply not be able to comprehend such a phenomenon. The Arab Legion Commander ordered us to stop singing, because it was getting on the nerves of his men.

Shabbat, 20th *Iyyar* 5708 (29th May 1948)
"And They Draw Near Unto the Gates of Death"
(Psalm 107:18)

Dawn rose, and most of the injured were transferred toward Lions' Gate. Once again a small number who were unable to walk remained behind. It was thus my misfortune to end up as part of the final convoy of four stretchers which left the Armenian School. Our escort included a corporal and six soldiers of the Arab Legion. They carried us through the Armenian Quarter where women glanced through their windows, acknowledging us in silent empathy.

We headed in the direction of the *Kishla* prison. Near the *Kishla*, three Arabs in civilian clothes approached my stretcher, exclaiming: 'Look, he is a member of the Stern Gang. Let's beat him up' This was done deliberately to get the Arab rabble worked up. I was immediately lowered to the ground. People shouted and a mob gathered. I was saved by the corporal who cried out, also in Arabic: 'Stop! He's in my care! It's against the law! Let them get on with it!'

We continued down to the market in HaShalshelet Street, filled with armed Arab gangs. We then turned into the Street of the Cheese Vendors. The Arabs carrying me shouted out to the Arabs nearby, who sprang on us cursing and spitting. The abuse did not stop, and they began to threaten us with their weapons, making as if to slice us in half with knives. Finally, one of the Arabs took out his Italian carbine rifle, cocked and aimed it at me. When I saw his finger press the trigger, I closed my eyes. At that precise moment, however, the corporal shoved him in the ribs and ordered the stretcher-bearers to quickly move on!

To the accompaniment of the hecklers screaming '*Deir Yassin*' down the road at us, we eventually reached the ambulance waiting for us in another street. My stretcher bearers attempted to deposit me in a nearby building that bore the flags of the Arab mobs. Their actions set off another round of arguments, this time between the officer of the Arab Legion and an Arab 'mobster'. The latter was armed with two bullet belts and appeared to belong to one of the Arab gangs. Finally, we four injured men were carried into the ambulance.

Once we were all inside, the ambulance drove for a short time through the city. Eventually we caught up with the main contingent of prisoners of war, who were waiting under heavy guard in buses and trucks by the Lions' Gate. We continued to drive in the direction of the Mount of Olives. There we halted in an Arab village near the headquarters of Abdullah Bak. Permission was granted to a group of Arab women to approach the ambulance and shout '*Deir Yassin*' at us.

We then set off once again on the road to Jericho accompanied by a convoy of outriders who amused themselves by pretending to fire live ammunition at us. This shooting spectacle was most enthusiastically received by every Arab community whom we encountered on the way to Rabat-Amon, Jordan. In several places we were, in addition, also pelted with stones.

The wife and two of the daughters of the Jewish *Mukhtar* traveled with us in the ambulance. Dr. Egon Riess [1917–89] shared a taxi with the *Mukhtar* and his two older daughters, one of whom was a nurse. Two female members of the medical service and two hospital orderlies made up the remainder of the convoy.

On reaching Jericho, the convoy drove into the police courtyard, where we were transferred from Israeli jurisdiction to Jordanian jurisdiction – more specifically from the *Eretz Yisraeli* ambulance to the Jordanian Red Crescent ambulance. We then drove over the Allenby Bridge. *En route* to Amman we lost track of the other buses and trucks. We were stopped a great deal – each time one of the four of us felt ill. It should be emphasized that our escort treated us very well. Especially worthy of mention is Dr. Rekes of the Arab Legion, who was in charge of the ambulance. By contrast, we were later told by our friends in the other convoys that their treatment had not been so good.

The total journey lasted five hours. When we finally reached the Arab Legion prisoner of war camp in Amman, we were escorted into the rooms used by the royal military band. This was a well-accoutered military band, similar in every way to any typical British military band of the period. To start with the Arab Legion treated us very well indeed. Even the food was not bad. However, this positive attitude lasted only for three days. We later learned that their approach was typical of Muslim etiquette. After our 'honeymoon' period, the situation went downhill on a daily basis.

– End of diary entries –

⇒   MEANWHILE, IN THE HOUSE OF THE RAV THE *NAZIR*

During the battle for Old Jerusalem, and at the time of her surrender, the *Nazir's* family were not aware of their son's fate. This is how Shear Yashuv's mother, Rabbanit Sarah Cohen, described their feelings at the time:

"The first women to return to west Jerusalem were girls who had volunteered as nurses in the Old City. On the Friday they returned to west Jerusalem and they contacted me to say that my son had been wounded. They added that he had been taken prisoner with all the other residents of the Old City. This was even though he was seriously injured. According to the terms of the surrender, he should have been taken to a hospital on the Israeli side in west Jerusalem, in order to convalesce properly. They also told me that in spite of his injuries, he continued to sing and to smile. And this is why the Arabs did not believe that he was seriously injured."

On hearing this news, the *Nazir* and Rabbi Goren immediately appealed to Chief Rabbi Herzog, begging him to do his utmost to obtain the freedom of their injured POW. At this time Shear Yashuv was still being held in the Armenian Monastery. As soon as Chief Rabbi Herzog heard this news, he went straight away – on the Sabbath – to see the Israeli-Jordanian liaison committee. He tried to impress upon them that as Shear Yashuv was severely injured, it was only right and proper that he should be one of those who were set free. But to no avail.

Many years later Rabbi Cohen recalled with a smile: "All these efforts on my behalf were well meaning but, far from helping, they seem to have actually harmed my prospects. For now the Jordanians got it into their heads that they had captured a most valuable prisoner of war, and for this very reason dug their heels in all the more, determined to hold on to me."

When his family finally realized that their son was going to be a prisoner of war in Amman, they were extremely concerned about his fate, as were the staff and students at Merkaz HaRav Yeshiva.

However, on Tuesday, 23rd Iyyar 5708 [1st June 1948], the *Nazir* learned in a most miraculous fashion that his son was still alive. This is how the *Nazir* records the experience in his diary: "For a week I was worried sick, but when I went up to the *duchan* to recite the Priestly Blessing, I heard in my heart the words (of the Patriarch Jacob, Genesis 45:28): '*It is enough; Joseph my son is still alive*.' This was confirmation for me that my own son, Eliyahu **Yosef** Shear Yashuv, was still alive."

In Captivity

"Lights flash – sparkle in the night silence.
Guards cock their weapons.
Sitting here in fetters, seeking salvation.
Far from home and in tears, I ponder revenge.

"On the road, traffic twists and turns
The Bedouin song ululates
Like echoes of a battle in rage
The sounds climb up our mountain

"A prayer arises to save us.
In silence it shouts for joy. It pours out its heart in
anguish.
My God! Save the fighters of the hills
From the battle that storms!

"Besmirched by the ashes of surrender
And servitude under the alien jackboot,
The captive wallows and recoils at each touch
Of the enemy who stands over him.

"In the still of the night, he crouches
And weaves dreams as hope
Slowly dawns – the fighter who has lost
Lies conquered and captive.

"Blessed be the light
that heralds Redemption!
Blessed be the light
that grows brighter,
proclaiming
Kingdom!"

Shear Yashuv Cohen
Tishrei 5708 [September-October 1948]
Umm el-Jimal POW Camp

In Captivity

Thursday, 25th *Iyyar* 5708 (3rd June 1948)
In the Hospital

"Most of our comrades had already been transferred to the POW camp in Transjordan. The camp was situated at Umm el-Jimal, near Mafraq, on the crossroads to Syria and Iraq. There were seventeen of us injured combatants who needed medical attention. But we had been abandoned in the large room used by the royal military guard band of the Arab Legion. This room was situated on the bottom floor of a two-story edifice. The top floor had been allotted to the Weingarten family, who had also been taken prisoner with us. In addition, there were Dr. Riess and two young female members of our medical services. The major in charge of the POW camp also resided on the second floor. This major used to visit us, always delivering 'positive' news, such as: 'Arab victories along the entire front.' We knew that negotiations were being held regarding our fate and that our side hoped to rescue us from the POW camp and bring us back home to freedom in our newly liberated homeland.

"On the whole, we were well treated by the guards. On the second day of captivity, approximately ten injured men were moved to a hospital in an affluent neighborhood. We were all photographed, after which some of us stayed there for treatment. The Arab doctor in this hospital looked like a butcher to us: there was always an unpleasant smirk on his face. Through the grapevine we learned that this doctor had served as district commandant in the army of Fawzi al-Qawukji [1890–1977] during the 1936–39 Arab massacres. Obviously this piece of information greatly affected how we felt about being in his care.

OPERATION WITHOUT ANESTHETICS OR DISINFECTANTS

"I was still unable to use my injured leg. This had now become a matter of urgency. According to the hospital, an infection had developed and I was told they needed to amputate. The doctor gave me a piece of paper to sign my consent to the amputation. I was on the verge of signing, when the Armenian nurse standing behind him made a negative motion with her hand, which implied: 'Do not consent.' For two seconds I agonized, and then decided to take her advice. A few days later she was proven right. Over the course of the next week, I dosed myself with huge amounts of sulpha (a penicillin substitute), consumed a great many onions, and in the end, my infection was cured!

"Dr. Wintzberg, who was destined to become a senior medical officer in the Israel Defense Forces (IDF), was also with us. He was a member of Kibbutz Gezer, and before that had served as a doctor in the Soviet Red Army. He was therefore very experienced in the treatment of injured soldiers. He immediately saw that I urgently needed an operation to remove the grenade fragments from my knee.

"The POW camp to which we had been transferred did not possess any anesthetics, but Dr. Wintzberg decided to go ahead with the operation, nevertheless. The pain was excruciating, like a razor going through your body and at one point I fainted from the sheer agony. The orderly poured ether over the site of the operation the whole time. After the operation the doctor stitched up the knee. He also sprinkled powder on the stitches to stop the oozing. Even though I never again regained full use of my leg, with God's help, I was now able to walk."

Shabbat *Parshat BeHukkotai* (Leviticus 26:3 ff)
27th *Iyyar* 5708 (Saturday 5th June 1948)

A SHABBAT OF HOLINESS

A week went by and then Friday night, Sabbath eve, arrived. As dusk seeped into the cavernous prison hall, the melancholy of exile also filled the chambers of our hearts. It was time to welcome in the Shabbat – and then, the door opened and who should enter, but Old Jerusalem's Jewish "mayor," Avraham Mordechai Weingarten. He was escorted by a guard officer of the Arab Legion, who deposited his charge and left. Mr. Weingarten told us that he had been permitted to take part in the Kabbalat Shabbat prayer service. Though a barrier had arisen between him and us, because of his attempts to negotiate a "deal" with the Arab gangs in the Old City, we overcame our feelings and treated him with respect. We even asked him to lead the prayers.

"Mr. Weingarten accepted our offer with alacrity. He set about praying with every fiber of his being, following the ancient Kabbalistic traditions of Jerusalem. When he reached the prayer, *Lecha Dodi* ('*Come my Love and meet the Bride*') by the Kabbalist, Rabbi Shlomo Alkabetz [c. 1500–80], his quivering voice seemed to encompass the very pain and anguish of eternity. And when he came to the lines: '*Royal Mikdash, Royal City, rise up and leave the midst of the turmoil*', he wept unashamedly like a baby, the tears flowing down his cheeks.

"We were shaken to the core. Even though we did not agree with his politics, at that seminal moment there was not one of us who did not experience in his bones the archetypal, primordial and atavistic love of Jerusalem which burst from his ruptured heart. We now realized that everything he did was infused with love, the love of Jerusalem between the walls. It was this love which epitomized the entire life of Abraham Mordechai Weingarten, the Jerusalemite *par excellence*.

LIFE IN THE POW CAMP UNDER THE ARAB LEGION

"It was on the festival of Shavuot when we read the biblical book of *Ruth*, part of which takes place in the land of Moab, that we were transferred to the Arab Legion POW Camp in Umm-el-Jimal in Transjordan, the biblical land of Moab. Here we joined our combatant comrades, as well as civilians from the Old City who had also been taken prisoner, and the remnants of Kibbutz Gush Etzion who had been captured some time earlier.

"I cannot say that we were not frightened, since we did not know what awaited us. However, it should be emphasized that the Jordanians treated us fairly, according to regulations laid down by the Geneva Convention. Every day, two officers were assigned to count the prisoners, and the lights went out at 21:00 every night.

"Gradually, ten synagogues sprung up in the POW camp, all housing Torah Scrolls which had been transported from the Old City and Gush Etzion. After a short time these ten synagogues were no longer large enough to hold the many *minyanim* [groups of at least ten men] of worshippers, so services were also held outside, under the dome of heaven.

"The Arab soldiers did not get involved in the running of the camp, so it was up to us to assume the mantle of internal leadership. Our leadership consisted of representatives from the Naharayim Electrical Company, the Kibbutzim Masuot Yitzhak and Ein Tzurim, civilians from the Old City, and representatives of the various field corps. The camp spokesman representing us to the Arab authorities was Yosef Blustein, who had directed the Naharayim plant; he spoke fluent Arabic. The leaders made sure that an *Eretz Yisrael*-type of atmosphere reigned in the camp.

This is what Yosef Blustein recalls:

"Rabbi Shear Yashuv arrived at the POW camp looking like a scarecrow. He was carried in on a stretcher and his knee was completely smashed. After the thirty day mourning period for the fall of the Old City, the youngsters who had fought for Jerusalem came to see me and demanded that I organize a memorial service for those who had fallen in defense of the Old City. I therefore approached the Jordanian camp commandant and asked for permission to arrange a memorial service. The Jordanians agreed to my request, but were on constant alert, surrounding the camp with soldiers armed with machine guns. The person chosen to recite the eulogy for the fallen of the Old City was Rabbi Shear Yashuv Cohen.

"His eulogy was incredibly moving. Here was a Jerusalemite actually reciting the funeral oration in memory of those who had fallen in defense of the Old City. After the eulogy we all burst into the *HaTikvah*, and in my view if you had not been present to experience our singing you have never experienced singing at all."

Rabbi Cohen takes up the story of life in the POW camp:

"There were two kitchens in the camp: one was kosher and one was not kosher. The Arab Legion provided us with 'starvation rations.' Our breakfast consisted of a mug of tea without sugar, half a packet of biscuits and two grams of cheese. Our lunch consisted of a watery type of weak soup, a small portion of non-kosher meat (to last us for two days) and another packet of biscuits. Dinner consisted of tea and half a packet of biscuits.

"When our government learned of these meager provisions,

they used to send us additional food on a daily basis. This consisted of sugar, rice, apples, tomatoes, onions, *pittot*, eggs or kosher meat (to last for two days) and, several times a week, canned fish. We also received cigarettes – all this, care of the government and our parents who had organized for this purpose. Clothes came in shipments donated from all over Israel. These donations raised our spirits and provided a real psychological boost to us POWs. Any money that we had brought with us was deposited in a communal kitty to be used for the joint needs of everyone. Whenever anything was needed, we would purchase it from the Jordanians, using the communal kitty.

"The camp was a 'tent camp' in which ten men slept on the ground in a small tent. Red Cross visits were not a regular occurrence, but, rare as they were, they always lifted our spirits. All mail communication was done through the Red Cross. Short letters written in English arrived on a fortnightly or monthly basis, though a large proportion of these were lost on the way. During the first few months of my incarceration in the POW camp I was hospitalized in a hospital tent."

A TYPICAL DAY IN THE LIFE OF A PATIENT

This is what Rabbi Cohen recorded in his diary as his impressions and experiences as a patient in the Jordanian POW camp:

"Morning. The sun rises to the east, which is bathed in a sea of red. On the road, a tail-back of slow armored cars from Iraq wend their way lethargically toward Jerusalem. To the north, the Hermon glistens in all its Lebanese whiteness. The guard at the 'Bren' post stretches and opens his eyes, rubbing them well, as if to rid them of all vestiges of sleep. This is how the tent camp awakes from its deep slumber. The morning chill rouses the sleeping men, forcing them to snuggle up even tighter in their beds. And so you close your eyes and meditate, conjuring up dreams and indulging in all kinds of wishful thinking.

"Suddenly, your reverie is rudely interrupted by raucous sounds that you cannot quite make out, the crashing noise of water in cans, immediately followed by the voice of the military policeman: 'Who has stolen the water? Whoever he is will be court-martialed!' No one answers. The sounds of cans clashing are now joined by the patter of feet and cries of: 'Hurry up and get a move-on.' This is the *meshuga* group that has only one thing on their minds: religiously performing their morning exercises and keeping fit at all costs.

"The shrill sound of a whistle cuts the air like a knife. Breakfast! The camp inmates rush to the queue. Like paupers at the gate they ogle the man doling out the tea. Each inmate hopes that the 'tea man' will grant him a generous dollop. But he reserves his favors for those whom he likes, while those who have for some reason or other displeased him end up with next to nothing.

"We patients are spared all this. For us they wheel in a white tray, which seems to have last been washed somewhere or other in Gush Etzion, piled high with a selection of 'dainties fit for a king' – worm-eaten biscuits and rotten eggs! These arrive courtesy of the renowned Abu-Akeb.

"With the 'meat' still stuck between our teeth, we cannot attend morning prayers, but instead have to put up with the doctors on their morning rounds. They move from bed to bed, muttering under their breath: 'And how are we today?' answering for us: 'OK.' Woe betide you if you dare to complain about your aches and pains. Because then they would pester you at night as well. They would massage your injury with their hands, rubbing it well. At that moment, you would start seeing stars in pain. Far better to remain silent.

"All you really want is a bit of peace and quiet but that is when the whistle blows once again: Roll Call! Abu-Akeb visits the tent, inquiring after our health, smiling like a benevolent parent. He delivers his morning speech, yells that we should "Please wake up!", and the roll call follows.

"Once the roll call is over the visitations begin. There is no doubt at all that the children of Israel are the most obliging of people. They turn your tent into a café, your bed into a gaming table, and your ears into a receptacle for all sorts of noise and gobbledygook. After all, you're 'important', for you're in a hospital . . . And then comes a dust storm, turning your eyes red with tears. You would like to close the tent windows, but you can't.

"At long last, the whistle blows again, this time for lunch. Trembling excitement in the camp! More wild cries: 'Row 8, kosher! Row 9, not kosher!' Armed with their mess tins, the guests in your tent gird their loins and rush to the line.

In the hospital tent, quiet at last, and in Umm el-Jimal, joy and gladness. From 13:00–16:00 is siesta time. The Lord has provided a cool, refreshing wind as the sun sets in the west. Those who are steady on their feet go out for a walk. Others sit in groups, and some conduct discussions on different subjects. Marxists and religious kibbutzniks shout at each other, gesticulating with their hands. They would love to argue the whole night, but suddenly comes the curfew whistle, sending them back to their tents.

"A typical night in the camp pans out as follows: the paraffin lamps are placed on pillars which look to us like gallows. Flickers of light enter our dark tents. The injured men lie on their beds, snuggling up under their blankets. The time for 'tall stories' is about to begin. Lying in our beds, we recount our experiences.

"We owe a special debt of gratitude to our comrade from the Old City of Jerusalem who plays a *'Gramuschka'* melody for us, heralding sad and melancholy songs. These sounds flow into each other, reminding us of home, birthplace and youth movement. Our eyes slowly close, while our ears are filled with sounds of chit-chat from nearby tents. These sounds mingle with the voice of the guard, as he stands by the barbed-wire fence, singing a wild desert song. Very slowly sleep takes over and submerges you in a world of make-believe, where everything is good – as in a dream."

THE CAMP CHAPLAIN

Between them, the Jewish POWs possessed a wide range of knowledge and learning. Our camp included engineers from the Naharayim Electric Company, rabbis from the Old City, and *kibbutzniks*. In order to keep the inmates from hanging about aimlessly, idling away their time, the rabbis and *kibbutzniks* organized study groups on every conceivable subject. The subject matter of these groups ranged from religious topics, with classes on Bible and Rambam, to lessons in math and foreign languages.

Rabbi Cohen played a pivotal role in organizing the classes on religious subjects. One of the POW inmates was a Chabad Hasid, Rabbi Ya'akov Cohen. He recalls: 'I became very attached to Rabbi Shear Yashuv Cohen, who arranged Torah classes for us. If you immersed yourself in Torah study life in the camp became far more bearable than if you just wandered around with time on your hands, your frustrations mounting by the minute.'

According to Yosef Blustein:

"When the residents of the Old City arrived at the POW camp, they had not washed for weeks due to a lack of water, and were covered with lice. There was a very great danger that the whole camp would become infested. The camp doctors told us that all the people from the Old City had to cut off their hair immediately, otherwise the entire POW camp would become infected.

"The problem was that the haredi men from the Old City refused to shave off their beards. We asked Shear Yashuv Cohen to intervene. He called them into his 'infirmary' tent and managed to convince them, with halakhic-legal arguments, that, given the severity of the situation, it was necessary for them to shave off their beards."

And this is how Shear Yashuv became a sort of unofficial chaplain to the inmates of the POW camp. In fact the Jordanians were so impressed that they gave him the title of *"Hacham."* This is the normal Sephardi title given to a "wise man and spiritual leader," the Ashkenazi equivalent of "Rabbi." Whenever they were in his presence, they would bow their heads as a mark of respect.

When a religious festival occurred, he would give a public talk relevant to the day. When appropriate, he would also give a eulogy to commemorate those fallen in battle. He knew English well enough to assist people who turned to him whenever they needed a written request for help from the Red Cross or Arab Legion. In addition, he became one of the editors of the POW newspaper, *"HaTayil"* (*"The Barbed Wire"*).

One day, a Jordanian officer came into Shear Yashuv's tent, saluted and said: "The Israeli Defense Force has appointed you as army chaplain to the camp." He later learned that his brother-in-law, Rabbi Goren, in conjunction with the Military Chief of Staff, had drafted him into the IDF, and appointed him *in absentia* as army chaplain to enable him to represent the POWs to the Jordanian authorities on religious matters. The day of his "draft" had been backdated to Feb. 1, 1948. This is the earliest record for the drafting of any IDF soldier.

Rabbi Cohen regarded the time when he was a POW army chaplain as a prelude to his later role as Chief Rabbi of Haifa. The diversity within the camp prepared him very well for his later role. Among the different types of prisoners were fighters for the Jewish Quarter of the Old City, some of whom were haredim with the typical Old Yishuv mentality. A second group consisted of left-wing kibbutzniks from Revadim, a socialist-Zionist pioneering kibbutz of HaShomer HaTza'ir in Gush Etzion. And there were also professors from the Naharayim Power Company. Rabbi Shear Yashuv served as a chaplain to all these groups. It is not surprising that one of his main tasks was to settle disputes among the members of these disparate groups.

Later, Rabbi Cohen himself declared that his election to the position of Chief Rabbi of Haifa was directly related to that very POW camp of 1948.

This is because Yosef Blustein, the POW representative to the Jordanian authorities, got to know Rabbi Cohen very well from their time together in the camp.

Many years later, Blustein became a leading light in the Haifa Labor Party. Thus, when the need arose to choose a new Chief Rabbi for the city, he turned to his dear friend of those bygone days and asked him to throw his hat into the ring. "And so this is how, after a lengthy process, *'from the strong came the sweet'* (Judges 14:14) – eventually! For, if I had not been taken prisoner, I would not have ended up as Chief Rabbi of Haifa."

ROSH HASHANA IN ARAB LEGION CAPTIVITY

The days sped by and in no time at all it was Rosh HaShanah. The following is Rabbi Cohen's description of the Yamim Nora'im (the ten "Days of Awe" between Rosh HaShanah and Yom Kippur) and the Festival of Sukkot, as experienced in the POW camp:

"By now we no longer harbored any illusions that the lull in the fighting would lead to our release from this place any time soon. The month of Elul was approaching fast, with the *Yamim Norai'im* just around the corner. From the beginning of *Elul*, we began to sound the *shofars* which had secretly been smuggled into us. A sense of homesickness hung forlornly in the air and would not go away. On the eve of the festival we longed for our homes and the atmosphere of Jerusalem, and this longing accompanied us wherever we went.

"This all changed at the beginning of the week before Rosh HaShana, however. From across the lines we received a gift from the new Yishuv of *Medinat Yisrael*. For, suddenly, on the other side of the road, in the glow of the glistening sun, appeared the grey and white colors of a Red Cross truck. Stuck into the grille at the front of its hood, the Red Cross flag fluttered in the sand storm, columns of dust rising up from the tracks left by its wheels. And, behind this truck, as if from nowhere, there suddenly emerged a convoy of heavier trucks, laden with a gigantic cargo.

"These trucks bore the insignia and serial numbers of the Israel Defense Force – the IDF. Our excitement knew no bounds. But, at the sight of the IDF insignia, our eyes filled with tears, while the eyes of the Arab Legionnaires were seething in fury. They held their weapons aloft, as they feasted their eyes on this mountainous abundance of goodies, piled up high in large IDF crates.

"We stacked our parcels on top of each other in a corner of

the POW camp, under the beady eye of the notorious camp sergeant, Abu-Akeb. He stood, hands on pot belly, his scheming eyes
not missing a trick as he supervised the whole operation. Our
spokesman Yosef Blustein had already apparently mesmerized the
sergeant with a word in his ear about the significant share he could
expect – ten percent of the total!

"The inspection was soon over, and our combatants quickly dis-
persed to their tents to dig into their parcels. Some stood around
their beds, thirsting for the news from Israel that had been written
down on bits of paper inserted in between the wrappings. Others
perused the newspapers in which the gifts had been wrapped,
a good way of smuggling in news. Most important for us were
the small scraps of paper bearing the Israeli flag and other Israeli
insignia, which were passed around in awe and reverence. The
heightened atmosphere of the tent camp was broken by the guards
blowing their whistles. We settled down on the ground in threes,
which is how we normally assembled for the regular roll call.

"A sudden silence prevailed. The order of the day issued by our
own camp leadership was read aloud: *'As the year 5708 comes to
its end and we enter 5709, a wire surrounds us. But this is not the
barbed wire [of the Nazi camps]. We are rather prisoners of war,
the very first POWs in Israel's history. May the coming year herald
victory and redemption.'* The POWs were proud to be interned in
a POW camp as combatants who were sure to be released one
day, and not as inmates of concentration camps bound for Nazi
destruction.

"These words filled our hearts like dew from heaven. They
were food for our body and balm for our soul. So we would, after
all, manage to get out of here. From the midst of the lion's den
we would arise and re-enter the gates of Zion. We would indeed
return to our families, who were looking forward to seeing us step
through the front door once again.

"We felt immense gratitude as we prayed for freedom and victory. At that moment the entire camp was uplifted. We were filled
to overflowing with a profound sense of brotherly love. For we
knew that we would never again be alone. In times of trouble, each
one of us would be there for his brother, whether as a friend in
need, or as a comrade in battle. We hugged each other and shook
hands, as we wished each other well for the year 5709: *L'Shana
Tova Tikatevu – L'Shana HaBa'ah B'Yerushalayim ('May you be
written and inscribed for a Good Year – Next Year in Jerusalem').*

"The festive food that had been prepared in advance was spread out in every corner of the tents. There was even sparkling raisin wine which had been prepared by the few survivors of Gush Etzion. Thanks to the vineyards of the Gush they were well versed in the art and science of wine-making. The wine had been poured into medicine bottles that had been saved. The white *pitta* bread was wrapped in canvas.

"Meanwhile, I had already gone over the order of the *shofar* blasts with the man chosen to blow the *shofar* the following day. He was a member of Kibbutz Ein Tzurim and had grown up in the *Bnei Akiva* youth movement. The *gabbaim* (sextons), also survivors of the Gush Etzion massacre, finished preparing the tents for the festival service.

"The camp was composed of three *minyanim*. The first *minyan* comprised the survivors of the Gush, who were joined by all those who had been active combatants. The second *minyan* consisted of the various Hasidic 'sects' from the Old City of Jerusalem – Bratzlaver and Karliner Hasidim, together with Perushim. And the third *minyan* was composed of Sephardim, including those from Kurdistan, who followed their own particular Sephardi tradition. We emptied two of the tents in the field hospital for this purpose, and then all was ready for the service.

An atmosphere of sanctity hovered in the air. The injured men took their seats – jerrycans – and wrapped themselves in *tallitot* that been sent over across the lines by the IDF Religious Department. The large crates of sugar that had arrived from home were used to cobble together a Holy Ark. This was covered with a *parochet* curtain, hand-made by the POWs themselves. In the center of the 'hall' we set up the *bimah,* on which the Torah reader, the shofar blower and the shofar supervisor (the *makri*) would stand. The Torah scrolls salvaged from the flames of Gush Etzion and the Old City were also placed there.

"The tent was packed full to the point of bursting, as more and more POWs formed themselves into groups and entered the tent together. The first to arrive were members of the Moriah Battalion, both 'troops' and 'reinforcements.' Then came those from Jerusalem who had guarded the City Walls. Next were the nine sole survivors of the '*Masada*' of Kfar Etzion, their hearts still aflame from the pain of the massacre. They were followed by members of the squadron that had served at the different positions in the larger area of Gush Etzion. These men had survived the de-struction wrought at the German Monastery and other positions, as well as in the hills. Etched on their hearts were the memories of comrades, great fighters and great human beings, who had fallen, justifiably proud and defiant in the face of the contemptible foe.

Also present were members of Kibbutzim Masuot Yitzhak and Ein Tzurim, fulfilling the image of a generation of Torah renewed with working-the-land. There were men who had settled Hebron and its hills, building bridges between the city of God and the city of the Patriarchs. They all carried with them the memory of families destroyed and comrades cut off in their prime. Their one desire was to rebuild and avenge their memories.

"The final group to enter the tent included the survivors of the Palmach platoon, which had fallen in defense of Kfar Etzion. The remnants of the Shomer HaTza'ir Kibbutz Revadim came in together. They had especially covered their heads in honor of this solemn occasion, and their deep set eyes brimmed with *Yiddishkeit*. For the light of *teshuva* [religious return and repentance] was shining on them.

"Our makeshift synagogue was packed full of inmates gathered together on the *Yom HaDin* ('Day of Judgment'), standing in supplication before the Almighty Creator. We all turned to face the reddening sun in the west which was about to set in the direction of Jerusalem [which lies to the west of the Kingdom of Transjordan]. We directed our hearts toward the Holy City and towards the *Kotel*, held captive in the hands of the enemy.

The *chazan* (prayer leader) began the service: *'Bless the Lord Who is blessed.'* Like the crashing of waves in a tempest-tossed sea, the sounds of our congregation at prayer rose and fell, cutting through the barbed-wire fences, heard even by the Arab soldiers who surrounded the camp in their guard huts.

"*'Blessed is the Lord Who is blessed forever and ever.'* The officer in charge was called Abu Ali. He came out of his sumptuous tent, carefully surveyed the congregation at prayer, muttered something under his breath, and returned to the quiet of his elegant abode. The *chazan* weighed every word carefully. The congregation prayed for Israel's victory, for Zion's freedom, for Gush Etzion to be rebuilt, for Jerusalem to be completely restored, and for the *Kotel* to be set free from captivity.

"After the evening service, we gathered in the 'synagogue' tent for comradely chit-chat and the festive meal. The words flowed freely and entered our hearts. We spoke about what that day meant to us. For we knew that this was the moment that our fate would each be individually inscribed by God for the upcoming year. We reaffirmed our respect for the honor of Israel, and held ourselves seven-fold responsible for her. And above all, as we waited for the Almighty to pronounce judgment over us the very next day, we reiterated our deep trust and faith in Him.

"Slowly, almost hesitantly, we finally opened our mouths and burst into a deep and meditative rendition of Lamentations 3:22, which lifted us out of our silence: '*The Lord's kindness never ends: His mercies endure forever*'.

"We followed this with the words from the *Mussaf* (Additional Morning Service) on Rosh HaShanah: '*Blessed is the man who never forgets Thee, and the son of man who draws his strength through Thee*'. And we ended with Psalm 84:5: '*Blessed is the man whose strength is in Thee*'.

"At dawn we rose for our usual morning roll call. As we sat in threes on the bare ground, our mustachioed commandant checked that we were all present. 'Have a good day', he added, menacingly, while counting each head with his stick. His paunch had increased by leaps and bounds during our sojourn as his guests. There was no doubt at all that he for one would definitely be praying fervently for our stay to be extended as long as possible.

"Once again, we assembled for prayer, our own voices intermingling with the sounds of the Sephardi *minyan*. When the time came for the blowing of the *shofar*, the entire congregation was overcome with awe. We wrapped ourselves in our *tallitot* and I was privileged to be invited up to the Ark to call out the sounds of the *shofar*. Before the *shofar* was blown, I addressed the congregation as follows:

"'Go and learn what distinguishes us from the nations of the world. For how do they celebrate New Year's Eve, the night which marks the start of a new year for their own '*minyan*'? They bring in their new year by engaging in wild, licentious behavior, and indulging in debauchery and riotous conduct. Is there no end to their drunken revels? Contrast this type of behavior with what do we do when our holy day, the *Yom HaDin*, arrives. We Jews immediately assemble in synagogues and study houses. We wrap ourselves in holiness and purity. We engage in soul-searching and bring the previous year to a close by recounting its blessings and curses.

"Then we recited the following Psalms: '*I cried out to the Lord because I was in a very dark place. The Lord answered me by showing me the bigger picture*' (Psalm 118:5). '*Guarantee Thy servant's wellbeing and do not let the godless oppress me*'. O, how we savored the significance of these words from *Psalm* 119:122.

'*God is king over the whole earth . . . God reigns over the nations*' (Psalm 47: 8–9). Then came our own special plea: '*Please uncover the glory of Thy kingdom upon us as speedily as possible. Restore us to our liberated borders, as jubilant prisoners of Zion now free once more. Lord of the Universe, bring us once more into Thy house.*' We concluded our POW Rosh HaShanah service for the year 5709 by reciting: '*Blessed are those who dwell in Thy house, ever singing Thy praises – Selah*' (Psalm 84:5).

⇒ YOM KIPPUR (THE DAY OF ATONEMENT) IN POW CAMP

"Ten days went by, and then the great day, *Yom Kippur*, was upon us. The camp doctor visited me in my tent and asked me whether it was necessary under POW conditions for the sick men to fast, and we came to an agreement. The weather was dreadful. All day long an icy gale raged over the steppes of Umm el-Jimal. The face of heaven alternated between white and brown. Heavy clouds of sand rose in the air and invaded the length and breadth of our camp, assailing us from all sides. Somewhere or other, tents were being swept away in the vortex of the sand and blown across the barbed wire fence. The latter was surrounded by guards, just in case the overcast weather would tempt us to take evil advantage of the poor visibility.

"As if by some miracle, just before the *Kol Nidre* prayer, the winds settled down, and the visibility cleared. We assembled once again in our 'synagogue' tents. We knew that this was the awesome moment when God would be deciding and inscribing our individual fate for the year. The profound significance of it all welled up inside of us. The *chazan* adorned himself in a white surplice, known as a '*kittel,*' wrapping his *tallit* around him. The choir had been specially trained for this occasion and encircled the *chazan*, waiting for the service to start. Silence reigned. The entire camp was assembled both inside and outside the tents of prayer. The *chazan* began intoning the '*Kol Nidre.*' The sun set into the ruby red sky. Somewhere to the west, *minyanim* in a free Israel were also intoning the '*Kol Nidre.*' We may have been in *Galut*, but our hearts were in the reddening west, where, just at that moment, the ash-colored mountains of Moab gently morphed into scarlet.

"The choir began to sing, accompanying the *chazan* in his traditional *niggun*. Suddenly, a gust of wind blew out the light of the gas lamp. We were plunged into darkness and could not make out the words anymore. The voice of the *chazan* grew stronger, together with our memories. The survivors of Kfar Etzion stood in a corner, trying to stem their tears that were floating to heaven. From the next tent we could hear the Bratzlaver and Karliner Hasidim interspersing their fervent prayers with *Kotel niggunim*. The Sephardim were also intoning their own unique *niggun*. The entire camp was at prayer.

"When we returned to our tents later that evening we started studying Talmud Tractate *Yoma* from the one and only *Shas* that had been salvaged from the Old City and her numerous Yeshivot. Suddenly we were interrupted once again by the Red Cross representative, this time bringing us letters from home. The next day was spent entirely in prayer. The vast majority of POWs fasted until the evening. When it was time for the final evening '*Neilah*' prayer, our fervor reached its peak.

"And when the *Baal Tekiah* blew the shofar, we burst out in unrestrained enthusiasm: *LeShanah HaBa'ah BiY'rushalayim HaB'nuyiah* ('*Next Year in Jerusalem, in Jerusalem rebuilt*)'. Our elation knew no bounds, as we began a spirited dance that swept us off our feet and virtually blew us away.

"That evening, back in our tents, we opened the letters that had arrived on *Kol Nidre* night, the previous evening. For on that 'Holy and Terrible Day', Jerusalem had sent us her warm and whole-hearted greetings. Meanwhile, we could hear the wheels of Arab Legion convoys wending their way from the Iraq desert road toward Jerusalem. Throughout the camp, however, the dancing was at its height: Next year in rebuilt Jerusalem!

THE SUKKOT HOLIDAY IN CAPTIVITY

"The Festival of Sukkot was approaching, the Tishrei festival *par excellence*. But we were extremely worried about how to observe the traditional *Sukkot* customs according to Jewish law, which many of us held very dear. For the essence of Sukkot is to build a *Sukkah* and obtain the *Arba Minim* (see Leviticus 23:4: the '*Four Species*,' consisting of a citrus fruit – *etrog*, palm branches, three myrtle branches, and two willow branches). But, how were we to find these four species in the heart of the desert, not to mention constructing a *Sukkah*?

"But then we had a brainstorm. A specially selected group of our young men used to work regularly in the grounds of the British camp commandant, about seven kilometers away from Umm el-Jimal. In the grounds of his house stood a number of eucalyptus trees. His wife allowed them to lop off a few branches from one of the trees. As if by magic these 'few branches' grew and grew, so that eventually there were enough to fill an entire truck. In the evening our young men returned to camp, together with their great pile, which provided enough *s'chach* to cover all the *sukkahs* in the camp. Thus was solved the problem of ample *s'chach*.

"My friend and colleague, Rabbi Shlomo Min-HaHar, was older than me and already a rabbi and recognized religious authority. Together with other colleagues who were well versed in Jewish law, we formed ourselves into a makeshift *Bet Din* [religious court or judicial panel], in order to rule on whether individual *Sukkahs* in the camp were '*kosher*' or not.

"What we did was to inspect each *Sukkah* in turn, dealing with relevant queries. It was a camp rule that after 'lights out' it was forbidden to leave the tent, on pain of being shot by the numerous sentries positioned around the camp. Therefore, the Arab officers did not allow us to move at nightfall from our tents in order to sleep in our *Sukkahs* [something considered by many to be obligatory in Jewish law], even if we then returned to our tents in the morning, ready for roll call.

"There was, however, one particularly devout young man from Kibbutz Masuot Yitzhak in Gush Etzion. He insisted on observing the *mitzvah* of spending the night in the *Sukkah*. How did he manage to do this? Next to the tent, he dug a hole exactly 10 'handbreadths' deep. Then he took some branches and covered his home-made *Sukkah* with *s'chach*. Every night, he would roll into the *Sukkah* from his tent and sleep in it, thus observing the *mitzvah* of 'sleeping in the *Sukkah*.'

"Incidentally, this was the first time in my life that I had come across a *Sukkah* that was precisely 10 handbreadths, no more or less. He was not able to make his *Sukkah* any wider, because the Arab soldiers did not let him dig a bigger hole. They were afraid that we might 'secrete' the hammers, hoes and spades provided by them for the job. They were concerned that we might use these garden tools to dig an escape tunnel, following in the footsteps of some of our fellow POWs in Latrun, Kenya and Eritrea! For this reason, they were suspicious of any kind of digging and placed difficulties even in the path of his tiny *Sukkah*! But this is the way the young man managed to observe the *mitzvah* of *Sukkot* to his satisfaction.

"The other POWs came across what looked like an iron fence that had been lying about, and hung blankets on it. Although these blankets did not fully cover the side of the *Sukkah*, we calculated that the distance from the bottom of this iron fence to the ground would not be more than the distance permitted according to Jewish law. This was the biggest *Sukkah* in the camp. It was made out of blankets and could hold dozens of POWs at one sitting alone. The engineers from the Naharayim Electric Company rigged up an electric cable inside the *Sukkah*, and hung lights on it. With colored paper we decorated the lights so that they resembled colored lanterns. Our *Sukkah* was now truly resplendent, adorned with all sorts of fruits that we had obtained, as well as these lanterns and paper chains.

"Now it was the turn of the '*Arba Minim*'. How did we manage to observe that *mitzvah*? The banks of the River Jordan are famous as a source of first class *lulavim* (palm branches). So we asked the Arab commandant if he would mind driving to the River Jordan and bring us back some *lulavim*. He agreed to do this for us, and this is how we obtained our *lulavim*. *Aravot* (willow branches) we managed to find in the vicinity of the camp. We gave the Arab soldiers money to buy the *hadasim* (myrtle branches) for us in the local markets. And *etrogim* (yellow, lemon-shaped citrus fruit) we received care of the army chaplaincy that was already up and running in Israel – and the joy was great.

"It was an incomparably beautiful sight to witness the venerable residents of the Old City standing inside the POW camp, *lulavim* in their hands, binding together the *Arba Minim*, so that every single inmate would be able to recite the customary *bracha* (blessing) over them. Whether they were engineers from Naharayim, kibbutzniks from Revadim, or ultra-Orthodox combatants from the Old City, each and every one of them stood in line inside the synagogue, waiting patiently to perform the *mitzvah* of reciting the blessing over the *Arba Minim*, according to their own particular tradition and custom. And then they followed this *bracha* with a second *bracha* – the '*Shehecheyanu*' in which we thank the Almighty for enabling us to reach this season.

"This was only the second time in our history that the *bnei Israel* (children of Israel) observed Sukkot in the desert. And, inside the maze upon maze of barbed wire, observed by the Arab guards who surrounded us, we Jews then performed yet another of the holiday commandments by marching in *hakafot* circles, wrapped in our *tallitot*, holding our *lulavim* and *etrogim* aloft. And even as we rejoiced in this custom, we wished we could be reunited once more with our families and loved ones.

SIMCHAT BET HASHOEVA ('THE WATER DRAWING' FESTIVAL) IN THE CAMP

"Meanwhile, Jews in synagogues in our new-old State of Israel were continuing to observe *Chol HaMoed* (the Intermediate Days of *Sukkot*) by celebrating the *Simchat Bet HaShoeva* ('*Water Drawing*' Festival). This day commemorates the 'Water Libation' Ceremony which took place when the Temple was still standing. In our camp synagogue, after the evening service on *Chol HaMoed*, venerable elderly Jews began humming to themselves, while their feet started dancing.

"Yehiel Vultz [my childhood violin teacher] took out the violin which he had brought with him from the Old City, tensed his bow, and allowed his hands to do the rest. It occurred to us that at this very moment people would also be dancing in synagogues in Jerusalem.

"However, whoever did not experience *our* own special POW *Simchat Bet HaShoeva* has never really experienced a *simcha* in their lives! And whoever did not witness the Arab *Debka* (a popular Middle Eastern dance) performed by these elderly gentlemen from the Old City, and by members of Kibbutzim Ein Tzurim and Revadim, survivors of Kfar Etzion, and Old City combatants has never experienced a true dance in all their born days!

"One of the youngsters from the Bratzlav Yeshiva in the Old City, a great expert in the '*Debka*', stood in the center of the *Sukkah* and sang the following words: '*He placed me in the desert. My heart was parched, and they cried out to each other: Holy, Holy, Holy*' (Isaiah 6:3). He sang this to a typical Middle Eastern Arab *niggun*, and quick as a flash, the Arab soldiers started to join in, celebrating together with us, stamping their feet, clapping their hands, and having a thoroughly good time.

"In short, the '*Hora*' that we danced around the *Sukkah* embraced hundreds of camp inmates. They were old. They were young. They were Kabbalists. They were aged Sephardim. They were aged Ashkenazim. They were young with black, curly forelocks. They were young, in short sleeves and undershirts. And they all danced together as one. And all of them were friends. And all of them were joyful.

"And what exactly was this joyful *simcha*? It was the *Simchat Bet HaShoeva*. And where did it take place? In the midst of the desert. And when did it take place? When we were imprisoned in a POW camp, after the fall of the Old City.

"And at the very heart of this *simcha*, in the midst of our rejoicing, we secretly hoped and yearned to return to Jerusalem so that in the future we could celebrate Sukkot there.

"It was time for lights-out. Everyone returned to his tent, humming a happy tune, in the hope that next Shabbat we would be in Jerusalem; next *Shabbat*, mind you, and not next year!"

"WHEN THE LORD ACCOMPANIED THE CAPTIVITY OF ZION" (PSALMS 126:1)

"The POW camp in Umm el-Jimal sends greetings to the *Yishuv* and to *Medinat Yisrael*. With the Lord's help, twenty three of us, former combatants and residents of the Old City and Gush Etzion have returned from the POW camp in Transjordan to *Medinat Yisrael* – from darkness to light. We are with you today, but our hearts are still over there with the hundreds of our comrades who were not so lucky. We are all praying for that great day when our comrades will also be redeemed and returned to their homeland."

The above is the beginning of the speech Rabbi Cohen delivered three days after his return from captivity, at the welcoming party organized by the "Committee for Soldiers" at the WIZO Club in Tel Aviv. The speech was quoted in the media.

Because he had been injured, Rabbi Cohen was among those fortunate enough to be included in the first group that returned to Israel from Jordanian captivity on 28th Marcheshvan, 5709 (30th November 1948). (Within three months all the others had returned as well.) At that time he was not yet aware of the efforts that had been going on behind the scenes to secure his release.

Not until many years later did he find out the details of this fascinating story from Moshe Dayan (1915–81) and from the ambassador, Moshe Sasson (1925–2006). Moshe Sasson's father, government minister, Eliyahu Sasson (1902–78), travelled to Jordan together with Moshe Dayan, in order to carry out a secret mission on behalf of the Prime Minister, David Ben Gurion. They were to meet with King Abdullah and negotiate an exchange of prisoners. As Moshe Sasson later explained, "The Bedouin have a custom that if a supplicant places his hand on the belt of his potential benefactor, his wish must be granted. Dayan said that he grasped the king's belt and promised that Israel would pay all expenses incurred regarding the POWs, and asked for their release." The King agreed, and set in motion the process to free the POWs.

The group that had been released was brought back via the crossing between Ramle and Ramallah, near Latrun. This crossing constituted the border between Jordanian territory and the territory held by the Haganah and *Medinat Yisrael*. From there the POWs were driven to Ramat Gan, near Tel Aviv.

Rabbanit Sarah Cohen relates: "I went to Ramat Gan to see my son. Our first meeting was extremely tragic: I barely recognized him. He was so thin, whereas previously he had been broad-shouldered. I only just managed to hold back my tears. He calmed me down, saying: 'Mother, I am fine, and everything is fine, except that I have a slight limp.'" And, indeed, when Rabbi Cohen returned to Israel it was confirmed that he had a permanent disability on account of his severe leg injury.

RAV TZVI YEHUDA

From Ramat Gan the POWs were taken to '*Bet Aharonson*' in the northern town of Zikhron Ya'akov. This later became the NILI Museum, but at that time was used as a convalescent home for the Military. The Intelligence Services wanted to debrief the POWs in a secluded environment, before they came into contact with other people. The following morning Rabbi Cohen was in for a thrilling surprise.

> "The next morning, as I was removing my *tefillin* after morning prayers, who should I see from the window but my rabbi and teacher, Rabbi Tzvi Yehuda, who was slowly making his way up the mountain. Later I found out that he had taken the first bus from Jerusalem and set off very early in the morning all the way to Zikhron Ya'akov in order to welcome me home. I ran out of the building and headed straight for him. He hugged and kissed me. He cried over me like a child, the tears pouring down his cheeks. After this outburst of emotion, he calmed down, put his hand in his coat pocket and took out a small pamphlet, entitled '*L'Mitzvat HaAretz*' ('*Regarding our Obligation toward Eretz Yisrael*').
>
> "This was the very same pamphlet which contained his article on the drafting of Yeshiva students. I had asked him to write the article and had promised to get it printed. Now, at long last, he wanted to give it to me, as I had not yet seen it. "On the inside

cover of the pamphlet, Rabbi Tzvi Yehuda had written an inscription as follows:

For my dear beloved friend whom I love and cherish, the initiator, advisor and the force behind this booklet. This pamphlet has been carefully set aside since the day it appeared, awaiting the return of the Lord's redeemed ones to Jerusalem . . . From your kindred soul and admirer of your great father, Tzvi Yehuda.

His mother, Rabbanit Sarah Cohen, continues:

"After that Shear Yashuv returned to Jerusalem, to a house full of people. The parents and relatives of our POWs had come to receive regards from their boys who were still incarcerated, and to hear how they were doing.

"Everyone was concerned with the fate of their own son, so that Shear Yashuv did not have time to eat or drink, only to reply to questions about their loved ones. He reassured everyone that everything was OK and that very soon more and more POWs would be exchanged. And, in fact, this is exactly what happened!"

CHAPTER EIGHT

Back Home

On his release from the POW camp in Jordan, Rabbi Cohen traveled to the United States for a series of medical treatments on his leg. These were not completely successful, with the result that he still needed to have his leg examined by a medical specialist from time to time. On this first of many trips to the United States, he traveled as a member of the earliest delegation of war heroes, for the United Jewish Appeal and IDF Chaplaincy. One of his tasks on the trip was to collect holy books for the IDF synagogues in Israel.

Mila Brenner (1921–99) went to sea at an early age, was promoted, and eventually helped create the fledgling Israeli Navy. He fought as a ship's commander during the 1948 War of Liberation and remained in the Israeli Navy until 1954. Later he became a businessman. He traveled as a member of this first delegation to the United States with Rabbi Cohen. He relates the following story:

> "Our trip to the United States took place a few days before Pesach. On the plane, I noticed a cardboard box under Rabbi Cohen's seat. I asked him to show me what he had inside. The rabbi opened the box, revealing a packet of *matzot* and hard-boiled eggs. 'What's this?' I asked. 'My food for America.' 'But we are traveling to a kosher place.' 'It may be kosher over there, but this is *more* kosher,' he replied.
>
> "These words had an enormous effect on me. And this is how I responded: 'Rabbi Shear Yashuv Cohen, I am happy to have found a teacher in you. Please teach me what prayer is all about, and something on Torah.' So we sat on the plane and studied together for many hours."

During the trip, Rabbi Cohen managed to collect a large number of holy books for the IDF synagogues. In addition, he embarked on a lecture tour, visiting several American Jewish communities which succeeded beyond his wildest dreams and marked the first of many future public appearances.

On his return to Israel, Rabbi Cohen continued to serve in the regular army, and specifically in the IDF chaplaincy, which his brother-in-law, Rabbi Goren, had just established. Rabbi Yitzhak Meir, who later became the mayor of Bnei Brak, described the process.

> "As soon as Rabbi Cohen returned from the POW camp and met with the General Staff for the first time, we insisted that he should be appointed IDF chaplain, even though he was not yet married. At the start of his career as chaplain, he served in the 8th Battalion, under the command of Major General Moshe Tzadok [1913–64]. Rabbi Cohen's very presence evoked respect, and General Tzadok always listened to him with deference, recognizing him as a person who should be taken seriously.
>
> "Rabbi Cohen never fought with his commanders, or with anyone else. He rather talked to every individual in a way that touched that person to the core. He spoke to everyone, of whatever rank, in the appropriate manner, and this was the source of his strength. He behaved the same way later under Lt.-Gen. Chaim Laskov (1919–82) upon becoming Chief Rabbi of the Israeli Air Force."

One year after the end of the War of Liberation, Rabbi Cohen and Rabbi Goren participated in negotiations with the Jordanians regarding the return to Israel of the corpses of the fallen Gush Etzion heroes.

One of Rabbi Cohen's roles as IDF chaplain was to visit the POW camp at Atlit (near Haifa) and compare the conditions there with the conditions of the Israeli POWs in Mafraq, Jordan, where he himself had been interred. He subsequently prepared a report for the IDF, entitled: *"POW Camp – Atlit."* From this report one can gauge the difference between conditions for the Israeli POWs in Jordan and the Arab POWs in Israel:

> "The camp itself is well ordered and purposeful, with good housing and ample supplies. When you enter the camp, you can see how busy the POWs are, and the work which they themselves undertake in order to control and improve their conditions. What really hits you is that the POWS are allowed to circulate freely among the soldiers who are there to guard them. They are even

A visit to the United Nations: Rav Shear Yashuv, in army uniform at right, next to David HaCohen, a leading Haifa politician. Sitting are Moshe Sharett and Abba Eban.

permitted to approach the commandant's quarters, almost unsupervised. When I asked the camp commandant about relations between the POWs and the soldiers, he explained that there were two battalions on site, a guard battalion and a battalion of soldiers, who were in daily contact with the POWs. This idea of separating the two functions is most original and certainly adds to the 'feel good factor.' However, it seems to me that all steps should be taken to prevent the POWs from circulating among our soldiers – for the safety of the POWs and soldiers alike. This is what we learned under the Arab Legion and in my opinion, the Arabs were right on this point.

"There is almost too much food for the POWs, far in excess of the amounts we received as POWs in Jordan. In Atlit there are kitchens and larders in every bloc. The kitchens are completely autonomous, which was certainly not the case in Mafraq. Here, in Atlit, the equipment and appliances are up-to-date and in good working order. Cooking is done using diesel oil so that the inmates do not suffer from smoke inhalation as we did from the wood-fire stoves used in Mafraq. Moreover, here they have four or five large pots, rather than a single huge pot (boiler) as we had in Mafraq. In the course of inspecting the conditions at Atlit I came to the conclusion that there was perhaps even too much food provided

*Visiting wounded soldiers in Tel HaShomer. Rabbi Cohen, at right, with Chief Rabbis
Uziel and Herzog. Second from left is Rabbi Goren.
(from the collection of photographer Abraham Arthur Rosman)*

for the POWs, because we found bread left over in the larders,
thrown away and discarded without being used, as well as sacks
of discarded grits . . . . To conclude, housing and nutrition are of
a far higher standard in Atlit than they were in the POW camp
in Jordan."

⇥ SEMIKHA (ORDINATION) AND THE CLOSE BOND WITH CHIEF RABBI HERZOG

During his military service Rabbi Cohen decided to complete his
rabbinic studies for *semikha* which he had begun before the War of
Liberation. After studying intensively at the Merkaz HaRav Yeshiva,
he was ordained as a rabbi by some of the foremost rabbis of the time.
These included Rabbi Eliyahu Mordechai HaLevi Valkowsky, Rabbi
Ya'akov Chai Zerihan, the then Sephardi Chief Rabbi of Tiberias, and
Rabbi Eliyahu Ra'm (1872–1959), the leading *shochet* of Jerusalem. Rabbi
Cohen was ordained by them all with flying colors! However, the most
emotional *hekhsher* of all, he received from the then Ashkenazi Chief
Rabbi of Israel, Rabbi Isaac Herzog. As Rabbi Cohen recalled:

"Although there was a close bond between our two families, he was strictly impartial during the examinations. I had to return to him three times, and he kept plying me with more and more questions and legal conundrums until, at long last, his mind was put at rest and he consented to give me *semikha*.

"After writing out the certificate and handing it to me, as I got up to leave, he said: 'Wait a minute; let's go downstairs and drink a *l'chaim* in celebration.' As his wife, Rabbanit Herzog, prepared the toast and we walked downstairs, he suddenly hugged me and burst out crying. With tears running down his cheeks, he told me that 'it is all because of you that I once broke Shabbat.'

"He went on to say that when the Old City had fallen and I had been on my way to the POW camp in Jordan, he 'broke' Shabbat in order to try to rescue me from what was feared to be the mortal danger of being imprisoned in the POW camp. He therefore phoned the Director of the Red Cross on Shabbat and asked him to intervene on my behalf. And now, at this moment, he was overcome with emotion, because he had closed the circle by being able to award me the '*semikha* of the sages.'"

This rabbinic ordination marked the continuation of the deep and meaningful relationship Rabbi Cohen enjoyed with Chief Rabbi Herzog. If anything, this bond became ever stronger over the years. Rabbi Cohen was now regarded as one of the family, and became a regular participant at the Torah classes conducted by the Chief Rabbi every Friday morning at his own home. One of these classes was conducted shortly after the Chief Rabbi and his colleague, Sephardi Chief Rabbi Uziel, jointly published a prayer for the peace and well-being of Israel. The prayer opened with the following words: "*Our Father in heaven, Rock of Israel and her Redemption, bless Medinat Yisrael, the beginning of the flowering of our redemption.*"

During that Friday morning class, Rabbi Cohen asked:

"Forgive me, revered teacher, but where is your source for saying that *Medinat Yisrael* is actually '*the beginning of the flowering of our redemption*?' While *Medinat Yisrael* clearly has much value in terms of the physical salvation of *Am Yisrael*, are we to say that this is *the* redemption prophesied by our biblical prophets and discussed by our Talmudic Sages?

"The Chief Rabbi smiled, pinched my cheek and replied: 'Apparently, you have forgotten the passage from the *Gemara* where this is explained. It states in Talmud Tractate *Sanhedrin*

IDF Rabbi Cohen, with Chief Rabbis Uziel and Herzog and his brother-in-law Rabbi Goren, during a visit to wounded soldiers in Tel HaShomer.
(from the collection of photographer Abraham Arthur Rosman)

98a: *'And Rabbi Abba said: 'There can be no more manifest sign of redemption than the passage from Ezekiel 36:8: 'But ye, O mountains of Israel, ye shall shoot forth your branches and yield up your fruit to My people, Israel, **for soon they will be home**.''*

Rabbi Cohen further relates:

"In the first years after the establishment of *Medinat Yisrael* there was a heated debate over the drafting of observant young women into the IDF. It was during this period that one day I drove as usual to the home of Chief Rabbi Herzog in order to take him to the regular class that he used to teach at the 'Machon Harry Fischel.' Standing nearby was one of the Jerusalem fanatics, who was obviously not quite right in his head. This man shouted out in Aramaic: 'Who do we have here, but a *zaken mamre* – one of those rebellious scholars – heaven forfend!'

"The Chief Rabbi was incredibly upset by this outburst, even though I tried to calm him down, by saying: 'The Chief Rabbi must realize that this man is mentally ill. Why is the Chief Rabbi so upset by the whole thing?' The Chief Rabbi replied: 'I am not upset by this particular man, but rather by our so-called great sages who are ignorant of Jewish Law. For the *Bet Din* of *Eretz Yisrael*

The Israel-Jordan Armistice Commission, discussing the return of the bodies of the Gush Etzion martyrs. Major Rabbi Cohen is at far right. Photo: from Bnei Tzion Publications.

has taught the *halakha* as it is and it is not permitted to disobey them.' The Chief Rabbi took a long time to calm down and only regained his composure when we arrived at the Machon and he started teaching his class."

⇛   IDF RABBI

After obtaining *semikha*, Rabbi Cohen decided to continue serving as an IDF chaplain. This was a stormy period for the chaplaincy. From the outset it assumed the character that we know today. But its status in relation to fighter command was not resolved without a struggle. The chaplaincy's ultimate success in negotiations on this subject was due primarily to the leadership skills of Rabbi Goren. According to Rabbi Cohen, on one occasion Rabbi Goren returned from private talks lasting for several hours with the Prime Minister, Ben Gurion. These were held at the general staff headquarters in *Gan Abraham* National Park, Ramat Gan. "Rabbi Goren returned from these talks, the blood drained from his cheeks, and ready to explode: 'I heard the type of things that the Sadducees [who did not believe in the Oral Torah] used to say during the Second Temple period. How can we possibly accept that?!'"

In his article: "*Religion in the IDF*," published shortly after the War of Liberation, but before the status of religion within the military framework had been finalized, Rabbi Cohen outlined his vision of the role of the IDF chaplaincy. During war-time, the principle of *pikuach nefesh*, the overriding priority of saving life, applied to many questions that arose on the Sabbath. But during peace time, a more precise definition of what was and what was not permitted in the army on Sabbath and festivals was required.

In those early days, the person entrusted with these sorts of decisions

Rabbi Shear Yashuv Cohen, the officiating IDF Rabbi in Arik Sharon's division, with his aide, in Suez during the Yom Kippur War.

was the commanding officer, who in most instances was not observant. And even if he wanted to adhere to *halakha* in these matters, he did not have the requisite knowledge to make an informed decision on serious *halakhic* questions, let alone offer a *heter* (legal permission) to override Shabbat when necessary.

Even worse, the commanding officer would often off-load the problem onto the shoulders of one of the rank and file, who happened to be religiously observant, but who did not always know enough and, in any event, lacked the authority to make the right decision in any given *halakhic* situation. It was thus deemed absolutely essential that the extremely important task of finding a way through the maze of *halakhic* queries and delivering a suitable practical solution to each one, be placed fairly and squarely on the shoulders of the IDF chaplaincy.

Nowadays, the situation is completely different. The IDF chaplaincy has invested a great deal of time and energy, as well as political pressure, to bring about the official integration of the requirements of the *halakha* into the structure of military command. In addition, *halakhic* decisions are no longer left in the hands of the commanding officer, or of the rank and file, but have become an integral component of the military defense of Israel.

Rabbi Cohen's first rabbinic experience was as a military chaplain. In this capacity, he conducted scores of weddings, supervised the *kashrut* in the military bases, and generally instilled Jewish values in the soldiers. Rabbi Cohen served in a number of different capacities, and was eventually appointed to the position of Chief Rabbi of the Israeli Air Force, a position which he held until the year 5715 (1954/5), when he was released with the rank of major. Even after his "release," however, he continued to serve in the reserves for over twenty years, until after the 1973 Yom Kippur War, despite his own war injury. During the Yom Kippur War, Rabbi Cohen served as the chaplain of the front command division, under the charge of his friend, Maj.-Gen. Ariel (Arik) Sharon (1928–2014), who later became the Prime Minister of Israel.

Rabbi Shear Yashuv Cohen, Chief Rabbi of the Israel Air Force

The Harry Fischel Institute for Talmudic Research (Machon Harry Fischel) and the Ariel Institutes for Advanced Torah Learning

"What is unique to Machon Harry Fischel and the Ariel Institutes is the appeal made by its first President, Rav Kook, our teacher and rabbi of saintly blessed memory, the light of Israel and its holiness, in his famous lecture (Hartza'at HaRav) that he delivered in 1921 to the sages of Jerusalem. The lecture begins with the words: 'To a life of creativity I call you.' These are sentiments he echoed in one of his well-known poems: 'Broad vistas, broad vistas, my heart yearns for the vistas of the Lord.'

The poem appeals to us not to remain confined within the 'four cubits of halakha,' but to open ourselves up to the 'vistas' – God's 'wide-open spaces' – and expand our horizons through our love of Torah, our love of the Jewish people, and our love of the Land of Israel. This is the approach of Machon Harry Fischel and the Ariel Institutes.

"The secret of greatness in a leader like Moses, who was both a prophet and a king, is that he went out to meet the people. The secret of his leadership was his involvement in the life of his brothers, and his willingness to come to the aid of the downtrodden. We try very hard to follow this path. We try to act justly and charitably toward everyone,

both near and far. We cultivate openness in Torah teaching and practice, not only through the 'awe of Heaven,' but also through expanding our awareness – not through self-mortification, but by daring to explore the larger picture and speaking to the people. This is the path we have taken at the Ariel Institutes.

"It is also the secret of the success of her alumni. They epitomize the verse in Psalms 119:63, 'I am a friend to all who fear Thee.' Their homes and their hearts are open to all those who truly seek God, while upon all is laced the spirit of love of Israel and love of the Land of Israel."

An excerpt from Rabbi Shear Yashuv Cohen's speech at the
73rd anniversary commemoration
of Machon Harry Fischel in 2005
The Ariel Institutes for Advanced Torah Learning

The Harry Fischel Institute for Talmudic Research (Machon Harry Fischel) and the Ariel Institutes for Advanced Torah Learning

⇛   PROJECTS ON LAW

The rebirth of the Jewish State after two thousand years of exile aroused in the heart of many the desire for an additional rebirth: the crowning of Jewish Law as the form of the official law in the new country, *Medinat Yisrael*. Therefore, during the first years after the establishment of the State, many books were published by some of Israel's foremost rabbis, offering a variety of proposals on how to formulate Israeli laws which would be in keeping with the Torah.

This approach enthralled young Rabbi Shear Yashuv Cohen. He realized that in order to formulate Israeli laws compatible with Torah teaching, the codifier had to be an expert in three types of law: *Halakha*, Israeli law, and international law. For this reason, while continuing to serve as an IDF chaplain, he also decided to study law at the Hebrew University in Jerusalem, and received the degree of Master in Jurisprudence from the Faculty of Law in 1955.

Many of his fellow students went on to become judges and experts in jurisprudence, including the former President of Israel's Supreme Court, Aharon Barak. At the Hebrew University Rabbi Cohen earned the nickname *"Hoshen Mishpat"* – the title of the fourth part of the 16th-century codification of Jewish Law (*Shulchan Arukh*) which deals with issues of monetary law and court procedures and which Rabbi Cohen was fond of quoting.

Rabbi Cohen's research thesis for his degree was *The Ketubah (Marriage Contract) and its Conditions*. Later he specialized in legal

Dedication of the Ariel Institutes building in Bayit VeGan, Jerusalem. From left to right: Rabbi Yosef Kapach, Rabbi Shalom Mashash, Rabbi Shlomo Goren, President Yitzchak Navon, Rabbi Shear Yashuv Cohen, Teddy Kollek, and Rabbi Yaakov Fink.

advice on rabbinic rulings and jurisprudence. Although he qualified as a lawyer he has never practiced in that capacity. Nevertheless, his law studies helped him in his research on the relationship between Jewish religious law and Israeli law. He developed these ideas at Machon Harry Fischel.

PRESIDENT AND DEAN

In 1953, Chief Rabbi Herzog, who was President of Machon Harry Fischel, appointed Rabbi Cohen as its Director after his wedding to Naomi, a granddaughter of Harry Fischel. (Naomi's father, Rabbi Herbert S. Goldstein, was one of the first Orthodox American rabbis.) The Institute had first been established in 1932 by then-Chief Rabbi Kook, as an institute for Talmudic research, a field that was generally studied in university humanities departments. Rav Kook wanted the institute to be unique in combining academic thoroughness with true "awe of heaven." The well-known American philanthropist, Harry Fischel (1865–1948) offered to sponsor the entire venture.

Rabbi Cohen's relationship with Rabbi Herzog deepened during this period, when he would accompany the Chief Rabbi to his weekly classes held at the Machon's Department of Dayanut – the first, and still the foremost, organized program for the training of judges for the Israeli religious courts. On the way Rabbi Cohen would chat with Rabbi Herzog on all aspects of Torah and consult with him on various matters.

Chief Rabbi Herzog died in 1959 at the age of 71. (Even many years later, Rabbi Cohen speaks of his grief at the death of his rabbi and teacher as if it were still fresh.) Under the aegis of Chief Rabbi Unterman, who was named President of Machon Harry Fischel, Rabbi Cohen continued to develop its Department of Torah Legislation, the aim of which was to arrange and codify Jewish Law in a way that would be easily understood by, and accessible to, contemporary jurists and lawyers. The vision was to integrate the theory and practice of Jewish Law into the law of the new State of Israel. His own Hebrew University background in the academic study of law helped a great deal in the development of this project.

Among those who initiated the Department of Torah Legislation back during Chief Rabbi Herzog's lifetime were Rabbi Meir Bar Ilan (1880–1949), the Mizrachi leader after whom Bar Ilan University is named; Dr. Zerach Warhaftig (1906–2002, Minister of Religions from 1961–74); and Yaakov Shimshon Shapira (1902–93, Minister of Justice from 1966–73). The Department also gained the enthusiastic support of the sixth Lubavitcher Rebbe (1902–94) and Rabbi Shlomo Yosef Zevin (1888–1978), editor of the *Talmudic Encyclopedia*.

In 1955 the Machon published a number of books. These included *Mishpatim LeYisrael*, dealing with contemporary criminal law and sentencing policy in Israel, and *Chukat Mishpat*, on the laws of selling, inheritance and estates, and more. These books are still regarded as seminal reference works for the practical application of Jewish Law in the contemporary world.

The Department's crowning glory, however, was the publication in 1962 of the *Halakha Pesukah*. This is a Code of Jewish Jurisprudence dealing with the section of the *Shulchan Arukh* known as *Hoshen Mishpat*. The *Halakha Pesukah* comprises a comprehensive summary of the development of Jewish civil law from the time of the *Shulchan Arukh* until the present day. It is based upon the works of hundreds of decisors and their responsa. Its aim is the integration of insights gleaned from the *Hoshen Mishpat* into contemporary legislation. In his introduction to the first volume of the work, Rabbi Cohen writes:

> "The political independence of Israel has still not brought about our much longed-for spiritual independence. Law and justice in *Medinat Yisrael* are still steeped in many foreign and alien legal systems imported from the Diaspora . . . The aim of our *Halakha Pesukah* project is to restore Jewish law to its former glory . . . and to clearly illuminate every aspect of life through the lens of

Torah. It is our aim to present Jewish law to Torah scholars and their Yeshiva students as plainly and as meticulously as possible . . . and to provide today's lawyers and judges with a tool, newly and clearly styled and formulated, so that, as the Bible states, 'they will know how to effect justice.'"

Under Rabbi Cohen's aegis, Machon Harry Fischel also developed a department for the publication of works of the *Rishonim* (leading scholars of the 11th–15th centuries), as well as manuscripts of still unpublished works in an integrated traditional and academic format. Rabbi Cohen was an active participant in this work and in 1965, together with Rabbi Eliyahu Prisman (1902–76), he edited the fourth volume of the *Sefer HaRaavi'ah*, a compilation of halakhic decisions and discussions by the famous *Rishon*, Rabbi Eliezer ben Rabbi Yoel HaLevi, who is often quoted in the *Shulchan Arukh*. A new edition of the first three volumes was published by the Machon in 1964.

Rabbi Cohen also published a new edition of *Yesod VeShoresh HaAvodah* (*The Foundation and Root of Divine Service*), written by the influential 18th-century Rabbi Alexander Ziskind of Grodno, an ancestor of Jane Fischel, Harry Fischel's wife. (Her maiden name, Braz, is an acronym for "*Bnei* [the sons of] R. Alexander Ziskin.") The world-renowned Chofetz Chaim is one of many rabbis known to have set aside time on a regular basis to study this classic. In addition, Rabbi Cohen initiated the project *Sanhedrei Gedolah*, the goal of which is to publish the rarer commentaries of the *Rishonim* on the Babylonian Talmud's Tractate Sanhedrin. Eight volumes of this project were published between 1967 and 1974.

⇒ THE ARIEL INSTITUTES FOR ADVANCED TORAH LEARNING

A short time afterwards Rabbi Cohen established the *Midrasha HaGvohah LeTorah*, under the auspices of Machon Harry Fischel. Although he was fully aware of the importance of publishing manuscripts of the *Rishonim*, and undertaking research into contemporary jurisprudence in light of Jewish religious law, he also realized that just as essential for the *Am Yisrael* were rabbis and rabbinic judges who could speak to them in contemporary language. For this reason he shifted the Machon's emphasis to the training of religious judges and rabbis, preparing them to go out and serve Jewish communities in Israel and the Diaspora.

Rabbi Cohen was thus following in the footsteps of Rabbi Herzog, strengthening the already existing training for religious judges that the Chief Rabbi had initiated.

This study program was a revolutionary concept for those days and was undertaken in conjunction with the Chief Rabbinate of Israel and the personal input of the Chief Rabbis. This was the first time in Israel that an Institute was specifically dedicated to the training of rabbis.

No less radical was the introduction of a final exam for the students, whether they were to become rabbis or judges. In order to receive *semicha*, they would have to sit for a written exam on all the *halakhot* (laws) that they had studied. These were the first exams for *semicha* of the Chief Rabbinate of Israel, and they were held at Machon Harry Fischel.

The Harry Fischel Institute was thus the flagship for the many institutes for rabbinical training that have since sprung up all over Israel, as well as for the introduction of the written examinations that many Yeshiva students now take every year for Chief Rabbinate ordination. The first examinations of this type in Israel were arranged by Rabbi Shear Yashuv during Rabbi Herzog's lifetime and with his blessing.

Another innovation introduced by Rabbi Cohen was the inclusion of the teaching of Bible, Jewish thought and other topics that would assist rabbis in their relationships with the community. Also included were courses in Jewish history, rabbinic literature, as well as homiletics (written and verbal presentational skills) and practical rabbinics.

This program and the introduction of *semicha* exams aroused considerable opposition in some sections of the haredi-religious public. Notices decrying the new program were posted all over Jerusalem claiming that training rabbis in this manner and the accompanying exams constituted an affront to traditional Torah learning. They heatedly argued that the only goal of the *Kollelim* (Torah study programs) had always been exclusively to study Torah, leading to the "graduation" of the individuals of the highest caliber to rabbinic positions.

Nevertheless, he obtained a great deal of support for the enterprise from some of the foremost rabbis in Israel, such as Chief Rabbi Isser Yehuda Unterman (1886–1976), who was then also the President of the Machon, and Rabbi Shlomo Yosef Zevin.

From abroad, support came from Rabbi Yosef Dov Soloveitchik (1903–93), known at Yeshiva University and throughout the modern Orthodox world as "the Rov"; Rabbi Emanuel Rackman (1910–2008), also of Yeshiva University, and later President of Bar Ilan University; and Rabbi Immanuel Jakobovits (1921–99), subsequently Chief Rabbi of the United Kingdom. Many of them sent their own students to study at Ariel.

In the beginning, the main role of the Ariel Institutes was that of a graduate school for rabbinical students from the Diaspora, providing them with additional preparation for their roles as spiritual guides and mentors to Jewish communities throughout the Diaspora. Later, however, it expanded and absorbed hundreds of young outstanding Yeshiva students from within Israel as well. Rabbi Yitzchak Ralbag, former chairman of the Jerusalem Rabbinate Council, relates:

> "Machon Harry Fischel became the best-known Institute in Jerusalem. Everyone knew that it was there that the greatest Torah scholars, the 'lions in the pack,' would study. Whenever one of the students was asked where he was studying, all he had to say was, 'At the Machon [the Institute].' Everyone understood that the reference was to Machon Harry Fischel. Studying there was the best credential for appointment to any post as a rabbi or *dayan*. This was entirely due to Rabbi Cohen, who had the wisdom and insight to elevate the Machon to such an exalted level that the most outstanding Torah scholars studied there."

Rabbi Cohen's institutions are imbued with a national-religious spirit in line with Rabbi Cohen's own religious outlook. At the same time they encompass within their framework people from every Orthodox background, including from the haredi-religious sector.

From 1978, the institutions established by Rabbi Cohen in Jerusalem and Haifa came to be known collectively as the "Ariel United Israel Institutes."

Many of Israel's leading rabbis have taught in Ariel, including Rabbi Aharon Chaim HaLevi Zimmerman (1914–95), one of the outstanding Torah scholars in the United States before he moved to Israel in 1972. Rabbi Zimmerman was a nephew of the famous Rabbi Baruch Ber Lebowitz (1864–1931) and hence had been schooled in the "Brisker" method. This is a highly exacting and analytical type of Talmudic study that focuses on precise halakhic definitions and categorizations, with particular emphasis on the legal writings of Maimonides. During his time at Ariel, Rabbi Zimmerman learned one-on-one with Rabbi Cohen.

Currently, Rabbi Zalman Nehemia Goldberg teaches at the Ariel *Kollel* for religious court judges. Rabbi Goldberg is a leading authority on Jewish Law, and member of the Rabbinical High Court in Jerusalem. The *Kollel* is presently headed by Rabbi Yaakov Wahrhaftig. Rabbi Eliezer Damari and Rabbi Yigal Tzefira also teach there.

The present Director of the Ariel United Israel Institutes is Rabbi David Tabachnik. Members of its International Board of Governors are some of the foremost rabbis and communal leaders of the Diaspora. Over the years, the Machon has trained many hundreds of rabbis and *dayanim,* who have gone on to fill senior positions in religious courts both in Israel and abroad. One of the alumni of the Machon was Rabbi

Avraham Shapira (1914–2007), Israel's Chief Rabbi from 1983–1993 and Rosh Yeshivat Merkaz HaRav from 1982 until his death.

Subsequently, another department was also added to the Machon: *Torah LaAm*. This department has published popular Torah literature which aims to bring Judaism to the broad public. Rabbi Cohen not only headed all these institutions, but also kept the Ariel Institutes going by traveling around the world to raise funds and recruit partners in these projects. During these trips he forged close ties between significant Diaspora organizations and *Medinat Yisrael*.

THE ARIEL INSTITUTES: ADDITIONAL PROJECTS

Under the supervision of Rabbi Shear Yashuv Cohen, the Ariel Institutes have published a number of Torah works, incorporating the latest scientific research. These included a modern edition of Rashi's commentary on the Torah: *Rashi HaShalem*. The two-volume English edition of this work, on Genesis, is known as the *Ariel Chumash: Rashi, Onkelos, Sources and Analysis*. Volume I (*Bereshit-Chaye Sara*) was published in Jerusalem in 1997. Volume II (*Toldot-Vayechi*) was published in 2001.

The institute has also produced scientific editions of the *Rishonim* and works on Jewish jurisprudence and the Jewish calendar. Ariel has collaborated with the Tzomet Institute in the publication of the halakhic journal *Tekhumin* dealing with modern questions of Jewish Law. In addition, Ariel has published some of Rabbi Cohen's own halakhic works including *Shai Cohen* and *Chikrei Halakha*. Perhaps the most widely known of all of Ariel's publications is the popular *Practical Talmud Dictionary*, written in English. Distributed by Feldheim Publishers, it is regularly stocked in Jewish bookstores to this very day.

Ariel Institutes also operate a busy and well-organized rabbinical court that adjudicates financial matters. In addition, there are a variety of courses for Torah-related professions, such as scribes (*soferim*) specializing in the writing of Torah scrolls, *tefillin* and mezuzot; *shochetim*, ritual slaughterers; and *kashrut* supervisors. The Nezer David Institute is also part of the Ariel Institutes, administered by Rabbi Harel Cohen. Over the years, it has published dozens of books and booklets on the teachings of Rav Shear Yashuv's father, Rabbi David Cohen, the *Nazir* of Jerusalem.

THE RABBI HERBERT S. GOLDSTEIN LIBRARY

The Machon was always famous for original manuscripts obtained – first by the founder, and then by other members – for its scholars to use in the course of their preparation of publications. But Ariel Institutes went a step further, building a large collection of publications, and making it available to the general public in the Rabbi Herbert S. Goldstein Library.

This institution also incorporates a music library that contains one of the largest collections of Jewish music in Israel equipped with state-of-the-art listening devices. This project was established at the initiative of Rabbi Shear Yashuv Cohen. The assembly of such a specialized collection is particularly appropriate in light of the importance of Jewish music in the lives of Rav Kook and the *Nazir*, both of whom also composed their own original compositions.

➣   RABBINIC CONFERENCES

Finally, Ariel organizes biannual study conferences for rabbis and their wives provide regular opportunities for in-house training. These seminars deal with contemporary issues relevant to Torah learning and to the State of Israel. Hundreds of Israeli rabbis regularly attend these study weekends with their spouses.

Rabbi Cohen places a special emphasis on the role of the rabbi's wife as a partner who shares in his life and work. The wives are invited to attend all the conference lectures and also have special sessions on a variety of relevant topics, including but not limited to their special role as the rabbi's wife. Many of these sessions are given by women with expertise in a variety of fields.

These conferences are organized by Rabbi Baruch Pachter, Rabbi of the northern town of Metullah, and Rabbi David Shapira of Bet HaKerem, Jerusalem. Rabbi Pachter relates:

> "The Ariel conferences have taken place for nearly 30 years, and create a very rare type of special feeling of unity. The rabbis and public figures who participate come from every branch of Orthodox Judaism. The subject matter is specially chosen for its relevance to issues faced by rabbis in their working lives. The lecturers include some of the foremost rabbis of the day, including past and present Chief Rabbis of Israel. Specialists are invited to lecture on the professional aspects of issues such as communication difficulties, economic problems and family violence.
>
> "To preserve the spirit of unity, we try to prevent the conferences from taking on a political nature, and we encourage each rabbi to express his views. This unity is also reflected in the prayer services held during the conferences, in which the *nusach* is different each time, as determined by the particular prayer leader.
>
> "Rabbi Shear Yashuv Cohen is the moving spirit behind all these

conferences, from choosing the subject matter to overseeing the sessions. Rabbi Cohen is involved in the entire event, and although his own views are well known, he makes sure that people with other views are allowed to give them expression. This is one of the many qualities that have earned him a special place in the hearts of the scores of rabbis who attend his conferences and study sessions every year."

⇶   WITH THE LUBAVITCHER REBBE

Even before he became involved with the administration of the Machon, Rabbi Cohen used to participate in the *Daf Yomi* (Daily Talmud Page) class in the home of Rabbi Shlomo Yosef Zevin. This class was also attended by other important Jerusalem rabbis, such as Rabbi Ovadia Yosef (1920–2013), who subsequently became the Rishon LeTzion, Israel's Sephardic Chief Rabbi (1973–83).

Rabbi Zevin's breadth of knowledge and clarity in expounding the texts greatly influenced the young Rabbi Cohen. But there was an additional significance to the close relationship between them. Rabbi Zevin, member of the Chief Rabbinate of Israel, combined his love for Torah in all its splendor, with an equally profound love for *Am Yisrael* and *Eretz Yisrael*, in accordance with the path of Chabad (Lubavitch).

Rabbi Zevin was one of Israel's leading Chabad rabbis, and established the movement's rabbinical court in the Holy Land. He was especially close to his teacher and master, the Lubavitcher Rebbe, and it was he who drew Rabbi Cohen to the Rebbe – a deep relationship that lasted for 30 years, until the death of the Rebbe in 1994. Rabbi Cohen regards the Lubavitcher Rebbe as one of the key influences on his own outlook, second only to that of his own father, the *Nazir*, and Rabbi Tzvi Yehuda Kook.

The relationship between the Rebbe and the *Nazir*'s family began many years earlier in Russia. During the Russian Revolution of 1917 Rabbi Menachem Mendel Schneerson, the future Rebbe, hid in the home of Rabbi Cohen's maternal grandfather, Rabbi Hanoch Henich Etkin, the rabbi of a small town called Luga, not far from St. Petersburg (later to be known as Leningrad).

The Jews of Luga were too poor to support their rabbi, so he earned his living as a bookbinder while his wife kept a guest house. The fact that the rabbi earned his living through manual labor was a positive factor in the eyes of the Communist authorities and they therefore left him alone and did not keep tabs on him.

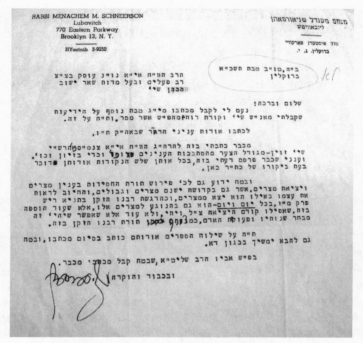

One of many letters from the Lubavitcher Rebbe to Rabbi Cohen on communal matters.

Later the Rebbe would tell Rabbi Cohen, "Your grandfather had one advantage in the eyes of the Bolsheviks: he was poor!" Thus, Rabbi Schneerson managed to elude the Bolshevik authorities by hiding in Rabbi Etkin's home for seven months, until he received a visa for Warsaw. There he married the second daughter of the sixth Lubavitcher Rebbe, known as the Maharitz, and eventually succeeded him as the venerated Rebbe of Chabad.

Another link between the two families came about through Rabbi Cohen's paternal grandfather, Rabbi Yosef Cohen, a well-known Chabad adherent. During Rabbi Shear Yashuv's first visit to the Rebbe, the latter spoke at length to him of the time he had stayed with his uncle during the *"the years of our suffering"* (Psalms 90:15).

During this first meeting the Rebbe exuded tremendous warmth and love towards the young Rabbi Shear Yashuv. That was when he made up his mind that he would pay the Rebbe a visit on every trip he made to the United States. On one of these occasions, in 1971, Rabbi Cohen accompanied the President of Israel, Zalman Shazar (1889–1974), to the Rebbe's home for the *Megillah* reading on Purim. Shazar had been a close childhood friend of the *Nazir*, and asked the Rebbe if he knew Rabbi

"My old good friend" – so said the Lubavitcher Rebbe about Rabbi Cohen, seen here visiting in Crown Heights with then-President Zalman Shazar.

Shear Yashuv. The Rebbe replied affably in Yiddish: "What do you mean? He is a very old good friend!"

The Lubavitcher Rebbe honored Rabbi Cohen more than once by inviting him to sit next to him during a *farbrengen* (Hasidic gathering). Rabbi Cohen also took part in one-to-one *yechidut* (private meetings) with the Rebbe. During one of these sessions, the Rebbe brought up the question of the *Nazir*'s strict vegetarianism: "I don't have any problem with you being a vegetarian because you are following your father. However, I am very surprised that your great father, a Kabbalist, exempts himself from the obligation to 'elevate sparks'[1] by eating meat." Rav Shear Yashuv recalls the incident:

> "At first, I was taken aback, not knowing how to answer such a great personage asking me a direct question about my own father and teacher. However, with God's help, I had a brainstorm: I asked

---

1. a Hassidic/Kabbalistic concept according to which sparks of holiness hidden in the physical world, including in animals, are "elevated" by having a blessing recited upon them and being eaten according to Jewish Law

the Rebbe if he had the book *Sdei Chemed*, an encyclopedia of halakhic responsa by Rabbi Hezkiya Medini [1833–1904]. The Rebbe answered, 'Of course, we ourselves published this book.' He went to a bookshelf, pulled out the book, and I opened it to the very spot where there is a discussion about distancing oneself from eating meat. There, the *Sdei Chemed* describes one of the scholars at the court of the *Arizal* [Rabbi Isaac Luria, 1534–72] 'who has for many years now abstained from eating meat, despite being derided by his friends, but God forbid that anyone should sneer at him; blessed is his lot.' The Rebbe read these words and accepted them as an adequate response to his question about my father and teacher. He smiled and said, 'My sons have defeated me' *(Bava Metzia* 59b), and he closed the book."

The substance of this session between Rabbi Cohen and the Rebbe became public knowledge among the Chabad community; some of the Hasidim had wanted to become vegetarians but were afraid of the Rebbe's reaction and this incident provided the legitimization they needed – a sort of *heter* (dispensation) to become vegetarian. One of these Hasidim was Rabbi Moshe Segal (1904–84) who had been Rabbi Cohen's commanding officer in the Underground *Brit HaHashmona'im* youth movement (see above, Chapter 4).

Rabbi Cohen recalls another *yechidut* session with the Rebbe. This was when the Rebbe was leading his famous campaign on the subject of "Who is a Jew." The Israeli "Law of Return" states that a Jew is one whose mother is Jewish or who has converted to Judaism. After the word "converted," the Rebbe wanted to add "according to Jewish Law."

During their meeting, Rabbi Cohen discussed with the *Rebbe* his own fears that – for economic or political reasons – *Medinat Yisrael* might not oppose the Conservative and Reform Jewish communities (who accept members who have not been converted according to the *halakha*). Rabbi Cohen added that maybe the time was not yet ripe for such a discussion and it might be a better idea to wait until the time was right. The *Rebbe* replied:

"There are matters that stem from the Torah itself, and are pre-scribed by Biblical Law. Carrying out conversions according to *ha-lakha* is one such matter. This law derives directly from the Torah, and needs an immediate response, not discussions about whether some will or will not accept it. Only on matters of Rabbinic law (*deRabanan*) is it possible to consider remaining silent."

One of their most dramatic dialogues took place during a *yechidut* session when Rabbi Cohen pressed the Rebbe on why he had not made aliyah and moved to Israel:

> "I told him that I apologized in advance, but that the soul of every Jew hung on my question. I said that I had not the shadow of a doubt that if the Rebbe were to move to Israel, the result would be an immense spiritual awakening throughout the world that would speed up the Redemption. The Rebbe answered that there were two reasons for his decision to remain outside Israel: 'One is that we know how to get there, but not how to return' – an apparent reference to the *halakhic* prohibition against leaving *Eretz Yisrael* – 'and we still have work to do here.'
>
> "The second reason he gave was, 'I have taken upon myself not to go anywhere from where I would not be able to reach the *Tsiyun* [the gravesite of his father-in-law, the sixth Lubavitcher Rebbe, whom he referred to as the 'Prince of our generation'] that same day.'
>
> "I dared to respond as follows: 'But there is a remedy for this, just as it states:*"Moses took the bones of Joseph with him"* (Exodus 13:19) to *Eretz Yisrael*. I meant that the Rebbe's father-in-law was also named Yosef, and that, just as in the Biblical story, he could reinter the remains of his revered father-in-law in Israel. The Rebbe remained silent for a time, and then his eyes suddenly filled with tears. A terrible fear fell upon me. I immediately apologized profusely in case I had in any way caused him pain, God forbid. I had only intended 'for the sake of heaven,' and who was I, after all, to tell our great teacher the Rebbe what to do! The Rebbe smiled, and we went on to a different topic."

The warm relationship between Rabbi Cohen and the Lubavitcher Rebbe also found expression in the many letters the latter sent him over the years on a variety of issues.

CANDIDACY FOR THE POST OF CHIEF RABBI OF THE UNITED KINGDOM

The Chief Rabbi of the United Kingdom and the Commonwealth, Rabbi Israel Brodie (1895–1979), retired in 1965, after serving in this role since 1948. From 1962, the President of the United Synagogue was the philanthropist, Sir Isaac Wolfson (1897–1991). He led a delegation of U.K.

Jewish notables who approached Rabbi Cohen in 1965, and asked him to put his name forward for the post of Chief Rabbi. Rabbi Cohen wanted to find out more, so he traveled to London and met with the leaders of the Jewish community of London, as well as with the Mayor of London.

On Shabbat, Rabbi Cohen was invited to preach to the members of the London Jewish community in a magnificent synagogue. The subject he chose was: "Do not enclose the Lord in splendiferous synagogues." The sermon led to huge repercussions throughout the Jewish community. Rabbi Cohen put forward the view that the construction of magnificent synagogues, while not accepting the inspiration of the Divine Presence in one's heart, misses the point entirely. "Do not imprison God in the synagogue," he implored. "Let Him enter into your home as a welcome guest, as part of the family. Let Him participate in your everyday activities, and even bear Him in mind when you pursue your hobbies."

The leaders of the community were divided. Some were inspired, and redoubled their efforts to have Rabbi Cohen chosen as Chief Rabbi. But their opponents said: "The fanatics have arrived from Jerusalem!" After a few days, Rabbanit Cohen, who had had grave reservations about the proposal from the outset, flew out to join her husband in London. The mood she encountered there increased her misgivings, and she said, "I didn't make Aliyah to Israel in order to end up living in England." She and Rabbi Shear Yashuv flew back to Israel. In the end, Rabbi Immanuel Jacobovits was chosen to fill the distinguished position.

➥   AS DEPUTY MAYOR OF JERUSALEM

By contrast, Rabbi Cohen's communal activities and public service were much appreciated in Jerusalem. Members of the National Religious Party, including a former member of Lehi, Shimon Barmatz (1922–2009), asked Rabbi Cohen to serve on the Jerusalem City Council as their party representative. According to Barmatz:

"As I was fully aware of the great gifts of my close friend, Rabbi Shear Yashuv Cohen, not only as a Torah scholar, but in day-to-day matters as well, it was clear to me that he was the right person for the job. I therefore approached him, and his response was: 'I have directed my strengths towards the tent of Torah. At the moment I am Director of Machon Harry Fischel, and I don't have the time for anything else.' My response was: 'When we were in the Underground together, you found the time to combine Torah study with public service. Just as you did then, you will manage to find time today!' Rabbi Cohen agreed."

After a number of years of service as a member of the Jerusalem City Council, Rabbi Cohen agreed to run as the head of the Religious Zionist

The Jerusalem City Council. Rabbi Cohen is sitting at the far left.

list in the Jerusalem mayoral elections. He consented because of "my love for Jerusalem and its rebuilding, and my desire to promote religious education in the city." This was the start of a very significant period of municipal activity for Rabbi Cohen. He was elected Deputy Mayor of Jerusalem, serving for a short time under Mordechai Ish-Shalom (1902–91), and then under Teddy Kollek (1911–2007), who was mayor for 28 years, until 1993.

Rabbi Cohen was therefore Deputy Mayor of Jerusalem during the heady days of 1967 when Israel's capital city was reunited, and until 1973. In total he served Jerusalem for 18 years, at the same time continuing as head of Machon Harry Fischel. As Deputy Mayor, Rabbi Cohen held the education and culture portfolios, which enabled him to support a variety of Torah and charitable institutions in the city. He oversaw the good work done by the Department of Torah Education in expanding Torah activities, as well as the funding of classes, study days and lectures on religious subjects. He also participated in sustaining the new-found unity of Jerusalem. On his initiative, the "TLT" project was established. These letters stand for *HaT'nuah LeHafatzat HaTorah*, The Movement for the Dissemination of Torah – under whose auspices institutions for Torah education were established throughout Israel, particularly in new-immigrant settlements. As Rabbi Cohen explains:

> "Even though today we live in Haifa, we retain an abiding love for Jerusalem. I received the opportunity to become involved in public work in Jerusalem. The problems we faced were acute. They

included maintaining the sanctity of Shabbat, relations with the non-Orthodox and similar matters. It was an enormous privilege to begin to serve the city of Jerusalem when it was still small, divided and split in half, and then to serve her as Deputy Mayor during those great days when the walls fell, when the Old and New Cities were reunited.

"It was a privilege to continue serving Jerusalem for many more years, when we cleaned out and created the Western Wall plaza and rebuilt the Jewish community of the Old City, Yeshivat HaKotel and other institutions. It was often extremely difficult for me to cope with the views of the Mayor, Teddy Kollek, who diametrically opposed me on so many fundamental issues dear to my heart – issues having to do with Torah and Judaism, the sanctity of the Old City, and our ongoing relationship with the Arabs. However, despite all, we managed to sustain a deep friendship."

It was during this period, when Rabbi Cohen held the education and culture portfolios in the Jerusalem municipality, that he secured *yechidut* sessions with the Lubavitcher Rebbe, *inter alia* in order to hear the latter's views on education. The Rebbe asked Rabbi Cohen to make sure to provide at least minimal Jewish education to every Jewish pupil. The Rebbe's views were clear and unequivocal: "We may not give up on even one Jewish child." The Rebbe could not accept the concept that a Jewish child, wherever he or she lived in the world, could attend a Jewish school without recognizing the *Shema* prayer. He also deemed it essential that every Jewish child know the verse: "Moshe commanded the Torah to us" (Deuteronomy 33:4).

After Rabbi Cohen had served as Deputy Mayor of Jerusalem for eight years, the Rebbe urged him to give up his political work and to immerse himself once again in the world of Torah. He advised him to concentrate on the Rabbinate and the Torah institutions that he headed. Rabbi Cohen heeded the Rebbe's advice and did not run in the 1975 elections for the City Council. Instead, he devoted himself to Machon Harry Fischel and its institutions, studied Torah, and wrote books.

RABBI COHEN'S RELATIONSHIP WITH RABBI SOLOVEITCHIK

Rabbi Cohen had a very meaningful relationship with another Torah giant of his generation, Rabbi Yosef Dov Soloveitchik (1903–93). On his trips to the United States, he would call on Rav Soloveitchik and attend some of his lectures on Jewish law and thought. He also consulted with him on matters of Torah and Jewish community. The high point of their relationship was the establishment of the *Midrasha* (the Institute of Advanced Torah Learning) under the general umbrella of Machon Harry Fischel; when Rabbi Cohen asked for Rav Soloveitchik's support, the latter acceded enthusiastically.

During the summer of 1974, Rabbi Cohen attended one of Rav Soloveitchik's lectures, addressed to a Yiddish-speaking rabbinical audience at the Moriah Synagogue on the Upper West Side of Manhattan. On becoming aware of Rabbi Cohen's presence Rav Soloveitchik introduced him to the audience and said [as summarized by a student who was present]:

> "I would like to introduce a very important guest, who honors us today with his presence at our lecture. This is Rabbi Shear Yashuv Cohen from Jerusalem . . . Rabbi Cohen is the only son of the great and famous *Nazir* of Jerusalem, of blessed memory, who was immersed in Torah and Kabbalah. The *Nazir* was a great thinker and enthusiast, a very gifted human being, capable of the most sublime emotions . . . He was altogether a man of holiness, who separated himself from all worldly matters, a true *Nazir*. Anyone gifted with the appropriate sense could see and feel how the soul of his great teacher and colleague, Rav Kook, illuminated and permeated everything the *Nazir* did, including his writings, for the *Nazir* was certainly Rav Kook's greatest student.
>
> "And so we are very privileged to have as our guest here today, Rabbi Cohen – the son as well as the pupil of the *Nazir*. Rabbi Cohen is a Torah scholar in his own right, as well as a great thinker. He encapsulates in his person the very essence of what I term the combination of '*halakhot* (Jewish law) and *halikhot* (day-to-day behavior);' neither his careful observance and teaching of Jewish law nor his pleasant demeanor come at the expense of the other. It is a major problem in contemporary Judaism that many behave as if there is a conflict between the two. But in Rabbi Cohen there is no conflict between *halakhot* and *halikhot*. Rabbi Cohen is a public leader and also heads Machon Harry Fischel, which has published many manuscripts written by the *Rishonim* . . . At the moment, he is also establishing a *Midrasha* there – an Institute of Advanced Torah Learning dedicated to the training of rabbis to serve in today's communities – which is the reason for his visit to us today. I would like everyone to know who it is who is with us today, and recognize and welcome Rabbi Shear Yashuv Cohen."

At a symbolic Hak'hel ceremony in Jerusalem: Rabbi Isser Yehuda Unterman to the right of Rabbi Eliyahu Pardes (holding the Torah scroll). To the left: Dr. Cahane, Rabbi Yitzchak Abuhatseira and to his left, Rabbi Shear Yashuv Cohen.

   REVITALIZING THE STUDY OF THE JERUSALEM TALMUD

Over a number of centuries and for a variety of reasons, the *Talmud Yerushalmi* (the Jerusalem Talmud, written in the Land of Israel during the first centuries of the Common Era) has been neglected in favor of the *Talmud Bavli* (Babylonian Talmud, completed in the 6th century CE). However, with the return of *Am Yisrael* to its land, many Torah scholars have also returned to the study of their own much-overlooked Jerusalem Talmud.

Rabbi Shlomo Goren, the brother-in-law of Rabbi Cohen, is credited with being among the first to encourage rabbinical scholars to renew their engagement with the Jerusalem Talmud (JT). Rabbi Goren wrote a commentary on a portion of JT Tractate *Berachot*, and then Rabbi Cohen took over the reins of the enterprise. So, in addition to his many other endeavors, he became the President of the Institute for the Study of the Jerusalem Talmud, the Talmud of *Eretz Yisrael*, headed by Rabbi Abraham Blass, and has taken it under the wings of the Ariel Institutes. The institute publishes JT tractates with a commentary.

Later, in 2004, Rabbi Cohen appealed to the members of the national-religious Torah world to devote themselves to the study of the Jerusalem Talmud, as a response to Rav Kook's appeal for a return to the Talmud of *Eretz Yisrael*. Rabbi Cohen wrote:

"Throughout the many generations of our Exile, the study and interpretation of the Jerusalem Talmud has been the lot of only a select few . . . Only in recent times have many of our foremost Torah scholars regarded the return to the study, interpretation, and dissemination of the Jerusalem Talmud as an inseparable part of the miracle of the restoration of Israel to her land after 2,000 years of Exile . . . The Torah of *Eretz Yisrael* is an entire, comprehensive way of life; the *Yerushalmi* encapsulates within its pages the life of the individual Jew living in *Eretz Yisrael*.

"We believe and pray that if we educate our younger generation according to the values of the Jerusalem Talmud, we will revitalize the study of Gemara and authentic faith. A new spirit will then pervade *halakhic* life in the Holy Land, with positive repercussions on the continuity of *Am Yisrael* both here and in the Diaspora . . . We are embarking on a historic path that will have enormous influence on Torah consciousness both in *Eretz Yisrael* and in the Diaspora. The message conveyed by the spiritual and educational values embodied in the Jerusalem Talmud should be regarded as the start of an enormous enterprise. We are the flagship!"

Many of the foremost religious Zionist rabbis of the time signed this appeal. These included Rabbi Mordechai Eliyahu (1929–2010), Sephardi Chief Rabbi of Israel from 1983–1993; Rabbi Dov Lior (b. 1933), Chief Rabbi of Hebron/Kiryat Arba and Head of the Council of Rabbis of Judea and Samaria; Rabbi Yaakov Ariel (b. 1937), Chief Rabbi of Ramat Gan; and Rabbi Shlomo Aviner (b. 1943), Rabbi of Bet El. To date, the Machon has published two tractates of the Jerusalem Talmud with commentaries: *Taanit* and *Moed Katan*.

Family

A Grandson's Tribute to his Grandfather
on his 80th Birthday

"Some time ago, in conversation with a friend, we got around to speaking about our respective grandparents and the very special inter-generational relationship that often develops. That chat helped me to put into words the special feelings about you that we, all your grandchildren, have for you. Wherever we are, we have your image before us, the image of everything you say and do, whether you are addressing the general public, at home or abroad, or, most importantly, when you address your own people, Am Yisrael. We notice the attention you pay to every detail.

"Wherever you are needed, there you appear as a preacher of gadlut, magnanimity, the big picture. Sometimes you are as zealous as Pinchas when he arose from the congregation and erupted like some mighty volcano; and at other times you embrace the whole of creation in your inimitable way, relating to every single person individually, drawing them closer to the light of Torah and shining its great torch into the most obscure corner – the Torah that embodies everything.

"Somewhere within us, Saba – grandfather – there is a place in which you dwell always. Wherever we go, your image accompanies us. In all our inner struggles and external challenges, there you are: in the eye of our inner soul. Your image began to grow within us when we were still very small. We have seen from afar how you conduct yourself both with giants of Torah and with leading world figures. We have also experienced you close-up in the bosom of the family. To me you represent total commitment to the word of God in the world, in the broadest sense, capable of encompassing the whole of creation. I see you, I live you and I learn from you."

From a speech delivered by Avishai Kraus, a grandson of Rabbi Shear Yashuv Cohen, on behalf of all the grandchildren, at a family gathering celebrating the 80th birthday of their grandfather in 2007

CHAPTER TEN

Family

In 1952, Rabbi Cohen met Naomi née Goldstein. Her father was Rabbi Herbert S. (Rafael Chaim Shimshon) Goldstein (1890–1970), one of the early pioneers of Orthodox Judaism in the United States. Naomi's mother Rebecca (Betty, 1891–1961) was a true "helpmate" to her husband, and much more. She actively participated in establishing several of the most important American Orthodox Jewish women's organizations during the earliest years of modern American Orthodoxy, concentrating especially on the field of Jewish education for women and girls. She was the second daughter of Harry Fischel (1865–1948) and his wife, Chaya Sheyna (Jane Braz (Brass), ca. 1865–1935).

Naomi (b. 1930) made aliyah in 1949, in order to study Jewish history at the Hebrew University in Jerusalem. Three years later, Naomi met her future husband Rabbi Shear Yashuv Cohen. In the summer of 1952, Naomi was staying with her parents, who were on a visit to Israel from New York, in her late grandfather's apartment inside the Machon Harry Fischel Institute complex (the Machon). This was the apartment where her grandfather had lived toward the end of his life. The neighboring apartment had originally been occupied by a younger brother of the great Rav Kook, Rabbi Dov Ber Kook, who had been appointed the Director of the Harry Fischel Institute.

After his death, his son-in-law, Rabbi Yaakov Kilav, inherited both the position and the apartment. The latter's son, the young Abraham Yitzchak Kilav (who eventually became a Rabbinical Judge on the Jerusalem *Bet Din*), became Bar Mitzvah at the Harry Fischel Institute's synagogue, and a *kiddush* was held in the Kilav apartment in honor of the event. Naturally, Rabbi Goldstein and his family were invited and, given the close friendship between the family of the *Nazir* and the family of Rav Kook, Rabbi Shear Yashuv was also invited. At that time, Rabbi Cohen was a young IDF chaplain and also a student in the Law Faculty at the Hebrew University.

According to Naomi:

> "After the *kiddush* we went back to our apartment and I immersed
> myself in a book. Mother came in and told me that guests had
> arrived and asked me to come to the living room. I did not really
> want to, but seeing it was my mother who was asking, I got up
> and went with her. This is how Rabbi Shear Yashuv Cohen met the
> person who became his wife of more than 60 years."

On the subject of Divine Providence present at every *shidduch*, Rabbi
Cohen recalls the words of the Gemara in Tractate *Moed Katan*, p. 18b:
"We learn from the Torah, from the Prophets, and from the Writings
that it is from God that a particular woman [is destined] to a particular
man." Rabbi Cohen explains the need for the three-fold repetition: "It
is natural for a person to think that it is through his own initiative that
he has managed to find a wife and marry her. This is why the Torah
emphasizes three times the belief in Divine Providence: 'From God is
a woman [destined] to a man.' This idea is expressed in Genesis 24:50,
Judges 14:4 and Proverbs 19:14."

Rabbi Cohen further recalls: "It is plain that Divine Providence was in
control of our destinies. For it transpired that during the three years that
Naomi had been living in Jerusalem as a student before I met her, many
mutual friends had been trying to get us together, either by inviting both
of us to Shabbat morning *Kiddush*, or to afternoon tea. However, on every
single occasion, one or the other of us could not make it."

Rabbanit Cohen elaborates: "Our meeting was delayed by Heaven, in
order to make sure that we would first mature in the same direction and
be ready to tie our lives together."

When the *Nazir* heard about the meeting between his son and Naomi,
he wrote in his diary on Tu B'Av, 8th August 1952, as follows:

> "With the arrival of the holy Shabbat of "Consolation," which
> comes straight after the Fast of 9th *Av*, and for a whole week
> after that, the radiant, smiling face of my dear grandmother, the
> Rabbanit of blessed memory, lit up my inner eye. And then the
> face of my grandfather, the *Gaon* of blessed memory, appeared to
> me in all its glory. They say nothing, but are happy, and I know
> that the matter is near and complete, all part of the divine plan."

After just two weeks of acquaintance, Rabbi Cohen and Naomi decided
to get engaged. On hearing the news, the *Nazir* wrote a poem of thanksgiving in his diary:

"O Lord our God, You have begun to shower beneficence on Your servant. My heart is full of gratitude on account of Your great Name. Many trials and tribulations have compassed me about. These have caused me great sorrow, and I did not know the whys or the wherefores, or what to make of it all. But now You have shone Your face upon me and heaped kindness and goodness upon me as tokens to Your child and servant that peace and quiet will be the lot of him and his family. *'Blessed is the person who trusts in You;' 'Give thanks to the Lord for He is good: may His mercy endure forever'* (see Psalms 84:12 and 107:1). Almighty God, please grant that Shear Yashuv will grow in Torah, strengthen Torah and spread the teaching of Torah throughout the world."

On 4th Shevat 5713 (20th January 1953), the young couple were married in the plaza behind the Yeshurun Synagogue in Jerusalem. The festive meal was then held at the Hotel Tel Aviv at *Kikkar Zion* (Zion Square). The wedding was attended by many of the "great and the good" of Jerusalem. These included, of course, the distinguished relatives from both sides of the family: from the family of the *Nazir* as well as from the family of Rabbi Herbert Goldstein, whose father-in-law had been the well-known philanthropist, Harry Fischel.

After Rabbi Cohen (then the Chief Rabbi of the Israel Air Force), consulted with his brother-in-law, Rabbi Shlomo Goren, (Chief Rabbi of the IDF), and with his future wife, Naomi – he decided to be wed in military style. He therefore appeared under the marriage canopy wearing his Air Force dress uniform, and as he walked down the aisle to the *chuppah*, a row of military officers lined each side.

Many guests were amazed by this decision. These included Rabbi Moshe Kalcheim, the father of Rabbi Uzi Kalcheim who later taught at the Ariel Institutes. He asked Rabbi Tzvi Yehudah Kook if it was "appropriate for a bridegroom to stand under the *chuppah* in military uniform, especially in Jerusalem, the Holy City, where the bridegroom usually wears his Shabbat best, such as a *shtreimel*." Rabbi Tzvi Yehuda answered that the bridegroom is likened to a monarch, and since the military uniform is a form of royal garb, these clothes were most appropriate for the occasion:

"The *shtreimel* only became imbued with 'holiness' *post facto*. While it is true that many *Torah* scholars and holy *tzaddikim* wear a *shtreimel*, and we certainly have great reverence for them, and are nothing but dust under the soles of their feet, the *shtreimel* is revered only on account of the merit of those who wear it. By contrast, the Israeli military uniform is intrinsically holy."

Rabbi Cohen arrives at his wedding wearing his Air Force uniform, standing next to his father HaRav HaNazir. Rabbi Tzvi Yehuda Kook is on the far left in the back.

Rabbi Cohen is betrothed to his wife Naomi under the chuppah. Chief Rabbi Herzog, the officiating rabbi, is on the right.

This response was another example of Rabbi Tzvi Yehuda's great love for the young Rabbi Cohen. After reciting one of the blessings under the *chupah*, he danced with the bridegroom as if he were his own son. Years later, Rabbi Cohen would relate that he would never forget "Rav Tzvi Yehuda's very personal dance with me on the night of my wedding."

A few days after the wedding, on 17th Shevat (2nd February), the *Nazir* wrote in his diary:

> "I love my new daughter as I love my own soul. My daughter-in-law, Naomi, came into my life by great *mazal* and good fortune. Naomi is meticulous in observing the Torah, and is a vegetarian, like my own son, whose very soul is linked to mine – and now they are one. May they always experience joy everlasting. We celebrated their wedding on the 4th of Shevat in splendor and beauty. Let it be a sign for the future, both for their own lives and for the glory of Israel."

The couple's only child, Eliraz, was born toward the end of their first year of marriage. Naomi had already thought of the name "Eliraz," as she later explained:

> "Firstly, the name reflected somewhat the personality of Shear Yashuv's father, the *Nazir*, whose main interest is in 'secret' wisdom (*raz*), the inner wisdom of Jewish mysticism. Secondly, the name 'Eliraz' is an anagram of 'Raziel.' By giving our daughter this name, we would be commemorating the name of David Raziel, the commander of the Irgun, who had been a student at Yeshivat Merkaz HaRav. Raziel had been a good friend of Shear Yashuv before he fell in 1941, while fighting on behalf of the British against the pro-Axis Iraqis. Shear Yashuv gave an additional reason for the name: Raziel is the name of the angel charged with protecting women in labor."

Naomi suggested that they should also give their new daughter a second name. This was 'Chaya,' after her own grandmother, Chaya Sheyna, the wife of Harry Fischel, and also after Rabbi Cohen's paternal great-grandmother. For Naomi this was not only a matter of commemorating the names of their relatives, but a "fail safe," just in case the child did not feel comfortable with her special name, "Eliraz." If she did not like that name, they would be able to call her Chaya instead. However, from the outset Eliraz was happy with her special name. And in fact, the name caught on, first among the *Nazir's* close circle, and later, further afield, and is now

ישיבת בני־עקיבא
כפר הרואה, עמק חפר
Telephone 063-22680 טלפון
חשבון בנק הדואר 43260
YESHIVATH BNEI AKIVAH
KFAR HAROEH, EMEK HEFER

ב"ה, כ"ד תשרי, ה'תשמ"ו

לכבוד
הרה"ג שאר-ישוב כהן
והרבנית שליט"א
המקום ינחם אתכם בתוך שאר אבלי ציון וירושלים

מו"ר

קראתי בעתון על פטירתה של האם הגדולה והמופלאה, הרבנית
מרת שרה ע"ה השלו'. מי עוד כמוני שזכה להכירה מקרוב, ובזכו שנים
שזכה להיות בן-בית מקורב לאביכם הגדול, נזיר-אלקים זצ"ל, שידע כאיזו
מסירות היתה אמכם עזר כנגדו, איך דבקה בכל נשימתה
לאמונתו, תוך נשיאה בעול האמת והנזירות, ובכל זאת נשמה טהורה
הלכה לעולמה, אינו דומה אשה זכה מעולמנו.
אשריה שזכתה לראות דור ישרים מבורך, וזכתה לרוות נחת
מצאצאיה, שזכתה לראות תלמידים מרובים עוסקים בכתבי קדשו
הנזיר אשר לו הקדישה את חייה.
בדברי הנחמות יתן לכם כח ועוז להמשיך בדרך הטוב והישר
אשר טבעתם בבית אבא-ואמא ולהנחיל מורשה יקרה זו לצאצאיכם
לאורך ימים ושנים.
בירושלים תנוחמו ולא תוסיפו לדאבה עוד.

בכבוד רב ובהוקרה
משה צבי נריה

Rabbi Moshe Tzvi Neriah's letter of condolence to Rav Shear Yashuv on the passing of his mother, the Rabbanit Sarah Cohen.

quite popular. Naomi therefore feels that she has added a new name to the Jewish people's treasury of names.

Eliraz grew up in Jerusalem, and when she graduated from high school, she decided to join the IDF. She served as an officer in the Education and Culture Division, with responsibility for the posting of lecturers to different units.

Today Eliraz lives in Efrat, a community in the Gush Etzion bloc. She has an MA in Communications, and a high school teacher's license, both from the Hebrew University. She has held many positions, including Head of the Department of Education of Efrat and its environs, and later as the Director General of the *Yesodot* Institute for the teaching of democratic ideals in the *mamlachti dati* (religious state) school system. Presently, she heads the Departments of Humanities and Social Studies in the pedagogical center of Israel's Ministry of Education. Eliraz has six children and eleven grandchildren, may they increase!

Rabbanit Naomi continued to pursue her academic studies after the wedding, studying Jewish thought and Jewish history at the Hebrew University of Jerusalem. Her special research interest has been Philo, or to give him his Hebrew name, Yedidya of Alexandria. Philo (1st century CE) was the first Jewish thinker whose extensive writings are still extant. It was her father-in-law, the *Nazir*, who encouraged her to specialize in Philo. He had always dreamed of restoring Philo's writings to their rightful place on the Jewish bookshelf, and even gave classes on Philo's teachings at Yeshivat Merkaz HaRav.

In 1971 the Rabbanit received her doctorate from the Hebrew University of Jerusalem for her thesis: *"Jewish Names and their Sociological Significance in the Hellenistic and Roman Periods in Asia Minor."*

At the beginning of her academic career she taught at the Michlala Seminary for Women in Jerusalem. She later taught in the Departments of Jewish Philosophy and Jewish Thought at the Universities of Tel Aviv and Haifa, as well as in the School of Education at Haifa University. She has written several books on Philo, and many scholarly articles on Philo and on other subjects, which have been published in learned academic journals. She has also written on topics of wider interest, such as education, feminism, and religion in Israel. Examples of her books on Philo include *Philo Judaeus: His Universe of Discourse* (Frankfurt am Main 1995), and *Philo's Scriptures: Citations from the Prophets and Writings – Evidence for a Haftarah Cycle in Second Temple Judaism* (Supplement to the Journal for the Study of Judaism 123, Leiden 2007). At present Rabbanit Dr. Cohen is a Research Fellow at the University of Haifa.

Rabbanit Cohen also takes great interest in public affairs. In recognition of her wide-ranging activities in Haifa, in 1982 she received the *Eshet*

HaMofet ("The Haifa Outstanding Woman of the Year Award"), and in 2010 she was one of the recipients of the *Yakirei Haifa* ("Outstanding Citizens of Haifa Award") – given every year to fifteen people in each of the major cities of Israel.

Rabbanit Cohen's communal work in Israel began when the couple still lived in Jerusalem. Rabbanit Sarah Herzog (1899–1979), the wife of Chief Rabbi Herzog, asked her to set up a "chapter" of young observant women to assist the activities of the older women of "*Omen Mizrachi Women's Organization*," which was later known as *Emunah*.

She relates:

> "I thought that I had managed to politely refuse Rabbanit Herzog's request, when I replied that I would think about it, certain that this would be the end of the matter. But after a fortnight I received a note from Rabbanit Herzog thanking me for agreeing to take on this task. I came to the conclusion that there was no choice: it was harder to turn down Rabbanit Herzog than to get to work to set up this new group.
>
> "I got my friends together and we founded the *Eden* chapter of *Omen*. Initially the criterion for joining was that one had a young child. The name '*Eden*' is an acronym for *Irgun Nashim Datiyot* ('Organization for Observant Women'). The root meaning of the word is 'base' or 'socket', as in the *Mishkan* (Tabernacle). *Eden* took off and, in no time at all, it became *the* leading religious Zionist women's organization in Jerusalem. Some years ago, it celebrated its 50th 'Jubilee' anniversary. Even though its membership has not been 'young' for some time, they are still carrying on their work on behalf of the community, and more enthusiastically than ever before."

For many years, Naomi has also been a member of the Board of the National Executive of *Emunah* itself. In the early days she regarded it as very important to set up organizations for young women, for that was a time in Israel's history when the majority of young women were immigrants (even if not all of them were new), and lacked any extended family nearby. We are talking about an era when women did not normally have a job outside the home.

Setting up and maintaining the kindergarten system, as well as other Israeli educational institutions, before this task was taken over by government agencies, provided the members of the religious women's organization with a sense of belonging and camaraderie, as well as contributing to their self-confidence and feelings of self-worth. When a woman was immersed in this kind of work, she no longer felt alone and isolated.

Furthermore, at a time when most people did not own a telephone, these monthly meetings provided a much-needed framework for the forging of new friendships and staying in touch. Every other profession: medical, teaching, or accounting, has its own professional organization to look after its members' interests. At that time in Israel's early history, there was no such organization for young Israeli housewives. The organization provided observant women with a sense of "togetherness," as well as giving them a collective voice with which to lobby government agencies in pursuit of women's rights.

Rabbanit Cohen was also one of the founding members of the *Shedulat HaNashim BeYisrael* ("The Israeli Women's Lobby"), and served on their Executive for many years. In addition, when the Orthodox women's organization *Kolech* ("*Your Woman's Voice*") was set up to strengthen the status of women in Judaism and in Jewish society, she was invited to lecture at its founding celebration, and was one of the signatories to its foundational document of 1998. Rabbanit Cohen served on *Kolech's* Executive Council from its inception until fairly recently.

But the pride and joy of all the Rabbanit's achievements is her pioneering work in the field of Talmud study by women. After moving to Haifa, when her husband was elected as its Chief Rabbi in 1975, Naomi responded to requests from her friends in the community to set up a class in *Gemara* for women.

During the first year, their teacher was a man, but he found it difficult to cope with so many women of high intellectual caliber who were completely ignorant of even the layout of a typical page of *Gemara*, not to mention the Aramaic language. So she took over the task herself, and her largely independent study – both solo and with a study-partner – recalls the adage (as she put it herself) that "in the land of the blind, the one-eyed man is king." Since 1978, therefore, she has been teaching *Gemara* to women. Together they have covered the entire Talmud Tractates *Ta'anit* and *Megillah* and, in addition, selected chapters from *Pesachim, Yoma, Gittin, Baba Metziah, Avodah Zarah,* and others.

⇒   HONORING PARENTS

Despite all his public commitments, Rabbi Cohen made every effort to participate regularly in his father's classes. These were attended by students from Yeshivat Merkaz HaRav, as well as by learned members of the general public. On Saturday nights there were classes on the rabbinic *midrashim* and on Tuesday the classes dealt with *Tikkunei Zohar*. On Hoshana Rabba, during the week of Sukkot, the *Nazir* used to hold a special class on the Kabbalistic work *Idra Zuta*. Rabbi Shear Yashuv would read the text aloud, and his father would provide the commentary. It is noteworthy that the *Nazir's* wife, Rabbanit Sarah, used to participate regularly in his classes.

Regarding his mother, Rabbi Cohen relates:

> "Mother never said anything that even hinted at *lashon hara* (slander or gossip). She never raised her voice, either to scold or to shout. All her words were soothing to the ear. Her spoken Hebrew was pure and polished; her conversational style was always serene, with no hint of complaint, or even a slightly raised voice. The *Nazir* used to say to his children: 'I have many periods of silence. Mother speaks. But whether the subject is religious or about everyday matters, her speech is always imbued with holiness. The real *tzaddik* in the family is your mother. Please pay careful attention to your mother. Treat her with great respect, and you will gain great merit.'"

And about his father:

> "I feel that the relationship between my father and me went beyond the normal relations between father and son. We were soul mates. Even when my father did not utter a word, he only had to look at me and I immediately knew what he wanted. For many years I had long heart-to-hearts with him that lasted for hours, even when I was young. If only I could have devoted more time to those conversations."

Rabbi Aaron Reichel – Director of the Harry and Jane Fischel Foundation in New York, a nephew of Rabbanit Naomi, and a sometime student at Machon Harry Fischel – also recalls the unique relationship between Rabbi Cohen and his parents:

> "The year in which I studied, *inter alia*, at the Machon in Israel was most memorable and left an indelible impression on me. The intensity of the study of the Torah and the unique atmosphere that permeated the Machon remain a source of continuing inspiration to me to this day. I was fortunate to have a unique experience with my relationship to the Cohen family that was strengthened during this period. Rabbi Shear Yashuv and his wife gave me a standing invitation to be their guests every weekend. But more than that,

my aunt, Dr. Naomi, would try to convince me to actually come over every weekend by telling me over the phone, in advance, what amazing and stimulating guests had already accepted invitations to grace their Friday night table each weekend.

"I also had the opportunity to accompany the Cohens, as part of the special Shabbat 'package,' on many of their Shabbat lunch visits to my uncle's parents, the noted *Rav HaNazir* of blessed memory, and his wife of blessed memory. Every Shabbat we would walk all the way from their apartment in Rehavia to the *Nazir's* apartment in Kerem Abraham, adjacent to Geula, despite my uncle's war injury that made walking somewhat uncomfortable. There I learned a lesson in *kibbud av v'em*, honoring one's parents, by observation. In an atmosphere of ultimate spiritual holiness, my uncle communicated with his father with the deference of a student to his revered rabbinical teacher, by speaking to him in the third person, the only time I had ever witnessed a son speaking to his father with such respect.

"I also attended the Rosh HaShanah and Yom Kippur services in the home of the *Nazir*, with my uncle leading the services as the principal *chazan*, or *shliach tzibbur*. I recall being taken aback as my uncle Rabbi Shear Yashuv chanted the services in the Ashkenazic pronunciation of the traditional Yeshiva world, in clear deference to his father and his father's older disciples and congregants, despite my uncle's strong identification with, and public personification of, the religious Zionist world, where as a general rule the Sephardi pronunciation was and remains the only one in use.

"By the time I spent my memorable year in Israel, the *Nazir* was quite advanced in age and found the delivery of his famous Saturday night lecture for a group of elite students from the Merkaz Harav Yeshiva very difficult. So his son (my uncle) deftly, subtly, and brilliantly assisted his father in the delivery of this lecture on the *Midrash* on the weekly Torah reading. Few people would have been able to do so in this manner, not to mention how few would have taken the trouble to do so."

THE NAZIR'S LAST DAYS

Rabbi Shear Yashuv gives a very moving description of the days before his father's death:

"Father became ill and his health deteriorated. On one of the most difficult days when even the doctors were in despair and saw no hope, father watched me walking around the house, steeped in anguish. On the eve of the Holy Shabbat, he called me to his bed and, with a radiant smile on his face, asked me: 'What are you afraid of? That your father is leaving this world? There is no need for you to be sad. You should be happy: this is what we have always longed for.' I pulled myself together and tried to overcome my sorrow. When I left the room I said to myself: 'Father and master, you are a great luminary. For you this may be a joyful occasion, but for us it is a matter of great grief.'

"On another occasion, when father was lying on his sickbed, I heard him singing: '*Shalom Aleichem, Malachei HaShalom, Malachei Elyon.*' This is a song sung to welcome the angels as Shabbat evening arrives. However, this was not Shabbat, but an ordinary weekday. I thought that the illness might be confusing him, because of the great pain he was suffering. Maybe he had forgotten what day it was. So I said: 'Father, today is not Shabbat!' He replied that he was aware of this, but that there exists a Kabbalistic custom that when a person is about to depart from this world, angels come to accompany his soul and at this time the verses that are normally sung on Shabbat are also recited.

"During our final conversation together, my father and teacher, *HaRav Nazir*, said to me: 'Why are you sorrowful? For a person who is fortunate enough to leave this world and, thank God, makes his final exit with reputation intact, there is no need for regrets. Does it not state in Ecclesiastes 7:1: '*Better than precious oil is a good reputation, and the day of one's death [is better] than the day of one's birth.*' This time too, I repeated what I had said before: 'For you this is an occasion for joy, but for us it is a time for grief, as we are to be parted.'"

When he was moved to the hospital, the *Nazir* was in agony from excruciating pain. In order to divert his attention, students from Merkaz HaRav, who used to come and help him in his old age, would sit next to him and sing: *Yibane HaMikdash* ("*May the Mikdash be Rebuilt*"). The *Nazir* would listen attentively and it was as if all his pain had vanished.

But, during the morning vigil of 28th Av 5732 (8th August 1972), *HaRav Nazir* passed away. Rabbi Cohen recalls his father's funeral:

"*HaRav HaNazir* was carried from the old *Sha'arei Tzedek* Hospital to the *Bet HaRav*, Rav Kook's home in the old building of the Yeshivat Merkaz HaRav. There, Psalms were recited, while his bier was placed on the table of a small room, the *Bet HaMidrash*, in which Rav Kook had taught his classes and which contained his large book collection. From there, the bier was carried to the *Nazir's* own home in Amos St. Rabbi Tzvi Yehuda Kook, who used to live near us, was sitting outside on the sidewalk (for he was a Cohen), sobbing uncontrollably, while we waited until the bier was carried out; and I was worried all the while that something might happen to him."

Word of the *Nazir's* death was received with great anguish. A vast crowd gathered and escorted him to his eternal resting place. Behind the bier walked many people who had known the *Nazir*, and many who had not known him. There must have been tens of thousands of people who followed his bier, exchanging their thoughts and comments on the amazing life of the *Nazir*. The greatest Torah scholars of that generation, the most learned rabbis, mingled with ordinary folk: together they all walked behind the bier through the Mea Shearim neighborhood and far beyond, until they reached the Mount of Olives.

Even after the death of her husband, Rabbanit Sarah Cohen continued to distinguish herself on the Jerusalem landscape through her communal work and her unique deeds of lovingkindness. Of his mother, Rabbi Cohen relates that:

"There was once a man from a good Jerusalem family who fell on hard times and became addicted to drink. As a result he lost his job and took up begging, but he used most of the money he collected from begging to feed his drinking habit. When my father died, I was no longer living in Jerusalem, but during one of my visits to the city, the young woman who lived with my mother and helped her when necessary, appealed to me: 'Rabbi, you must do something: I am scared of being in the house. There is a drunkard here who keeps disturbing us. If things carry on like this, I'll be forced to leave and your mother will have no one to look after her.'

"I went into the house and opened the door of the *Bet HaMidrash* – the room which my father had used both as a small synagogue of prayer and as a place of learning. There, on the very desk at which he had taught his classes and had written new insights on the Torah, were rows of silver coins. And, sitting at the desk, was the poor beggar himself, who was almost completely drunk and reeking of alcohol, which you could smell from a long way off. And there, on the desk itself, were his total 'takings'. It became immediately apparent that this was where the beggar was running his 'bank' – on top of the table in my illustrious father's *Bet HaMidrash*. And while he counted, he took another swill, and while he drank, he counted his coins.

"This spectacle shook me to the core, and I told him off immediately: 'What do you think you are doing?' I said. This really scared the wretched fellow, who dropped his bottle as fear and shame overcame him. I went to my mother in the next room and said: 'Mother, things can't go on like this: if you really want to support this fellow, I am willing to help him find a room somewhere else, and we can pay his rent.'

"My mother's answer was both simple and amazing: 'If I ask him to leave, no one will know who he is. No one is aware that he comes from a really good family, from a wonderful home. It is completely out of the question! There is no other way but to let him continue to come to us: this is now the only home he knows.' There was nothing for it: the man was allowed to carry on coming to stay in my parents' home almost up to the last year of my mother's life. And when mother finally had to go into hospital, and he realized that she would never be coming back, it was as if his whole world collapsed before his very eyes. This is just one example of the very many special acts of kindness performed by my mother of blessed memory."

Rabbi Abraham Yitzhak Rosenbaum, Director of Machon Harry Fischel, adds the following story:

"A certain individual arrived from Eilat, with his young daughter of six or seven. He left the child with Rabbanit Sarah and went wandering around the streets of Jerusalem. Several days went by, and the man conveniently 'forgot' to come back and pick up his daughter! One day, I visited the house and found the Rabbanit standing and washing the child in the shower, as well as shampooing her hair. I asked the Rabbanit who was then nearly 90 years old: 'Do you really think that you should be doing this kind of work at your age?' The Rabbanit answered: 'And who do you suppose I should send the child to? As far as her father and mother are concerned, she is like an orphan to them: she doesn't have a mother or father anymore!'"

Rabbanit Sarah – may her soul rest in Paradise – went to the next world many years after the death of her husband, the *Nazir*. She died on the night of *Hoshana Rabba*, 21st Tishrei 5746 (6th October 1985). This was the very night when scores of visitors had in the past visited the *Nazir's Sukkah* to participate in his classes on the *Idra Zuta* and listen to the sacred *niggunim* melodies composed by the *Nazir* and Rav Kook, accompanied on the violin. They would also take part in the singing and dancing of the regular participants, which were often in full flow in the *Sukkah* by the time they arrived. The sad news reached her son, Rabbi Cohen, when he was in the midst of Sukkot festivities in his own *Sukkah* in Haifa.

We conclude with the words of Rabbi Harel Cohen, Director of Machon Nezer David in the Ariel Institutes:

"It is remarkable that despite his myriad other duties, so many years after the death of both his father and mother, Rabbi Cohen continues to personally oversee the arrangements for the annual memorial services for them, which take place at our own Machon, as well as the annual Torah seminar held in memory of the *Nazir*."

"To Jerusalem, Thy City…" (From the *Amidah* Prayer)

"My Jerusalem is the city of Torah. Every nook and cranny overflows with yearning and longing for the traditions of our fathers. It is a city in which the air is filled with the sounds of Talmudic students returning home after their late-night study. Jerusalem is famed for the modesty of her Torah scholars and simple folk alike. They all devote their lives to penetrating and perusing the very depths of the Torah, paying attention to every last detail.

"Jerusalem is a city of layer upon layer of tradition. At times you stand with mouth agape at its zealous inhabitants' refusal to change a thing, while at other times, your heart rejoices at the refreshing audacity of the creative minds in her midst, the cream of Jerusalem's great centers of learning.

My Jerusalem is also a city of the self-sacrifice and sheer tenacity of her builders and leaders. Every one of Jerusalem's many neighborhoods is a shining example of pioneering and boldness. No district is without its own story of sacrifice, blood, sweat and toil of the brave generations who have guarded her walls, and who broke through to its unwalled open spaces and new horizons.

Jerusalem is a city carved out in stone by builders who shed their blood in order to create a fresh vision for future generations of Bible students – dreamers who hear the echo of prophecy. It is a city of Talmudic scholars who have returned to take part in its rebuilding.

My Jerusalem is a city of warriors, heroes of the Underground groups fighting hostile and implacable foes. Although these intrepid fighters disagreed with each other on tactics, on this they firmly agreed: the identity of the joint enemy and unconditional love for their comrades, whoever they were, as well as for all the inhabitants of the city.

"Even regarding the enemy, only on the very rare occasions when their understandable pain temporarily clouded their generosity of spirit, were incredibly high standards not maintained.

"My Jerusalem is a city of wisdom and science. The libraries amassed in the homes of her citizens contain a far greater wealth of literature per capita than you will find in any other city in the world. Jerusalem is justly proud of her sages and scientists. She is home to great thinkers, philosophers and scientists, and many types of schools and institutes of higher education adorn her hills.

My Jerusalem is a city of religion, mysticism and spirituality, the Bet HaMikdash, *the Holy Sanctuary, where the sound of prayer never ceases – of the midnight Tikkun Chatzot lamentation over the destruction of the Temple, of the dawn Vatikin prayer, of the early morning Shema just as the sun's rays surface to the east of the Temple Mount, home of the Bet HaMikdash.*

"My Jerusalem is a city of never-ending minyanim. There is always a minyan in progress. An endless variety of congregations, communities, prayer services and styles string together to form a crown of praise to the King of the Royal Mikdash-Sanctuary. Their different harmonies come together in a hymn of thanksgiving to the Almighty for choosing Zion and Jerusalem as His home and Temple – His very own, special holy City.

*I profoundly love this city. I love her because she
is a city of contradictions and conflicts. I love her for her
twists and turns, her hopes and despairs, her yearning and
agonies, her ups and downs. I love her for her fallings-out
and patchings-up. I love her as do all her* banim *and* bonim
*(her children and builders), every single one of whom
cleaves to her totally. For, in the midst of the squabbling,
the in-fighting and the dissent, one thing unites all
Jerusalemites: their unique love of Jerusalem, a love like no
other.* 'Seek the peace of Jerusalem; may they prosper that
love thee.' *(Psalms 122:6)"*

Rabbi Shear Yashuv Cohen
BaMahane IDF Magazine
28th Iyyar 5732 (Friday, 12th May 1972)

"To Jerusalem, Thy City…" (From the *Amidah* Prayer)

➡ THE SIX DAY WAR

On Monday, 26th Iyyar 5727 (5th June 1967) the "Six Day War" broke out. The Israelis swiftly liquidated the Egyptian air force, and the IDF proceeded to capture the Sinai Peninsula. In spite of Israel's repeated warnings and pleadings to King Hussein of Jordan not to join in the war against Jerusalem, after Egypt announced to the world that it was winning the campaign, the Jordanian Arab Legion joined the other Arab states and began to massively bombard Jerusalem. The IDF had no choice but to take on the Jordanian assault and launch their own counter-attack, with the net result that the eastern part of Jerusalem fell into our hands.

At the time, in 1967, Rabbi Cohen was serving as the Deputy Mayor of the Jerusalem municipality, and throughout the fighting he was to be found in the municipality "situation room." When the battle for Jerusalem began he asked a favor of Major General Rafael Vardi (b. 1922), who was the liaison officer between the IDF and the municipality. If the war spread to the Old City in the eastern part of the city, he, Rabbi Cohen, wanted to be a member of her liberating force.

In 1948, as an injured soldier, he had been the last Jew to be removed from the Old City. At that time, he had promised himself that, being the last one out, he would be the first back in. On Wednesday, 28th Iyyar (7th June) Rabbi Cohen stayed up all night on the top floor of the old Municipal Building in Jerusalem, only just making out the Old City, and praying for the welfare of the soldiers. In the dark of that night he could clearly discern the explosions from the street fighting over Jerusalem.

Rabbi Cohen's brother-in-law, IDF Chief Rabbi, Rabbi Shlomo Goren, did not sleep a wink, either:

With his brother-in-law IDF Chief Rabbi Shlomo Goren, lighting Chanukah candles in the Machkemah building adjoining the Temple Mount

"My *shofar* had been destroyed during the day. But since I knew that we were on the verge of liberating the Old City that day and reaching the *Kotel* (the Western Wall of the Temple Compound), when dawn broke at around 4:00 in the morning, I ran as fast as I could to the home of my father-in-law, *HaRav HaNazir*, and knocked at the door. I told him that I needed a *shofar* because we were going to liberate the *Kotel*. My father-in-law began to weep uncontrollably. Then, as the special *shofar* was tucked away in a secret place high up in one of the cupboards, he climbed onto the table, took it out and handed it to me. I took the *shofar* from him and ran as fast as I could, this time in the direction of the Rockefeller Museum. And from there I walked up toward the Lions' Gate."

Rabbi Goren was right. That very day, 28th Iyyar (the very same day that the great Rav Kook, the first Chief Rabbi of Israel while still under the

Rav Shear Yashuv, flanked by his father, the Nazir, and Rabbi Goren

Mandate, had made *aliyah*, and set foot on the soil of the Holy Land), the 55th Paratroopers Brigade, led by Lieutenant General Mordechai "Motta" Gur (1930–95), took back the Temple Mount and the *Kotel* – this time from the hands of the Arabs.

Holding a *Sefer Torah* in one hand and his father-in-law's *shofar* in the other, Rabbi Goren joined the combatants in liberating the Old City. And when the hardened combatants, veterans of an untold number of battles, heard Rabbi Goren blowing the *shofar* at the Western Wall, they broke down and wept like children.

However, Rabbi Cohen did not realize his dream of being the *very* first civilian to enter the Old City, for his father, the *Nazir*, and his teacher, Rabbi Tzvi Yehuda, were there before him! Rabbi Goren had driven them both to the spot in his own jeep.

These two venerable rabbis were the first to announce the liberation of the Old City of Jerusalem and the site of the ancient Temple. They followed immediately on the heels of the combatants, while the IDF were still cleansing the Old City of every trace of the Jordanian Legion. Here is Rabbi Cohen's personal account of that very special day of the reunification of the two parts of Jerusalem:

> "On Wednesday morning, 28th Iyyar, a soldier came into the office and saluted. He reported that Major General Vardi remembered my request to be one of the first people to enter the Old City, and had dispatched him to transport me by jeep to the *Kotel*. When we

Standing behind his brother-in-law Rabbi Shlomo Goren on the day the Western Wall was liberated.

arrived, Rabbi Tzvi Yehuda and my illustrious father were already there, standing next to Rabbi Goren. Rabbi Goren proceeded to lead the assembled gathering in a prayer that was simply not of this world. It was one of those very rare occasions, and altogether one of those unique, unforgettable 'once in a lifetime' experiences.

"Those of us who were lucky enough to be present at this momentous occasion will remember it for the rest of our lives. It was as if the heavens had opened and we were seeing visions of the Divine. Our prayer was the normal afternoon *Mincha* prayer, but on this occasion it was intoned by all present in pure and utter devotion. The hearts of all of us were full of joy and gratitude, as tears flowed down our cheeks. Every single soldier, whether observant or not, joined at this moment in the recitation of Psalm 126: '*A Song of Ascents: When the Lord accompanied the captivity of Zion on their return – we were like dreamers...*'" [from the Psalm recited on *Shabbat* and other festive meals].

⇛   "...WE WERE LIKE DREAMERS"

The first Shavuot holiday after the liberation of Jerusalem took place exactly one week later, on Wednesday, June 14. The road to the *Kotel* was opened, a plaza had been cleared in front of it, and access was granted through the Zion Gate. To those many tens of thousands of pilgrims, it was as if they had been reborn after a hiatus of almost twenty years. The never-ending crowds of people going to and from the Old City on that first Shavuot after the liberation and reunification of Jerusalem brought home more than anything else that this time Jerusalem had been truly liberated and reunified!

This is how Rabbi Cohen recalls the moments when he took part with tens of thousands of *Am Yisrael* on their first Shavuot pilgrimage to the *Kotel* in a reunited Jerusalem:

> I was extremely fortunate to be caught in the midst of that mass of people, because I happened to chance upon the great, unforgettable *Tzaddik* of Jerusalem, that devoted and generous *mensch*, Reb Aryeh Levin (1885–1969). Reb Aryeh had been one of the best-loved students of the great Chief Rabbi Kook. And Reb Aryeh was also happy to see me. He warmly embraced me, and so we walked together for some time without speaking, silent and deep in thought. And then he began to talk in Yiddish – almost in a whisper: 'My whole life I have not been able to understand what is meant by those words of Scripture: *When the Lord accompanied the captivity of Zion on their return – we were like dreamers . . . .'* But now, now, I understand!'
>
> I asked him: "What do you understand?" Reb Aryeh replied: "It is characteristic of a dream that in a single instant a person can see events that have actually taken place over a long period. In a dream you can sometimes see something that has *lasted* for many years, but you actually *see* it in a single instant. In the twinkling of an eye the whole picture becomes clear to you. Through a 'dream moment' you comprehend a whole era, a whole history, a whole story. In that very instant you experience the entire existence of generations past. . . .
>
> "This is exactly what is happening to us now. We are just about to enter the Old City, walking on foot to the *Kotel*. Are we not 'like dreamers'? At this very moment we are connected to the many millions of Jews who have prayed throughout the generations for what we are experiencing right now. Right now, we can see everything. We can 'see' the long years of *Galut*, the Shoah, the Underground [where I visited you and others in Latrun Prison], the War of Liberation, and, most recently, the Six-Day War. This very second, while you and I are walking together to the *Kotel*, everything is happening as if in a dream."

With his father, the Nazir, and an IDF soldier on the day the Kotel was liberated.

Reb Aryeh proceeded with great emotion: 'Because, this is it! It is happening now! How fortunate we are to merit this moment, the moment of the rebirth of Israel, the moment when *Am Yisrael* are once more in control of the City of Jerusalem. How fortunate we are to be worthy of reaching these times: the times of the 'beginning of the redemption.' And if we all do *teshuva* right now and repent (and with the Lord's help may it happen speedily), there is no doubt that redemption will soon be complete."

At that moment I comprehended that it was Reb Aryeh from

The first prayer after the liberation of Hebron and the Machpelah Cave during the Six Day War. Left of Rabbi Cohen is Rabbi Mordechai Piron.

the Old *Yishuv* of Jerusalem who was seeing clearly that the liberation – the retaking and the reunification of Jerusalem – was the culmination of the vision and dream prayed for by many generations of Jews throughout the ages, as encapsulated by the Psalmist's vision of the return of *'captivity of Zion'.*

Rabbi Cohen also celebrated the following festival in the liberated Old City. On the festival of Sukkot, some four months later, he was a guest in the *Sukkah* of the newly-built Yeshivat HaKotel. At that time, so soon after Jerusalem had been liberated, it was the only *Sukkah* inside the Old City.

THE "PEACE FOR JERUSALEM" SHABBAT

The day after Jerusalem was liberated and reunified on 29th Iyar 5727 (Thursday 8th June 1967) the Chief Rabbinate convened under the leadership of the Ashkenazi Chief Rabbi of Israel, Rabbi Unterman. It called on all synagogues to introduce a celebratory Thanksgiving Prayer on the following Sabbath, Shabbat Parashat Bamidbar (when the beginning of the Book of Numbers is read aloud).

The Chief Rabbinate also called on everyone "to preserve the very special re-awakening that had been aroused during the war." In years to come, *Yom Yerushalayim* (Jerusalem Day) was actually celebrated on the date of the liberation itself, 28th Iyar, and not on Shabbat Parashat Bamidbar.

In 5768 (2008), Rabbi Eliezer Shefer, the Head of the Union of Synagogues in Israel, asked Rabbi Shear Yashuv to write a special thanksgiving prayer that would unite the entire people of Israel in honoring Jerusalem and praying for her well-being. This prayer would be recited on the Shabbat immediately preceding Jerusalem Day, the Sabbath to be known as *Shabbat Sh'lom Yerushalayim*, the "Peace for Jerusalem"

Sabbath. Rabbi Cohen wrote a prayer, which was distributed to synagogues and communities in Israel and throughout the world, for festive recitation every year on that special Sabbath. In 2009, a special melody was composed by the conductor and composer, Elli Jaffe, for Rabbi Cohen's prayer.[1]

⇒ RAV SHEAR YASHUV'S PRAYER FOR JERUSALEM

תפילה לירושלים

אָבִינוּ שֶׁבַּשָּׁמַיִם הַבּוֹחֵר בְּצִיּוֹן וִירוּשָׁלַיִם, אֲשֶׁר אִוִּיתָ לְּךָ אֶת עִיר הַקֹּדֶשׁ, בָּרֵךְ כָּל בּוֹנֶיהָ, בָּנֶיהָ וְדוֹרְשֵׁי שְׁלוֹמָהּ, וּשְׁלַח בְּרָכָה וְהַצְלָחָה בְּכָל מַעֲשֵׂי יְדֵיהֶם. וּפְרֹושׂ עָלֶיהָ סֻכַּת שְׁלוֹמֶךָ, וְקַיֵּם בָּהּ מִקְרָא שֶׁכָּתוּב: לְמַעַן צִיּוֹן לֹא אֶחֱשֶׁה, וּלְמַעַן יְרוּשָׁלַיִם לֹא אֶשְׁקוֹט, עַד יֵצֵא כַנֹּגַהּ צִדְקָהּ, וִישׁוּעָתָהּ כְּלַפִּיד יִבְעָר. וּבְנֵה אוֹתָהּ בְּקָרוֹב בְּיָמֵינוּ בִּנְיַן עוֹלָם, וְכִסֵּא דָוִד עַבְדְּךָ בִּמְהֵרָה לְתוֹכָהּ תָּכִין. בָּרוּךְ מְנַחֵם צִיּוֹן וּבוֹנֵה יְרוּשָׁלַיִם מֵעַתָּה וְעַד עוֹלָם, אָמֵן כֵּן יְהִי רָצוֹן.

Our Father Who is in Heaven,

He Who has chosen Zion and Jerusalem,
the Holy City which You desired for Your Seat –
bless all the sons and builders of Jerusalem together with all those who seek her well-being,
and send blessing and prosperity in everything they do.
Spread over the city Your Tabernacle of Peace, and fulfill in her the prophetic verse:
For the sake of Zion I will not keep silent, and for the sake of Jerusalem I will not keep quiet –
until her righteousness goes forth like a star, and her salvation burns like a torch;
and build her soon in our days as an eternal building,
and erect speedily in her the throne of David Your servant.
Blessed is He who comforts Zion and rebuilds Jerusalem from now and forever, Amen.

---

1. The prayer can be seen and heard here: http://www.youtube.com/watch?v=TbZOBYdNgsU.

CHAPTER TWELVE

Chief Rabbi of Haifa

On being appointed Chief Rabbi of Haifa, my main concern was to have a close relationship with all the residents of the city, and not just with the religiously observant. I therefore introduced regular classes in places not exactly famed for their pro-Torah sympathies. I taught one class on the popular Mishna commentary Pirkei Avot (Ethics of the Fathers) at the Haifa Workers Council. The second class took place at the office of the Union of Journalists, on the subject of the Jewish Laws of Avoiding Gossip and Libel. After having attended this class for a few years, one of the journalists remarked: "Honored Rabbi, we are now in the fifth year of your Chief Rabbinate, and I have to say that ever since you have been here, 'red' (Communist) Haifa has become 'black' (Haredi)." My response was, "Actually, my dear friend, you are wrong: 'Red' Haifa has not become 'black', but 'whiter than white'."

Rabbi Shear Yashuv Cohen,
in an interview with the authors
Haifa 2013

כתב רבנות

בהתאסף ראשי עם יחד שבטי ישראל על דעת כבוד הרבנים הראשיים רבני השכונות ורבני הקהלות של עדת חופה רבתי, ובמעמד שרי התורה ושרי הקהילה, ראשי הורי מנהני וחברי מועצת העיר ראשי המועצה הדתית חבני וחברי המועצה ראשי הקהל וראשי העדות וחברי מועצות הקודש ורבצ'בי חורה בתוכם עיר הברזולי.

בינו עולמים לברר... כבוד ה' אלקי הרואת לכל בשר איש על העדת אשר יצא לפניהם אשר לא... אשר יעלאם אשר כיאב... הוא יין תמיבת לעשר יין לדוד... שנה ימות אלקים... שבן האת ותלקישים ישו לברואת העולם אחרי מלאת כא שנים לבריאת ישראל... לריעעלים העולמים.

נועדי קהל עדת ישורון, למסור כתב רבנות זה לכבוד מעלת מורנו הרב הכהן מיהר רבי

אליהו יוסף שאר ישוב כהן

אשר יעדר בינ יי בבית התפלה מרב ראשי לחופה המחין ולבן... על כסא הרבנות הראשית בעיר... הקהל עדה... על שבעי מע הירא... להוריל חורה להאזירת ולהנחות את ארין הישוב... הנע התורה דרך האמת והשלום.

על ... ועל דעת הקהל קבלנו עלינו כי יורע רבני... ישראל... בני האת ונליה ... אשר ישב בה את את המעלה אשר... לכל אשר עין... על פי יבא ... יעשר מפי יעשר... מלתה וכל עיב.

יהי רצון מלפני אבינו שבשמים לשרות את כוכב שלומי על דעת כבוד רבני... ידו על ... להכין אותו ולתמך על מדלכת התורה, והעברית שכינה הקדושה על כל... לידי ולגו ישראל. ויקיים בו ... אני ואת בריתי אתם אמר ה' רוחי אשר עליך ותברי אשר שמתי בפך לא ישושו מפך ומפי זרעך ומפי זרע זרעך אמר ה' מעתה ועד עולם.

בסימן ובמזלא טוב יהיה הברכה הזאת לישראל שכן, לבטח יבא לעיין ונאל אמן.

Chief Rabbi of Haifa

⇛ THE ELECTION OF THE CHIEF RABBI OF HAIFA

In 1970, the Chief Rabbi of Haifa, Rabbi Yehoshua Kaniel
(1895–1970), a former student of Rav Kook, passed away. The "elders"
of the city of Haifa, which had, from the days of the British Mandate,
enjoyed the reputation of being *the* secular Israeli city *par excellence* –
were unable to find a suitable replacement to unify the disparate sections
of Haifa society. By then, Rabbi Cohen had completed his term as Deputy
Mayor of Jerusalem and had resumed his administrative duties at the
Machon Harry Fischel and Ariel Institutes, as well as his Torah writings.

It was at this stage that Yosef Blustein, by this time the Deputy Mayor
of Haifa, turned to his old friend, Rabbi Cohen. The two men had become
well acquainted during their time together as POWs in Jordan, as has
been mentioned above in Chapter 7. Blustein, then an engineer from the
Rutenberg plant of the Palestine Electric Company in Naharayim, had
been taken prisoner when the plant was captured. As he knew Arabic,
he had been appointed as the "secular" spokesman for the POW inmates,
while Rabbi Cohen had worked alongside him as Communal Rabbi.

Many years had elapsed since then, and Blustein had by this time
become a very powerful figure in the Haifa Labor Party. So, when a new
Chief Rabbi was needed for the city, Blustein had a word with the Mayor,
Yosef Almogi (1910–91: Mayor 1974–75). Almogi asked Blustein to sound
out Rabbi Cohen, his friend of bygone days. This is what Blustein said to
Rabbi Cohen:

> "I remember the special relationship you had with every single
> prisoner of war. You treated everyone in exactly the same way. You
> had to deal with *Lubavitcher* Hasidim, religious Zionists, members
> of the Underground Irgun and Lehi, the ultra secular HaShomer

Rabbi Shear Yashuv Cohen with Rabbi Yehuda Tzedakah and Rabbi Shlomo Zalman Auerbach

HaTzair [taken prisoner at Kibbutz *Revadim*], professors from the Haifa Technion [captured while working at the Naharayim Electric Company] and last, but not least, members of the ultra-Orthodox and anti-Zionist *Neturei Karta*. Haifa is a very special and unique city, also made up of many different types of people. Therefore, there is no doubt in my mind that you, and only you, are the right man for the job of Chief Rabbi of our special city."

Rabbi Cohen told Blustein that he would consider his proposal, and the lobbying began! First of all, two members of the Religious Council in Haifa, Yehuda Azrieli and Eliezer Alter, met with Rabbi Cohen and also urged him to stand for office. They were followed by the great Hasidic *Rebbe* known as the *Seret-Vizhnitz*. He was enjoying a vacation with one of his followers in the "French Hill" area of Jerusalem, and encouraged Rabbi Cohen to take on the role. "If you stand for office, the entire Haredi community will support you," he assured him. After this, Rabbi Moshe Blitental, Chairman of the United Religious Front of Haifa, informed Rabbi Cohen that he also had the backing of the *Gerer Rebbe*, Rabbi Yisrael Alter, who said, "If the *Nazir*'s son runs, we'll support him." The Rebbe, in his youth, had studied Kabbalah with Rabbi Shear Yashuv's father, the *Nazir* of Jerusalem.

Rabbi Shlomo Yosef Zevin, the editor of the Talmudic Encyclopedia, and a member of the Chief Rabbinate Council of Israel, also gave his enthusiastic support. He wrote an enthusiastic letter to Rabbi Cohen, part of which reads as follows:

> "I was very happy to hear that you are a candidate for the position of Chief Rabbi of Haifa. I want you to know you have my full support and blessing, and when you are elected, with God's help, may you be privileged to fulfill the important, albeit difficult task that will be yours as Chief Rabbi."
>
> I have known you well from your early youth and am acquainted with your outstanding qualities and your encyclopedic knowledge of Torah. You were educated and raised in sanctity and in the company of some of the foremost Torah scholars of the generation. Your illustrious family stems from a long line of distinguished rabbis excelling in all areas of Torah practice and thought. I have always known that you were destined for great things."

Former Chief Rabbis Unterman and Nissim also favored his election. In fact, Rabbi Unterman (who from 1964–72 preceded Rabbi Goren as Ashkenazi Chief Rabbi of Israel) wrote a reference on his behalf to the leaders of the Haifa community. He praised Rabbi Cohen's great scholarship and personal qualities which would, in his view, be great assets in his role as Chief Rabbi of Haifa. After Rabbi Shear Yashuv agreed to run for the office, Rabbi Unterman's Sephardi counterpart, Rabbi Yitzchak Nissim (Chief Rabbi from 1955 to 1972), wrote to him:

> "I was very surprised that his Honor has decided to stand for the office of Chief Rabbi of Haifa. For there are several Torah institutions under your aegis that are blossoming and demand your full attention. Who will take over your excellent work? At the same time there is no doubt that you are eminently suited to the position of Chief Rabbi of Haifa. You have the great gift of being able to bring people closer to the love of God, to Torah and to the practice of the commandments. If you have decided to take on the task you have my full support and blessing and I pray to God that you will fully succeed in the task which has been entrusted to you."

The other major candidate in the election was Rabbi Yaakov Rosenthal (1924–2010), head of the Haifa Rabbinical Court. The vote took place at the Municipality Building and Rabbi Cohen was duly elected Ashkenazi Chief Rabbi of Haifa and subsequently Chief Justice of the city's Rabbinical Courts. His Sephardi counterpart was Rabbi Eliyahu Bakshi Doron who later became Sephardi Chief Rabbi of Israel (from 1993 to 2003).

Rabbi Cohen's teacher, Rabbi Tzvi Yehuda Kook, wrote to him after the election in his unique style:

> "To my dear beloved, to my wonderful and extraordinary Shear Yashuv Eliyahu HaCohen *shlita*, now the esteemed teacher and rabbi of the sacred city of Haifa, may it be rebuilt speedily in our days; may you flourish for many years to come, *mazal tov* and *siman tov*, and be blessed by the Lord Most High. . . .
>
> "From the very bottom of the depths of my heart and soul I herewith express my sincere and joyous blessings at your rightful election, with God's help, to the position of Chief Rabbi of the Holy City of Haifa. May all the pleasant ways that the Lord has bestowed upon the Torah scholars of Israel, and that they bestow upon each other, rest upon you and upon all your enterprises and deeds as the spiritual leader of this great and holy community. Finally, in everything you do, may the holy *Shekhina* (Divine Presence) accompany you."

⇒   LEGAL RULINGS ARE NOT ENOUGH

Rabbi Cohen's first goal upon being appointed the Chief Rabbi of Haifa was to try and make the Torah as accessible as possible to everyone and not only to the observant sections of the city. He did this through engagement with all parts of the community. In one of his first speeches as Chief Rabbi, he defined the role of a rabbi by means of a parable that he had heard from his father, the *Nazir*, who himself had heard it from Rav Kook. The parable is based on the law that if a tree stands within the city walls, with its topmost branches outside, the ground under the branches is considered as part of the city for various laws. The Mishnaic formulation of the law is, "Everything follows the spread of the branches" (*Maaserot* 3:10). Rabbi Cohen then quoted Rav Kook as follows:

> "A rabbi is similar to a tree: his essence must be planted deep, his own roots firmly planted in the house of the Lord. But he will only succeed in all his activities if he manages to 'follow the spread of the branches.' For these branches provide shade for those poor souls who have spent a great deal of time wandering around in the barren wilderness and are no longer in touch with their Jewish selves. But eventually even these worn-out souls will surely hunger after the word of the Lord and thirst after the waters of Torah."

Rabbi Cohen cited this parable when the Lubavitcher Rebbe asked him why Rav Kook and the *Nazir*, both steeped in Kabbalah, refrained from writing their Torah thoughts in the traditional Hasidic/Kabbalistic style. Rav Shear Yashuv asked his father, who told him to answer the Rebbe in his name and in that of Rav Kook as follows:

> "With us, everything follows the 'spread of the branches.' That is, if we want to reach out to Jews who are not rooted in Torah, we have to speak to them in their own language and style. In our case, we must strive to communicate in the modern, intellectual style that appeals to the contemporary reader."

Rabbi Cohen described this special method of interrelation on a number of occasions and in different venues:

> "I believe that this method can achieve a great deal. We should speak to all Jews as if to beloved brothers or sisters for whom we want only the best, making it clear from the outset that our aims are therapeutic rather than punitive. For instance, can we really criticize the survivors of the Shoah who have lost their faith and stopped practicing Judaism? Or, is it right to deal harshly with those who grew up without any Jewish background whatsoever, such as those from Soviet Russia? Certainly not! The very fact that they have made *aliyah* to Israel is surely in itself one of the greatest miracles of our generation. Now that they are here with us, it is essential to open our doors as wide as possible and give them the warmest of welcomes home 'through ways of pleasantness and paths of peace.'"

Rabbi Cohen also used to illustrate this message by retelling a story that he had heard in the name of the Gerer Rebbe, Rabbi Abraham Mordechai Alter (1866–1948), author of the famous *Imrei Emet*: "A father and his mischievous child live in a house where there is a ladder whose rungs are unstable and about to break. Whenever the child approaches the ladder, his father moves the ladder away and punishes the child. However, on one occasion the father is not paying attention, and the child climbs up the ladder, falls off and breaks his leg. Will the child be punished for this? Not at all. The father will lovingly lift the child onto his shoulders and take him to the doctor or to the hospital."

Rabbi Cohen explains that this is similar to our own preferred relationship with contemporary non-observant Jews. "They have already climbed up the ladder and fallen off. Spiritually speaking they are completely broken. These people do not need punishment: what they need is a large dose of empathetic, loving engagement. We should put all our efforts into bringing them back into the fold, and having them do *teshuva* out of love." Rabbi Cohen points out that the Lubavitcher Rebbe, with whom he was in frequent contact, also preferred this method of engagement and was always at pains to teach his students never to abandon or neglect even one single Jew.

⇒ THE COMMUNITY RAV

Rabbi Cohen describes his early days as Chief Rabbi:

> "During my first year in Haifa, I was approached by the Rabbi of Haifa's Ahuza neighborhood, Rabbi Binyamin Ze'ev Benedict (1913–2002), one of my greatest supporters before the elections. Rabbi Benedict said: "In my opinion, the sermon given on Shabbat Shuvah[1] is a special and unifying event involving all the members of the community who even study its sources in advance. As you are the Chief Rabbi, I would like you to have the honor of giving the sermon instead of me." I thanked him very much, but insisted that he give the sermon there as usual and that I would preach in another synagogue at a different hour. This conversation strengthened the already-existing deep bonds between us and they continued for many decades to come".

The members of the Ahuza neighborhood fondly remember the classes and regular *minyanim* in the synagogue in his home on Friday evening and Shabbat afternoon, including classes on the relevant Torah portion. Following the tradition of his father, the *Nazir*, Rabbi Cohen also taught a class on *Midrash Rabba* on Saturday night. And on Hoshana Rabba eve he would teach *Idra Zuta*. The community also describes the special way he used to celebrate Purim in his home. Although he continued the tradition of his father and refrained from drinking wine, this in no way impeded the joy and merriment of the holiday. His home was always full of a variety of people – men, women and children – carrying gifts of food for Purim, known as *mishloach manot*.

On Chol HaMoed (the intermediate days of Sukkot and Pesach), Rabbi Cohen would hold the traditional "Meet and Greet the Rabbi" session in

---

1. lit., the Sabbath of Return, between Rosh HaShanah and Yom Kippur. Its Haftarah is the Biblical passage from Hosea 14:2–10: '*Return [Shuvah] O Israel to the Lord your God,*' encouraging repentance and requesting God's forgiveness.

his home. All Haifa residents, whether observant or not, were invited to come and visit. Another memorable occasion in the city was his Pesach Seder meal, to which he invited many leading citizens. Professor Reuven Yaron (1924–2014), a world-renowned scholar,[2] describes it as follows:

> "The Seder with the Rabbi in his home was simply one of a kind. It was an evening of extraordinary and far-ranging study and learning, going well beyond the scope of the Haggadah itself. This was an opportunity for deep and meaningful conversations on the import of Seder Night. The Mayor of Haifa joined in the customary Pesach *'leaning'* as did the other distinguished guests – a colorful cross-section of every background and standard of religious observance."

Rabbi Cohen often officiated at wedding ceremonies for Haifa citizens and would serve as Cohen for the ceremony of the Redemption of the First-Born Son. Educator Ephraim Frish, Haifa Distinguished Citizen awardee in 2008, tells the following story as an example of the special relationship between Rabbi Cohen and his community:

> "When my eldest grandson was born, it was taken for granted that we would ask Rabbi Cohen to be our *Cohen Podeh* (redeeming Cohen), and he gladly agreed. After the ceremony the Rabbi did not return the customary five silver coins to us, but only asked in passing the exact name of the child and his father. We told him their names, and shortly afterwards, we received a silver goblet from Rabbi Cohen on which was engraved, 'To Ariel ben Yechiel, from the *Cohen Podeh.*' . . . Years after, it was to be the very same Rabbi Shear Yashuv Cohen who ordained our grandson as a rabbi. In our eyes things had gone full circle."

What is it like when one visits Rabbi Cohen in his office at the *Bet Din* (religious court)? Sessions with him there are frequently interrupted by phone calls of all types. For instance, a woman whose mother has just passed away calls to inquire about the religious laws of mourning; the

---

2. He studied law with Rabbi Cohen at the Hebrew University. Before that, he had studied at Aberdeen University, Scotland, where he also taught for a while, before doing a D. Phil at Oxford, later becoming, from 1967 to 1971, the 9th Dean of the Law Faculty of the Hebrew University, and subsequently the Chair of the Israel Broadcasting Authority, the Director of the National Library of Israel, and the Director of the State Archives.

rabbi gently reads out the relevant passage from *Gesher HaChaim* (*The Bridge of Life*), by Rabbi Yechiel Michel Tukechinsky (1872–1955), a classic Jewish book on death and mourning. Another woman phones: her *get* (religious divorce) has been held up for six years, and in his role as *dayan* (religious court judge), Rabbi Cohen has been helping her. She wants to invite him to officiate at her son's wedding. He agrees on the clear understanding that no money will exchange hands. Next, he makes an evening appointment with a distinguished medical professor at Rambam Hospital. A non-observant man, he had told the Rabbi that he wants to divorce his wife and Rabbi Cohen decides to meet with them and try to restore domestic harmony.

"You see," says the rabbi, "this is what being a rabbi entails: it's not just about giving rulings on legal matters, on what is or is not permitted. While you have to pay meticulous attention to even the thorniest of legal question, you have to do it in such a way that you radiate warmth and make people feel good throughout the process."

"RED" HAIFA TURNS WHITER THAN WHITE

As mentioned above Rabbi Cohen spent many years teaching classes on Torah in the very heart of non-observant Haifa. He also initiated projects to strengthen Haifa's general Jewish identity. In his own inimitable way he lectured widely on Jewish culture and tradition and published articles providing the Torah's viewpoint on contemporary topics. He also opened a Community Cultural Center and was commissioned to teach a weekly Bible portion class to be broadcast on *Kol Israel* ("Voice of Israel"), Israel's national radio station.

Rabbi Cohen believes non-observant Jews do not need to be coerced to observe the Torah's commandments. Nowadays, unobservant people are halakhically defined as "babes in arms who have been taken captive." They have never had the opportunity to learn about Torah theory and practice and should therefore be drawn closer to Judaism through empathetic engagement. On the other hand, he is of the opinion that Israeli state law should, wherever relevant, preserve the religious character of the country:

> "Just as the State has laws that make it compulsory to behave in a certain way, so should there be laws that govern behavior in the public sphere in accord with Jewish religious tradition. The cessation of commerce and industry on Shabbat and the laws of personal status [marriage, etc.] must accord with the Halakha.

"But this must not be only a legislative matter. We must also explain Torah so that people come to understand the *value* of Jewish law and practice. For instance, just as there are restrictions on store-opening hours during the week, we can properly explain why they must be closed on Shabbat as well. Similarly, if we want to preserve our continuity as one people and have Jewish grandchildren, it is vital for everyone to comply with the requirements of the laws of personal status.

"Synagogues should play their own part by welcoming strangers warmly into their midst and helping them find their way. Synagogue doors should be open to them as long as they do not desecrate Shabbat there or violate other Jewish traditional practices."

Rabbi Cohen provides examples of how he himself reaches out to people who are estranged from Jewish observance:

"With the non-observant couples at whose weddings I officiate, I have a preliminary chat at my home. I try to have them visualize in their mind's eye the beauty of Judaism: the lighting of candles, Shabbat *Kiddush*, sitting together at the table on Friday night, studying words of Torah – food for the brain – singing, telling stories and so on. It is only at this point, when their appetite is already whetted, that I then explain that every beautiful picture needs a frame and that in our case the frame consists of the 39 types of work that are forbidden on Shabbat and thus help preserve the content of the day."

Rabbi Cohen's hard work bore fruit and he became much appreciated by all sections of the Haifa community. He was asked to become President of the Bnei Tzion Organization and appointed a member of the Board of Trustees of Haifa University. During the Second Lebanon War in the summer of 2006, the Mayor of Haifa, Yona Yahav, asked Rabbi Cohen to open a special session of the City Council Assembly with a passage from Psalms appealing to God to give victory and protection to their bombarded city. Despite not having access to a bomb shelter or an available secure room in his own home, Rabbi Cohen opted to stay in Haifa throughout the entire conflict.

After 33 years of service as Chief Rabbi, in honor of his 80th birthday, Rabbi Shear Yashuv was awarded the accolade of Honorary Citizen of Haifa. He noted at the time:

With the Lubavitcher Rebbe

"The Holy One Blessed be He supported me in my election and in all the sacred endeavors with which I have been involved in this city. Thanks to the Lord, I can finally state unreservedly that 'red' Haifa has now become whiter than white, in fulfillment of Isaiah 1:18: *'Even if your sins are presently as scarlet, one day they will be as white as snow.'*"

BIRKAT COHANIM: THE PRIESTLY BLESSING IN HAIFA

One of the most significant rulings during Rabbi Cohen's tenure as Chief Rabbi, with wide repercussions among many foremost Torah scholars of the generation, concerned the recitation of the Priestly Blessing in Haifa. On his arrival from Jerusalem in 1975, Rabbi Cohen discovered that the majority of Ashkenazi synagogues in the north, following the Diaspora custom, recited the Priestly Blessing only during the Mussaf service on Shabbat and festivals. As a Priest himself, this situation pained him greatly, and so he set about looking into the question in depth, seeking to find out why the Cohanim of the city did not fulfill this daily Torah commandment.

After studying all the relevant halakhic literature, Rabbi Cohen was astonished to discover that there was no genuine source for the Ashkenazi practice of curtailing the Priestly Blessing in northern Israel. He saw that in many Haifa synagogues where both Ashkenazim and Sephardim prayed, the latter tended to recite the Priestly Blessing on a daily basis in line with their custom throughout northern Israel. This led to disputes between Ashkenazim and Sephardim. Anarchy reigned, with each tradition trying to impose their own particular custom on their synagogue.

Rabbi Cohen and congregational leaders in Haifa wrote to the foremost rabbis both inside and outside of Israel to help them come to a decision. Among those approached for a response were Rabbi Shlomo Zalman Auerbach (1910–95), the Lubavitcher Rebbe, Rabbi Tzvi Yehuda Kook, Rabbi Mordechai Eliyahu, and Rabbi Avraham Shapira. (The latter two later served together as Chief Rabbis of Israel from 1983 to 1993). Rav Shear Yashuv asked them whether he should work to strengthen the practice of the Priestly Blessing throughout Haifa.

By far the most positive response came from Rabbi Cohen's own former teacher, Rabbi Tzvi Yehuda, also a Cohen, who deemed it essential to perform the Priestly Blessing on a daily basis. He cited the example of his own father, Rav Kook:

> "Rav Kook would take me to *duchan* [recite the Blessing] every day at the Hadrat Kodesh Synagogue in the Hadar neighborhood of Haifa's Carmel district whenever he vacationed in Haifa . . . Many other city elders also told me that they had themselves witnessed Rav Kook recite the Priestly Blessing every day, whenever he was on holiday here in the Carmel, staying at the Segal Guest House."

Other leading rabbis also responded positively. Rabbi Eliyahu wrote: "It is a great mitzvah of immense importance to carry out the Priestly Blessing on a daily basis, even in localities where this is not customary." Rabbi Shapira, a Cohen, agreed: "It is essential to bolster the mitzvah of observing the Priestly Blessing on a daily basis." Rabbi Auerbach's ruling was more conservative: "If it is not yet customary to recite it in a particular locality, do not change. However, if it is the custom to *duchan* in Yeshivot or Kollelim, do not take the minority practice into account." The Lubavitcher Rebbe's reaction was to follow the adage, "Allow Israel to behave in the way it is accustomed to behave." He explained orally that he personally supported the new initiative but chose to follow the precedent of the *Baal HaTanya*, R. Shneur Zalman of Liady (1745–1821), who wanted to establish a daily Priestly Blessing in the Diaspora but in the end decided not to.

Rabbi Yitzchak Yaakov Weiss of the Satmar Hasidic community opposed Rabbi Cohen's ruling, stating that Haifa neighborhoods where the Priestly Blessing was not already recited on a daily basis should be regarded as following their local *minhag*, which should therefore not be altered. However, Rabbi Binyamin Zilber of the Council of Torah Sages and Rabbi Elazar Brizel of the Karliner Hasidim did not agree, ruling that in Haifa and northern Israel the Priestly Blessing should be recited daily.

In 1979, as a result of these halakhic discussions and responses, Rabbi Cohen wrote a letter to all the rabbis of Haifa and northern Israel, inviting them to a meeting to discuss the question of whether Haifa should, like most of the rest of the country, adopt the practice of daily recital of the Priestly Blessing. Rabbi Cohen chaired this meeting with Rabbi Bakshi-Doron, the city's Sephardi Chief Rabbi and the minutes were published on Tu B'Shvat, 12th February 1979. The decision was that, as there had been no fixed custom one way or the other, the Priestly Blessing was thenceforth to be recited daily in every synagogue in Haifa.

This ruling led to a profound and extensive debate throughout the Torah world. Rabbi Tzvi Yehuda wrote to Rabbi Cohen, expressing his great satisfaction:

> "A thousand thanks and blessings to you, my most dear, beloved friend, Rabbi Shear Yashuv Cohen, Rav of the Holy City of Haifa, son of the saintly Cohen, Rabbi David . . . I cannot thank you enough for having gladdened me by informing me that you have merited to reinstitute this mitzvah in Haifa . . . May you go from strength to strength and I bless you with the love of the Priestly Blessing [which states that God commanded the Priests "to bless Israel with love"]. It is especially meritorious to re-establish a Biblical commandment where it has been neglected or abandoned."

The response of the great halakhic leader Rabbi Shmuel Vosner of Bnei Brak (who died in April 2015 at the age of 101) was cautious. He declared, in contrast with the above-mentioned Rabbi Weiss, that it is "not an actual change in custom," and that those who had now started to recite the Priestly Blessing on a daily basis may continue to do so, while those who had not need not be compelled to change.

In the end, not every synagogue accepted the new ruling of Rav Shear Yashuv and the other Torah authorities, though many synagogues in Haifa do follow it and recite the Priestly Blessing every day. Some synagogues do not recite it daily, but only during the Shabbat morning *Shacharit* service and the *Mussaf* service that follows it.

⇒   PURIM: WAS HAIFA A WALLED CITY?

When Rabbi Cohen arrived in Haifa, the custom was to read the Purim *Megillah* (Scroll of Esther, describing the story of Queen Esther and the Purim miracle) only on one day, 14th Adar, the "regular" day of Purim. This was in contrast with other cities in Israel that may have been "walled during the times of Joshua bin Nun," where the practice is to observe two days of Purim and to read the *Megillah* on the 15th of Adar (Shushan Purim) as well.

Rabbi Cohen researched all the sources he could find and unearthed corroborating evidence of Haifa's "walled city" status. He discovered that modern Haifa is actually built on an ancient *Tel* (heap of ruins) called *Tel Shikmona*. Archeologists from the Haifa Municipality Department of Museums had been excavating the area from the 1960s and had just discovered the 3000-year-old ruins of a city dating from the time of the biblical Joshua ben Nun. The oral tradition was thus proved to be based in fact. The archeologists discovered that the oldest extant remains were dated from the Late Bronze Age (1550–1200 BCE). They concluded that the ruins must have been abandoned before the 7th century CE as no remains have yet been discovered from the later "Early Arab" period.

Rabbi Cohen wished to strengthen the custom of reading publicly only on 14th Adar, while individuals would read again on 15th Adar, albeit without the benediction. Chief Rabbi Mordecai Eliyahu agreed with him, but Rabbi Yosef Shalom Elyashiv, renowned halakhic authority in the Haredi community, felt that the ancient Haifa custom of reading on both days should be restored.

In practice, most synagogues in Haifa nowadays read the *Megillah* only on 14th Adar, with a few synagogues reading it on the 15th as well. Rabbi Cohen himself hears the *Megillah* reading on the night of 15th Adar at the Lubavitch Chabad Center near his home.

⇒   RECITING *HALLEL* ON ISRAEL INDEPENDENCE DAY EVE

As a child, Rabbi Cohen had been raised and nurtured by people for whom love of Israel was taken for granted: His father, the *Nazir*, Rav Abraham Isaac HaCohen Kook, Rabbi Tzvi Yehuda Kook and Rabbi Yaakov Moshe Charlap. Rabbi Cohen grew up imbued with the vision of those many rabbis who established *Yom HaAtzma'ut*, Israel Independence Day, as a day of praise and gratitude to the Almighty for the miracles granted us that day in 1948.

In one of his articles Rabbi Cohen expressed his view that the miracle of national independence represented far more than the simple declaration in 1948 of *Medinat Yisrael* as a sovereign state. In his view the real miracle of *Medinat Yisrael* was not so much her birth, but the fact of her *continued existence* in the face of unremitting hatred from the rest of the world. Thus, the miracle was a "never-ending" one, beginning on 5th Iyar 5708 (14th May 1948), when Israel's leaders declared Israel an independent sovereign state in *Eretz Yisrael*. "Therefore," he wrote, "though we are far from pleased with the attitude of the State and its institutions towards the preservation of all that is holy to the Jewish People and our heart is pained at this situation, we may still not deny or play down the miracle that God performed for us on this day."

Rabbi Cohen recalls a conversation with Rabbi Tzvi Yehuda on the subject of learned Torah scholars who deny any religious significance to the State of Israel. Rabbi Tzvi Yehuda used to call them "faithless *tzaddikim*: they are undeniably righteous and men who believe, but deep down, they simply have no faith." Rav Shear Yashuv asked him to explain:

> "Rav Tzvi Yehuda arose from his chair and took a book from the bookcase, opening it to Tractate *Sotah*, p. 48b, which cites Zechariah 4:10: *'Who has despised the day of small things?'* The Gemara explains that this means, 'Why will the tables of the *tzaddikim* be destroyed in the world to come, thus denying them their full reward? The answer is: The 'small things,' i.e., their lack of genuine faith in God.' Rabbi Tzvi Yehuda's voice thundered as he added: 'The Gemara calls them *tzaddikim*, so they are truly righteous men, but they still might not believe in God's miracles.'"

Rabbi Cohen relates a similar story involving his own father, the *Nazir*:

> "When the Satmar Rebbe, Rabbi Yoel Teitelbaum, who was sharply opposed both to Zionism and to the State of Israel, wrote his book *VaYoel Moshe*, one of his followers wanted to sell it to my father. My father told him to leave the book with him and he would make up his mind after reading it. After reading the contents, he returned the book. The Satmar Rebbe heard about this, and two weeks later, the man again turned up at my father's house and said: 'The Rebbe would like to give you this book as a gift.' My father replied: 'I don't want it: give it back to your Rebbe and tell him from me that even a man of God is permitted to repent.' He meant his words to be hard-hitting: On the one hand, he praised the Rebbe and called him 'a man of God,' while on the other, he told him he must repent."

Rabbi Cohen agreed with his brother-in-law, Rabbi Goren, that *Hallel* (Psalms 113–118) should be recited not only during the day of Yom HaAtzma'ut, but also on the night of the festival, introduced by a blessing as is the custom on Pesach night (but on no other night). This is what Rabbi Cohen himself does when he prays in a family *minyan* or in a special prayer service. However, in public Rabbi Cohen follows the latest ruling of the Chief Rabbinate of Israel which is to recite the Hallel only during the daytime.

⇛ BUILDING BRIDGES WITH THE DIASPORA

In addition to the practical matters with which he had to deal as Chief Rabbi of Haifa, Rabbi Cohen did not neglect his important work of strengthening ties with Diaspora communities overseas. His first undertaking was the founding of special courses to train rabbis for communities around the world, as described above in Chapter Eight. In addition, Rabbi Cohen often made annual visits to a variety of Diaspora communities, in order to strengthen their Jewish identity. He also represented the Israeli Government on a number of missions with organizations such as the United Jewish Appeal, Israel Bonds, the Jewish Agency, the Jewish National Fund and *Bnei Brith*. Under their auspices he traveled to England, France, Holland, Switzerland, Scandinavia, the United States, South America, and even as far as Australia and the Far East. He was always welcomed with open arms.

On one of these visits to Japan, he was faced with an important halakhic issue. Rabbi Cohen planned to leave Japan on Thursday night to spend Shabbat in Minneapolis, Minnesota. He would be crossing the International Date Line on his journey, meaning that in Japan, Shabbat would already have begun, while it would only be Friday morning in Minneapolis. The question was: Is Shabbat an obligation of the individual, who must count six days and then rest? If so, Rabbi Cohen would have to observe the Sabbath as if he were still in Japan. Or, should he keep the Sabbath according to the community in which he planned to spend the day, i.e., together with the Jews of Minneapolis?

Rabbi Cohen phoned Machon Harry Fischel in Jerusalem and discussed the issue with the scholars there. His own view was that he was not obliged to observe Shabbat by Japan time, but rather according to Minneapolis, where he would be joining the local Jewish community. Rabbi Cohen asked the Machon to contact Rabbi Shlomo Zalman Auerbach, who agreed that one must keep the Sabbath wherever s/he is. He said that if a Jew happens to be in a locality where Shabbat has not yet come in, s/he should consider himself as operating under weekday time. For "time" is a concept combined of person and place, and it is this combination that sanctifies it. The law of counting six days and then receiving Shabbat on the seventh day refers only to cases in which the precise time for Shabbat is unknown, such as when one is alone in a desert. Still, to be on the safe side, Rabbi Auerbach advised Rabbi Cohen to take an earlier flight from Japan – which he did.

ON THE CONVERSION OF RUSSIAN IMMIGRANTS

One of Rabbi Cohen's most important milestones in his relations with Diaspora Jewry was his visit to the former Soviet Union as a member of the International Rabbinical Delegation. This visit took place a short time before the Soviet Union finally fell apart in 1991. Together with Chief Rabbi Israel Meir Lau, Rabbi Simcha HaCohen Kook (the Chief Rabbi of Rehovot), and rabbis from Europe, the delegation spent a week in the Soviet Union. The week was packed full of special events and emotional encounters with the Jewish population which, for 70 years had been completely cut off from any vestige of Jewish life.

The delegation even held more formal meetings with the Soviet Government leadership asking for improved conditions and education for the Jewish population. The Soviet government encouraged the rabbinical visit because it sought to appear to change its approach to Jews and Judaism in a desperate last-minute attempt to prevent the disintegration of the Soviet empire.

During their visit to the USSR, Rabbi Cohen and his colleagues came face to face, for perhaps the first time, with the widespread alienation and estrangement of nearly an entire Jewish community from the traditional Jewish way of life. This was, of course due to the Soviet regime's implacable opposition to matters of religion and sanctity.

The specific issues that came up in the course of the trip, such as attitudes to civil (as opposed to religious) marriages, mixed marriages, and above all, the conversion to Judaism of non-Jewish Russian immigrants to Israel, still rock the Torah world. This is because more than one million people from Russia have immigrated to Israel since the fall of the Iron Curtain, revolutionizing the Israeli landscape.

Given the huge Russian exodus to Israel, the pivotal question that has engaged Rabbi Cohen for the past 20 years and more is the conversion of Russian immigrants. According to official data, around a quarter of the over one million Russian immigrants are not considered Jewish according to Jewish Law. Once in Israel, many of them approach government institutions and rabbinical conversion courts to begin the conversion process that will help them to integrate fully into Israeli society. In the last few years concern has arisen in rabbinic circles about this trend which has also become a matter of public debate. Many of the Russian immigrants who convert for this reason do not continue to observe the Torah and its commandments after their conversion.

It is suggested that when these potential converts make a solemn vow to accept the "yoke of the Torah and mitzvot," a necessary condition for conversion, some of them do not actually mean what they say and their "conversion" is simply a ploy to become part of Israeli society with all its benefits. A stormy Torah debate has been raging on this question and no consensus has been reached regarding candidates for conversion whose commitment to religious observance is in doubt. Some rabbis have even gone so far as to claim that a number of conversions that have already taken place should be retroactively deemed null and void.

During Rabbi Cohen's 25 years as a chief rabbinical judge on a Conversion Court, this issue has come up on many occasions, and he has written and lectured extensively on this subject. Rabbi Cohen makes a distinction between a *goy gamur* ("100% Gentile"), whether living in a Jewish Diaspora community or in Israel, and a Gentile who has already entered Israel under the "Law of Return," either because s/he is married to a Jew or has a Jewish father. It is his opinion that strict precautions are necessary in the case of the former and it must be ensured that they will punctiliously observe the 613 commandments incumbent on a Jew. If it is doubtful that this is the case they must not be allowed to convert.

But regarding Gentiles who have come to live in Israel and are married to Jews and may already have Jewish children, conversion is important in order to stem the tide of assimilation and mixed marriages in future generations. After all, Rabbi Cohen, explained, "their children go to school with our children, and their teenagers mix with our teenagers." These prospective converts should be received after having expressed commitment to religious observance, even if it is feared that after their conversion they will not observe the precepts. Rabbi Cohen emphasizes that it is important to remain in contact with them after they have converted and try to encourage them to observe the mitzvot.

In formulating this ruling Rabbi Cohen based himself on the *responsa* of Rabbi Chaim Ozer Grodzinsky (1863–1940), one of the Torah giants of the pre-Holocaust generation in Lithuania. Rabbi Grodzinsky rules that if, at the time of conversion the convert did not accept the "yoke of mitzvot," the conversion is to be considered null and void. However, where the convert has accepted this "yoke" at the time of conversion, even if it is possible that after conversion he may desecrate Shabbat in order to earn a living, we should still go ahead with the conversion.

Rabbi Cohen quoted former Chief Rabbi Uziel's decision, which goes even further:

> "It is both permitted and a mitzvah to accept converts, male and female, even if we know that they will not observe all the mitzvot. This is because we have confidence that in the end they will come to observe them, and it is incumbent upon us to open our doors as wide as we can, in order to turn this possibility into a reality. Even if they don't end up observing the mitzvot, it will be their own sin, and as long as we have done our best, we will not be responsible."

Rabbi Cohen also relied on the views of former Chief Rabbi Unterman, who, although he had not personally experienced the huge wave of *aliyah* from Russia, had nevertheless met with immigrants from Soviet Russia who had managed to get through the Iron Curtain. The question of their conversion thus occupied his thoughts. With great foresight, Rabbi Unterman had predicted the huge waves of *aliyah* from Russia that would take place in the future. He therefore laid down in advance the halakhic foundations on which conversions were to be permitted in cases of "mixed marriages," even when there were well-founded misgivings about their future intentions to observe the Torah. In coming to this decision, Chief Rabbi Unterman also based himself on the halakhic ruling of Rabbi Grodzinsky cited above.

According to Rabbi Cohen every convert who appeared before him when he headed the Conversions Court accepted the yoke of the mitzvot and undertook to observe the precepts of the Torah:

> "We would ask them, for instance, what is entailed in the keeping of the Sabbath. We would try in all cases to get them to describe the entire process: preparing the kitchen on the eve of Shabbat, lighting the candles, reciting the prayers with which we welcome in the Shabbat, the evening prayer, Kiddush, the *zemirot* songs, Grace after Meals, the Sabbath Shacharit and Mussaf prayers, the end of Shabbat and the *Havdalah* blessing.
>
> "We would ask female converts to explain how they would run a kosher kitchen, or about *Taharat HaMishpacha* (Family Purity laws), from the spiritual as well as the practical, point of view. If I was satisfied with their responses, I did not ask any further questions, but duly began the conversion process according to Jewish law. . . . If, however, they show contempt for the *Bet Din*, and approach us merely to deceive us, God forbid, we are duty

bound to reject them. And the *dayan* carrying out the conversion must himself totally understand the subject with his whole being.

"If the prospective convert has not accepted the mitzvot orally, or if the *dayan* conducting the conversion has not explained their essential principles, the conversion is invalid. If the conversion candidate lives somewhere where kosher food is not available, or works in a place in which Shabbat is desecrated, the conversion process must be stopped. But if the candidate has already been converted in the proper manner, but has since stopped observing the mitzvot, s/he is nevertheless still regarded as Jewish. We must always assume that when they took on the obligation of adhering to Judaism they were sincere. Unfortunately, however, they apparently could not resist temptation, and were led astray by malign influences – but we assume that deep down inside they were completely sincere when first assuming the "yoke." Incidentally, we know of many cases where female converts are more scrupulous than their Jewish husbands and try to encourage them to observe the mitzvot."

Rabbi Cohen becomes emotional when recalling a son of one of the families he had converted, where it was questionable whether they would actually be observant. This man went on to study at the Ariel Kollel, and was subsequently appointed as Chief Rabbi of a European country. Rabbi Cohen adds:

"I had another convert who studied at Ariel. He was sent to me by Rabbi Tzvi Yehuda, who wrote, citing the words of Samuel I 1:27, *'For this lad I prayed.'* With God's help we converted him and he sanctified God's Name. Later, to my great grief, he was killed in one of Israel's battles, dying *al Kiddush Hashem*, for the Sanctification of God's Name. May his memory be for a blessing."

Rabbi Cohen warns against being overly zealous in conversions. If the immigrants who want to convert are pressured and their "yoke" made too burdensome, over and above what is required by Jewish law, they will simply turn to non-halakhic conversion such as those offered by the Reform and Conservative movements. This will only strengthen this type of conversion in Israel, harming the cause of legitimate conversions carried out according to Jewish Law. In general, Rabbi Cohen opposes the inclusion of Reform and Conservative representatives on municipal Religious Councils, which are run according to strict Jewish Law.

However, in keeping with his general outlook and personality, he is quite emphatic that great "love of Israel" be shown to all Jews.

Rabbi Cohen relates that he once "jokingly remarked to my friend, Rabbi Norman Lamm (b. 1927), the President of Yeshiva University in New York, that until I visited America I didn't know I was 'Orthodox'; I only knew that I was 'Jewish.' Orthodox, Reform and Conservative were all concepts that arose out of disputes that had taken place in Germany in the 19th century but are not related to Israel, thank God."

Generally speaking, Rabbi Cohen believes that though the case for Torah values should be put vociferously, it should not be done in such a way that those who disagree leave the fold and forsake *Klal Israel* for good. In this, Rabbi Cohen was following in the footsteps of Rav Kook, who opposed the formation of separate communities in 19th century Germany and felt that everything should be done to maintain the unity of *Klal Israel.*

⇒   ON THE FREEING OF TERRORISTS IN EXCHANGE FOR ISRAELI HOSTAGES

Rabbi Shear Yashuv Cohen does not hesitate to express his opinion on various issues in the public arena. One topic that arises from time to time is that of the release of Arab terrorists imprisoned in Israel, some of them for murdering Jews, in exchange for Israeli soldiers or civilians held in terrorist captivity. His opinion on this matter is based on the fact that the Talmudic principle "Captives are not be redeemed for more than they are worth" (*Gittin* 45a) is not held to be absolute. Torah scholars over the generations have ruled that there are cases when captives are redeemed for ransoms that would ordinarily be deemed too high. For instance, the Gemara cites the case of R. Yishmael ben Elisha, who was redeemed by R. Yehoshua ben Chananya (d. 131 CE) for a very large amount of money (*Gittin* 28a) because of R. Yishmael's importance to the community as a whole. Similarly, captives in danger of their lives must be redeemed even if the ransom is exorbitant.

Rav Shear Yashuv therefore holds that the rules governing such cases are not absolute and are dependent on the circumstances. "The problem of redemption of captives," he stated in 2009, "is not one for Torah scholars, but rather for the Shabak [General Security Service], the Mossad, and the government . . . It is most definitely a security and diplomatic issue under the purview of the heads of state and the army."

⟹　EFFORTS TO FREE JONATHAN POLLARD

In late 1985, Jonathan Pollard began a life sentence in American prison on the one-count charge of passing classified information to a friendly country – Israel. The sentence was considered inordinately harsh, as spies who had been convicted of far more severe offenses had been sentenced to shorter prison terms. Though at first, the State of Israel did not recognize Pollard as an Israeli spy, Rabbi Cohen and the Rishon LeTzion, Chief Rabbi Mordechai Eliyahu, whom Pollard considered his rabbi, initiated efforts to have him released. In 1995, these efforts intensified, and even Prime Minister Yitzchak Rabin asked U.S. President Bill Clinton several times to pardon him.

Rabbi Cohen wrote a special letter to Clinton, asking for Pollard's release and providing a unique and personal guarantee. The letter read, in part, as follows:

> "We understand that one of the reasons for Pollard's extended incarceration is the fear that he could cause damage to important United States interests. We do not believe that this is possible, given the long time that has passed since his service [in the Navy as an intelligence analyst]. In any event, the Chief Rabbi [Eliyahu] and I are prepared to take him under our care and responsibility and guarantee his [public] silence and his lawful behavior after he is released from prison."

However, in his response dated 13th September 1995, Clinton rejected their request: "Mr. Pollard committed a serious crime that posed a threat to our country. After carefully reviewing the arguments on both sides, I concluded that the extraordinary remedy of executive clemency is not justified in this case." It subsequently emerged that despite the many efforts of Jews around the world, American administration officials, and especially the heads of the security services, urged Clinton to reject the request for clemency and keep Pollard incarcerated.

In 1998, Israel finally acknowledged Jonathan Pollard as an Israeli spy, which led to intensified efforts to obtain his release. Toward the end of President George W. Bush's Presidency, Rabbi Cohen took part in a delegation comprising members of the Israeli Chief Rabbinate and other public figures, who met with Pollard's father, Morris, in order to discuss the best strategy for his son's release. After this meeting, the Chief Rabbinate of Israel appealed to President Bush to grant clemency to Jonathan Pollard upon the end of his term in office in 2009. This request, too, was rejected by the U.S. administration.

Rabbi Cohen also played a part in the official request of the Israeli government to President Obama to grant clemency to Pollard. This letter was handed to President Obama by members of the U.S. Congress, and Prime Minister Binyamin Netanyahu thanked Rabbi Shear Yashuv for his efforts in this regard.

Thank God, Pollard was released from prison on November 20, 2015, after serving 30 years, although, at present, major strings are still attached. He is not even being permitted to move to Israel! It is to be hoped that he will soon regain his physical health and, no less important, find a satisfying goal to sustain him in the difficult years ahead.

➣   HALAKHA AND TECHNOLOGICAL INNOVATIONS

It has been part of Rabbi Cohen's *modus operandi* as Chief Rabbi of Haifa to keep up to date with the global revolution that has taken place as a result of advances in science and technology. Together with *Agudat HaMad'anim Shromrei HaTorah* (The Association of Orthodox Jewish Scientists), *Irgun HaMehandasim HaDatiim* (The Association of Orthodox Engineers), and the Jerusalem-based Yad HaRav Herzog Institute for Advanced Talmudic Research, he initiated the establishment of *HaMachon HaMadai-Technologi LeBa'yot Halakha* (The Scientific Technological Institute for Halakhic Issues).

This institution concentrates on contemporary issues and problems of Torah and halakhic observance in modern industry and public services. A select team of halakhic experts, scientists and engineers examines the specific questions from every angle. They are constantly in touch with the most renowned Torah scholars and technological experts. Rabbi Cohen has chaired the working committee of the Institute and has lectured on its behalf at several national conferences of The Association of Orthodox Jewish Scientists in the United States, the United Kingdom and Israel.

Rabbi Cohen has given halakhic rulings on different issues arising from technological developments. As a result of the precision available through science, such as medical technology that can pinpoint the exact moment of death, and based on a Chief Rabbinate ruling that death is determined by the cessation of brain stem activity, Rabbi Cohen supports organ donation. However, there must be no connection whatsoever between the doctor who certifies the death of the patient and the doctor who later carries out the transplant. Rabbi Cohen practices what he preaches: he himself carries an ADI card, attesting to his consent to donate organs.

Another halakhic issue in the context of scientific development is whether citric acid is kosher for Pesach. Citric acid is used to add flavor to fruit juices, jams, candies and other food products. In the past, citric acid was produced from lemons and other fruits, but now it is produced commercially from wheat flour. After a thorough investigation, Rabbi Cohen concluded that there is not the slightest trace of *chametz* i.e., leaven forbidden on Pesach, in the citric acid produced in the Haifa Bay area by modern commercial methods and that therefore citric acid is kosher for Pesach. He explained:

> "For starters, the flour used to start the process does not ferment, and even when mixed with water, this is only for six minutes and so does not reach the stage of fermentation where it would be regarded as *chametz*. Secondly, the starch in the flour is then separated out from the sugar and the starch alone cannot become *chametz*. Finally, the citric acid is not produced from the starch itself, but from fungi that are nourished by a substance, one of whose components is that same substance produced from the starch that did not become *chametz*."

This painstaking halakhic clarification was adopted by the Kashrut Department of the Chief Rabbinate of Israel in a written ruling in 2001.

⇒ PRE-NUPTIAL AGREEMENTS

During the last few years, a wide-ranging halakhic debate has been under-way regarding pre-nuptial agreements aimed at preventing pre-divorce difficulties and disagreements. The agreement considers and resolves in advance all the aspects of divorce from the halakhic perspective in a manner that will be binding in a civil court. A pre-nuptial agreement would prevent the husband from refusing to give his wife a *get* (Jewish divorce) or the wife from accepting a *get*. This would be done through a prior signed agreement to the effect that the recalcitrant party would have to pay a fixed sum of maintenance to the injured party on a monthly basis. In addition, arrangements would be made in advance for custody of any children of the marriage, as well as the allocation of assets.

Many support this type of agreement as a preventative measure against possible blackmail or extortion tactics which might hamper the granting of the *get*. In addition, the agreement prevents disputes over the allocation of financial and property assets. Others oppose this agreement on the grounds that it will have to be enforced by the secular judiciary whether in Israel or in the Diaspora, which is not answerable to the local *Bet Din*, thus weakening the latter. Opponents are also concerned that the agreement might make divorce too easy, and that it might involve a "forced *get*," compelling the husband to grant the *get* against his will, which is explicitly forbidden according to Jewish Law.

In a number of articles, Rabbi Cohen has explained that the guiding principle on such issues is expressed in Tractate *Ketubot* 5a: "*The Rabbis have looked after the daughters of Israel.*" These words inspired the Sages of Israel on several rulings having to do with marriage, domestic harmony and the family. It is on the basis of these Talmudic words and spirit that Rabbi Cohen supports the usage of pre-nuptial agreements, which he considers to be an implementation of these words of our Sages. It is via enactments of this sort that Torah scholars can extinguish the fires of contention and create harmony even in cases where the couple eventually gets divorced. In this spirit Rabbi Cohen formulated a pre-nuptial agreement based on a clear monetary basis. It is entitled *Tenaei Ketuba* ("Conditions of the Marriage Document"), as follows:

> "We, the undersigned witnesses, do hereby attest and confirm that the bridegroom said to the bride after the betrothal and before the marriage: 'I have no legal claim whatsoever on your chattels, or on any simple or compound interest or profits ensuing therefrom . . . Likewise, I also undertake to give the bride, if she asks me to do so when she is my spouse, a *get*, within thirty days from receipt of her request in writing, if she so wishes. Furthermore, if I do not grant this immediately, I undertake to immediately pay her maintenance according to the conditions of the *Ketubah* [marriage contract] – both the *Ketubah* and the marriage dowry itself and any index-linked interest. In addition, I will also immediately pay her maintenance based on the legal concept of *meukevet mach'mato*, generously and commensurate with her honor and status. In full compliance therewith I now hereby undertake this obligation by means of a *kinyan sudar* (the transfer of a symbolic object), according to both Jewish law and Israeli law. And as proof thereof I hereby affix my signature.'"[3]

One of the conditions of the agreement is that when the *Ketubah* is signed, two witnesses, as well as the bridegroom, must sign the pre-nuptial agreement. According to Israeli law the agreement must be signed in front of a registrar of marriages or a notary, in order that the agreement

---

3. For the Hebrew text, see: Rachel Levmore, "*Min'i Einayikh Midim'ah: Pre-nuptial Agreements*," Jerusalem, 2009. It should also be noted that a more detailed form has since been created by the Rabbinical Council of America, readily available on the Internet at http://www.theprenup.org/

be fully valid both in the eyes of the Israeli family law courts and in the eyes of the *Bet Din*. Rabbi Cohen also strongly suggests handing over to the relevant *Bet Din* the ruling regarding the amount to be paid as dowry and maintenance, according to the *Ketubah,* so as to grant the process significant halakhic validity.

⇒   THE PRIZE FOR TOLERANCE (1989)

Rabbi Cohen's efforts to bring observant and non-observant Jews closer together in Haifa were recognized at national level when he was awarded the Tolerance (*Sovlanut*) Prize in 1989. This very special tribute is awarded annually in commemoration of Yitzchak Kahan (1913–85), President of the Israeli Supreme Court from 1981 to 1983, to a personality who has made special efforts to encourage tolerance and acceptance between observant and non-observant Jews in Israel. The judging panel praised Rabbi Cohen for:

> ". . . his many years of devoted dedication to the fostering of tolerance and empathetic engagement between observant and non-observant Jews. Every day he practices what he preaches, demonstrating real commitment to his rabbinic office. His door is open to the entire community and he is always ready and willing to tackle any issue which arises. By pursuing 'paths of peace' he has managed to bring observant and unobservant Jews together."

The award ceremony took place in the Israeli *Knesset* (Parliament) on behalf of *HaTenuah LeEretz Yisrael Tovah* ("The Movement for a Good Israel"). Sephardi Chief Rabbi Mordechai Eliyahu was the speaker who bestowed the honor on Rabbi Cohen. To illustrate what *sovlanut* really means, Rabbi Eliyahu told the gathering a story about a rabbi of the previous generation who had taken his students to a railway station and asked the engine driver to explain how the engine works.

Astonished at rabbinic interest in the subject, the driver nevertheless explained to them that: "You have to fill the tank with water, stoke it with charcoal, heat it up and only when the water boils do you start moving." The rabbi then asked: "But what happens if you open the tank?" The driver answered: "If hot air escapes, then the engine won't budge." The rabbi told his students: "That's the moral. The journey can only begin where there is warm empathetic engagement between one another, while at the same time our very human tendency to 'boil over' is kept well under control." Rabbi Eliyahu continued:

"Rabbi Cohen is following in the path of his father, the *Nazir* of Jerusalem, who suffered great hardship, which he bore (*saval*) with patience and restraint. The *Nazir* schooled himself to pursue a life of holiness and sanctity, immersed in studying and teaching. By ignoring the slings and arrows of his opponents he lit up the world by his presence, carrying it forward onwards and upwards.

"It is probably worth defining the word *savlan*. What is a *savlan*? A *savlan* is not someone who is soft or who constantly compromises. A *savlan* is not someone who always gives in. A *savlan* is a person endowed with the gift of 'empathetic engagement,' which helps him meet others in their own place, wherever they are at the time. No one expresses this better than the prophet Micah, who shares with us three seemingly simple rules of life. These three encapsulate the entire 613 mitzvot incumbent upon us (*Makkot* 24a). Micah says (6:8): '*What does the Lord require of you? You should behave justly, love chesed (kindness) and walk humbly with your God.*' These three attributes have been joined together in the personality of our very dear friend from Haifa, Rabbi Shear Yashuv Cohen."

"Let us take these three attributes one by one: '*You should behave justly.*' Rabbi Cohen sits with me on the *Bet Din* as a dayan – a senior religious judge. His rulings are always unswervingly just, in accordance with Jewish Law, and he constantly penetrates the very heart of Torah, without deviating to the right or to the left. He also embodies '*love of chesed*,' not only by nurturing countless students through education and training, but also by always putting himself out to find them work. He further demonstrates the injunction to '*love chesed*' by giving charity to others in such a way that they do not even know that he has done so. And all these things he does by '*walk[ing] humbly*.'"

The then Mayor of Haifa, Aryeh Gurel (1918–2007: Mayor 1978–93), added:

"I know from my own experience that Rabbi Cohen is a real *savlan*. Haifa is a city already renowned for its tolerance between Jews and non-Jews. However, what is far more difficult is to encourage empathetic engagement between Jew and Jew. Rabbi Cohen's input into this ongoing work is truly enormous. It is almost impossible to overestimate the significance of his own personal role in establishing parameters of constructive engagement between all the Jews in this city during his time here. In addition, Rabbi

Cohen is very sensitive to wrongdoing of any kind, and to the importance of doing the right thing at all times . . . I think that to have reached this level of humanity, a person must himself have undergone a very profound internal struggle. In this day and age, we sorely need spiritual shepherds of his caliber. We, the people of Haifa, are proud of our Chief Rabbi, not only in his role as Chief Rabbi, but even more as a decent person."

In 1983, after many years of service on the Chief Rabbinate Council of Israel, Rabbi Cohen stood for the first time as a candidate for the position of Ashkenazi Chief Rabbi of Israel. He did not win, and in 1993 he stood again. This time he obtained a great deal of support from over 150 Yeshiva heads and rabbis, including those from the Religious Kibbutz movement, as well as public figures. These included Rabbi Moshe Tzvi Neriah (1913–95), Rabbi Uzi Kalcheim (1935–94), and Rabbi Yaakov Ariel, the Chief Rabbi of Ramat Gan. The other two candidates were Rabbi Simcha HaKohen Kook (b. 1930) and Rabbi Israel Meir Lau (b. 1930), who proved to be the successful candidate.

Even though they had competed against each other for this high office, the three candidates remained friends. On becoming Chief Rabbi, Rabbi Lau appointed Rabbi Cohen as Chair of the "Israeli Supreme Rabbinic Commission for Dialogue with the Vatican." He also asked him to represent the Israeli Chief Rabbinate at interreligious dialogues between the relevant religious and spiritual bodies. This role will be discussed in more detail in Chapter 14.

In 2007, when Rabbi Cohen reached the age of 80, the rabbis of Israel contributed a *Sefer Torah* (Torah Scroll) in his honor at a ceremony organized by his rabbinic colleagues at the Ariel Institutes. It was held at Kibbutz Ginossar on the shores of the Sea of Galilee, famed as the "cradle" of the Palmach, the original elite fighting force of the Haganah.

This *Sefer Torah*, written "in appreciation of [Rabbi Shear Yashuv's] contributions to *Am Yisrael*, *Torat Yisrael* and *Eretz Yisrael*," was dedicated by 200 rabbis from all over Israel. They donated it to Ariel Institutes for use during their conferences, and it is still in the organization's possession. The scroll's two "Trees of Life" (wooden poles on which the parchment is wound) were donated by none other than Chief Rabbi Israel Meir Lau and his brother, Naftali Lau-Lavie (b. 1926), in honor of their father, Rabbi Moshe Chaim Lau (1892–1942), who was murdered at Treblinka extermination camp.

This very special *Sefer Torah* was carried aloft along the paths of Kibbutz Ginossar by all three rabbis: Rabbi Lau, Rabbi Kook and Rabbi Cohen. Despite their earlier rivalry, all three were now united in joy and

Rabbi Shear Yashuv reciting a chapter of Psalms at the signing of the peace treaty with Jordan

friendship. At the dedication ceremony Chief Rabbi Lau said of Rabbi Shear Yashuv: "He represents a wonderful blend of the two biblical tribes of Issachar and Zebulun [representing the partnership between those who study Torah and those who support them]. Like Issachar, Rabbi Cohen promotes Torah through his lectures, books and articles. But, like Zebulun, he has spent decades obtaining the financial support that enables numerous Torah scholars to carry on studying at the Ariel Institutes."

After Rabbi Shear Yashuv failed to be elected Chief Rabbi, he happened one day to chance upon the very wealthy Eliyahu Reichman in the Jerusalem neighborhood of Shaarei Chesed. Rabbi Cohen explains how Reichman consoled him:

> "He told me, 'You certainly know that your own teacher, Rabbi Charlap, also sought to become Chief Rabbi, and lost. But you don't know something important that happened after that. I acquired a very precious telegram written by the Chazon Ish, addressed to Rabbi Charlap, in which he wrote, 'A hearty Mazal Tov on not being elected! Signed, Yeshayahu Karelitz [the Chazon Ish].'"

Rabbi Cohen served for so many years on the Chief Rabbinate Council of Israel that he became known as the "Elder Statesman of the Council."

⮑ THE PEACE ACCORD CEREMONY WITH JORDAN (26TH OCTOBER 1994)

In 1994, following ongoing contacts between Prime Minister Yitzchak Rabin and King Hussein of Jordan, a peace treaty was signed between the two countries. During the preparations for the signing ceremony King Hussein told the Israelis that he intended to invite a *Qadi* (a Muslim religious judge) to recite passages from the Quran at the ceremony, thus lending a religious dimension to the proceedings. On hearing this Rabin's Bureau Chief, Eitan Haber (b. 1940), asked Rabbi Cohen, on behalf of the Prime Minister, if he would recite a short Biblical passage during the ceremony, seeing as he had been a Prisoner of War in Jordan during the War of Independence.

The signing ceremony took place near Eilat, on Israel's southern border crossing with Jordan. And so, as Rabbi Shear Yashuv faced the mountains of Moab and recited Psalm 121, the participants all rose to respect the age-old words: *"A song of ascents: I will lift up my eyes to the hills. From where will my help come? My help comes from the Lord, maker of heaven and earth."* Rabbi Cohen read the words in Hebrew, then in English, at which point tears began flowing down the cheeks of President Clinton, who knew the Psalm well.

Subsequently, Rabbi Cohen explained that he had chosen to recite that specific Psalm while facing the mountains of Moab, in order to declare that the Jewish People's trust is not in peace treaties or in flesh-and-blood leaders, but only in the Holy One, Blessed be He. Rabbi Cohen's prophetic words have recently taken on a special significance, with Arab regimes that once appeared to be so stable collapsing like ninepins, one by one. The result is that peace treaties with countries that at one time seemed to be so secure turn out to have been built on sand.

⮑ ADDRESSING THE VILNA PARLIAMENT, LITHUANIA (1997)

In 1997, the Lithuanian Parliament organized a celebratory event to commemorate the 200th anniversary of the death of Lithuania's greatest Jewish figure of all time, the Vilna Gaon (1720–97). The Lithuanian government decided that the 200th anniversary of his death was the appropriate moment to "adopt" the great Torah scholar as a hero of Lithuanian culture. They asked the heads of the Vilna Jewish Community to invite Rabbi Cohen on their behalf to address their Parliament on the unique qualities of the Vilna Gaon.

Rabbi Cohen was unsure whether to accept the invitation, given the active and murderous participation of the Lithuanian people in the implementation of the Shoah. Over 96% of Lithuania's Jewish population had been murdered, many of them by their Lithuanian neighbors. He therefore discussed the matter with Rabbi Shlomo Wolbe (1914–2005), the renowned spiritual supervisor of Yeshivat Be'er Yaakov in central Israel. Rabbi Wolbe, an expert in the Lithuanian ethical *Mussar* movement, expressed great reservations about the whole idea of Rabbi Cohen's trip. But he added that if Rabbi Cohen could be totally straight with the members of the Lithuanian Parliament and truly spoke from the heart, it might be worth accepting their invitation.

On these terms, Rabbi Cohen decided to accept the invitation. His speech to the Parliament was translated into Lithuanian and also broadcast around the world in English. Rabbi Cohen started by simply talking about the Vilna Gaon, the man. Then, directing his gaze at the Members of Parliament, he said: "But if the Gaon of Vilna had been alive in Lithuania at the time of the Holocaust he would have been the first to be handed over by you to the Nazis." He concluded with the words of Psalm 124: "*A Song of Ascents of David . . . If it had not been the Lord who was on our side when the world rose up against us, they would have swallowed us up alive.*"

After returning home, Rabbi Cohen confessed that he had been afraid that the Lithuanian MPs might have interrupted his very pointed speech. They might have even walked out. But to his surprise, his words made such a great impression on them and the other members of the audience that the President of Lithuania rose to his feet, followed by all the Members of Parliament, and stood in place throughout his reading of the Psalm (in English). They did not sit down until Rabbi Cohen descended from the podium and returned to his seat.

➤ HONORARY DOCTORATE FROM BAR ILAN UNIVERSITY (1999)

Rabbi Cohen's lectures and his dissemination of the spirit of Judaism all over the world, including at universities such as Harvard, granted him academic recognition. In 1999 he was awarded an Honorary Doctorate from Bar Ilan University and its Board of Trustees. The award was made in recognition of:

> ". . . his outstanding achievements in the field of Torah and his role as a trusted emissary of Israel throughout the entire world . . . Throughout the many long years that Rabbi Shear Yashuv Cohen has served as a Torah authority and as a public figure who lights up his surroundings, particularly noteworthy is his balanced, mea-

sured and tolerant attitude toward issues affecting the relations between religion and state."

Another institution that honored Rabbi Cohen was *Michlelet Shaanan*, the Religious Academic College for Education in Haifa. Rabbi Cohen was elected as President of its Board of Trustees and he is an honored guest at all its official ceremonies. Members of the Board are in touch with Rabbi Cohen on all manner of issues.

In 2002 Rabbi Cohen reached the age of 75, the official retirement age for Chief Rabbis in Israel and asked to be relieved of his duties so that he could return to his Institutes and devote himself once again to writing and promoting Torah. But the Mayor of Haifa, Amram Mitzna (b. 1945) asked him to stay on for another five years. Mayor Mitzna explained his reasons in a letter to the Chief Rabbinate in Jerusalem,which included the following accolade:

> "With his uniquely friendly and kind demeanor, Rabbi Shear Yashuv Cohen is accepted by every sector of Haifa society, whether they be Haredim, religious-Zionist, or the non-observant majority. He is much sought after as a speaker. He is a gifted lecturer and always attends events held by the municipality. As a rabbi, he is actively involved in all the different types of educational institutes in the city and always aims for empathetic engagement and reconcilia-tion. Our honored Chief Rabbi and his blessed, multi-faceted work is at the heart of all areas of the Rabbinate: kashrut and Shabbat, complex personal problems that he is constantly being asked to sort out, and more. He works to reconcile husbands and wives, parents and children, and friends who have fallen out. And he himself is a shining example of how to behave in all circumstances, as well as in our peaceful relations with leaders of the minority religions, including the sizeable Arab minority residing in Haifa."

The exceptional relationship between Chief Rabbi Cohen and Mayor Mitzna is exemplified by an incident that occurred after the murder of Prime Minister Yitzchak Rabin on 4th November 1995. The Mayor invited Chief Rabbi Cohen to speak at a large rally organized in Haifa. However, some of the city's youth groups announced that if Rabbi Cohen came, they would stay away. But Mayor Mitzna held firm and said that if Rabbi Cohen was not allowed to take part, he himself would also stay away. Rabbi Cohen cites this story about Mayor Mitzna as a positive example of how one man tried to put a halt to the negative mindset that swept over Israel during that somber period of her history.

➤ HONORARY CITIZEN OF HAIFA

On his 80th birthday, 4th November 2007, the city of Haifa awarded Rabbi Cohen its most important mark of esteem, bestowed only upon a very few individuals. He received the award of Honorary Citizen of Haifa in a festive ceremony at the Town Hall, attended by leading dignitaries, the Ashkenazi Chief Rabbi of Israel, Mayor Yona Yahav, and the "great and the good" from all walks of life, including many from the minority ethnic and religious communities. The Secretary-General of the Religious Council of Haifa, Rabbi David Metzger, said in anticipation of this momentous occasion:

> "Before Rabbi Cohen came to Haifa, the city was known as 'Red Haifa.' However, Rabbi Cohen took on the task of being everyone's rabbi, and his presence as our Chief Rabbi has transformed our city into a place of serenity, tranquility and empathetic engagement. Under his inspired leadership, Haifa has also witnessed the burgeoning of Yeshivot and Kollelim. So now, after all his hard work over the years, we can proudly proclaim that the earthly Haifa has truly been transformed into the 'heavenly Haifa.'"

Even on his 80th birthday, the Mayor did not want him to step down. However, in 2011 Chief Rabbi Cohen finally did step down and, with God's help, he has now resumed his administrative duties at the Ariel Institutes and Machon Harry Fischel, and continues to write, study and disseminate Torah.

The Struggle
for *Eretz Yisrael*

"Chanukah has come around again and all over Israel candles light up our doorways and windows. Once again, our hearts miss a beat as we recite the annual Chanukah blessing, thanking God 'Who performed miracles for our ancestors in those days of yore . . .' We then add another blessing of gratitude to our Creator: '. . . Who has kept us alive, helped sustain us and enabled us to reach this time.'

"But I cannot help asking this year if our blessing is just empty words. Do we really mean what we say? Deep down, are we truly grateful to God for helping us to "reach this time"? Let's listen hard to what our Chanukah candles are telling us about this difficult year that we have experienced [the year of the Disengagement/Expulsion from Gush Katif].

The sputtering flames hold a secret. They whisper that this past year has not proved to be, as we had hoped, a better year than its predecessor. It did not bring us the much hoped-for redemption or salvation. The Land thirsted for our blood – pure Jewish blood that saturated the earth of both our homeland and the Diaspora. Israel's cry arose from the ground and pierced the air. We experienced a difficult and painful year, in which our own Government of

Israel uprooted dozens of Jewish communities from the soil of their Holy Land.

The government sent the State's pride and joy on a most despicable mission. The army was ordered to violate its unique sanctity. Thousands of Jews wander as refugees in their own Land, subsisting in "tent cities," hotels, and hostels. Their dignity was trampled underfoot, their sustenance was stolen . . .

In the doorways and windowsills, our Chanukah lights flicker, telling the story of Zion 'between the Walls,' of the trampled and demeaned Temple Mount . . .

Our own dimming Chanukah flames also remind us of another, brighter flame: the flame of liberation, which led us to rebuild our Holy Land, the land in which our roots are embedded. Although the light is covered with dust, the odd flicker gets through here and there. The flames are also replete with anger. They whisper to us in burning anguish, blazing in fury at those who would lower our standing and diminish our national character, who have returned to rule us after it had appeared that a new era was beginning to dawn in Zion – an era of a new spirit in our heart, the spirit of the candles: faith, dedication and selfless devotion to duty.

This is why, as we celebrate Chanukah of 5776 (2005) and embark on the new year of 2006, we do not experience joy in our hearts, nor our customary gratitude to God for having been 'privileged' to be 'living at this time and season.' This season we will not be able to recite a blessing thanking God for the good, since we have already made a blessing thanking Him for the bad. We have accepted Heaven's decision in love and faith that even these bad things will turn out for the good in the end, with God's help.

"This year, as in years gone by, we will recite the customary blessing, 'Al HaNissim,' with joyful thanks to the Almighty for having performed the miracles of Chanukah,

not only for our forefathers during the reign of the evil King Antiochus Epiphanes (175–164 BCE), but also for us, today, 'in these days and in this season.'

"Let us all therefore join in blessing our Creator for having 'kept us alive and helped sustain us' from the Hasmonean era up to this very day. Let us thank Him for the heroism of the Hasmoneans that has not left us; let us recite together a blessing for the sparks of light that glow even in the embers of our darkness. Let's give thanks for even the tiniest scintilla of heroism wherever it appears. Let's praise God for the heroism of Israel and the Jewish people, for the heroism of our IDF soldiers, past and future. Let us be thankful for the heroism of all those uprooted brethren scattered throughout our Holy Land that they love and that has been promised by God to us and to our future generations forever."

Rabbi Shear Yashuv Cohen
BeNatznetz HaNerot,
"What the Candle Flames Tell Us"
in *Kumi Ori,* vol. I, 2005

The Struggle for *Eretz Yisrael*

➔ THE FIGHT AGAINST THE PARTITION
OF JERUSALEM

As mentioned previously, Rabbi Cohen was raised in an environment in which love of *Eretz Yisrael* was paramount. He was fortunate enough to have as his immediate teachers some of the foremost Torah scholars of Israel: HaRav Kook, his own father the *Nazir*, HaRav Tzvi Yehuda and Rabbi Yaakov Charlap. As such, Rav Shear Yashuv strongly supported the building up of Jewish communities throughout *Eretz Yisrael*.

Following the Six Day War, Rabbi Cohen listened spellbound together with his father, his brother-in-law Rabbi Goren, and members of the IDF and the press, to the words of his dear teacher, Rabbi Tzvi Yehuda Kook: "From here we shall never budge."

Rabbi Tzvi Yehuda's terse statement stemmed from the fear that weakness on the part of Israeli governments might lead them to hand over areas of *Eretz Yisrael* that had been retaken during the Six Day War. These areas had been illegally occupied by Arab countries in violation of both the historic rights of the Jewish people to *Eretz Yisrael* and United Nations resolutions.

Rabbi Tzvi Yehuda's apprehensions were soon proven to be wellfounded. Shortly after Jerusalem and parts of Judea and Shomron (known by the world as the West Bank) were restored to Israel, the first of many proposals was made to hand over these important areas of the Jewish homeland to the Arabs. As Deputy Mayor of Jerusalem at that time, Rabbi Cohen took part in some of the early struggles to retain the unity of Jerusalem.

Less than a year after the liberation of Jerusalem, Mayor Teddy Kollek was already calling for the city to be divided along demographic lines. Rabbi Cohen wrote a strong rejoinder entitled: 'Teddy Kollek's Bitter Error,' in which he appealed to Kollek to reconsider:

> "Jerusalem, our great, united and perfect city, is not up for division. Even during the Biblical era she was never divided among the 12 Tribes. This is because Jerusalem belongs in her entirety to the whole of *Klal Yisrael*, to the entire Jewish people . . . and therefore for a Jew to even consider carving her up between Israel and other nations is simply inconceivable. Jerusalem belongs to us. Every single stone, alley and street belongs to the holy mountain of Zion. And Zion is, as you know, the heart of our people and nation, the root of our soul.
>
> "Can a heart be divided? You can't subdivide a heart; you cannot form a partnership in a heart, or slice it into half, thirds, or quarters . . . We have absolutely no authority to make any compromises whatsoever in the name of so-called 'demography,' based on whatever temporary ethnic make-up happens to reign in our Holy City.
>
> "God help us should we ever associate ourselves with concessions suggested by various representatives with their own religious and political agendas, who have tacitly gone along with the Arab character of the Holy City of Jerusalem ever since the establishment of the State – and who now raise a hue and cry when she is restored to its true owners, the Jewish people."

During the years immediately after 1967, when Jerusalem was reunified, Rabbi Cohen worked tirelessly to assist the Jewish communities in the new neighborhoods of the Old City and eastern Jerusalem. These replaced the old Jewish neighborhoods destroyed by the Arabs during their illegal occupation after 1948.

⇒   RABBI COHEN'S OPPOSITION TO THE WITHDRAWAL FROM SINAI

After the Yom Kippur War of 1973, when Rabbi Tzvi Yehuda Kook became the spiritual mentor of the *Gush Emunim* movement, most religious Zionists extended their support to all the Jewish communities re-establishing themselves in Israel.

After the first such communities were built in Judea and Shomron, the Gaza Strip and Sinai, Israel's Torah scholars debated sharply whether it was halakhically permissible to cede any part of *Eretz Yisrael* to the Arabs in exchange for their signature on a peace treaty. In 1980, as Chief Rabbi of Haifa, Rabbi Cohen published an unqualified ruling on the issue:

"It is totally and utterly forbidden to hand over any area of *Eretz Yisrael* to non-Jews. This is not a case of *pikuach nefesh* (in which giving up territory would save lives), if we can reasonably expect that with God's help we can win any future wars and retain these areas. If it becomes evident, without a shadow of a doubt, that not giving up a particular area of *Eretz Yisrael* would result, God forbid, in the utter destruction of our sovereignty, and might even endanger the very existence of the State, only then can we consider saving *Klal Israel* by temporarily withdrawing from the relevant areas, with the idea of retaking them at a later date.

"Furthermore, this type of emergency withdrawal should never entail any agreement acknowledging the rights of non-Jews to our precious and beautiful Land. Our Land belongs to *Klal Israel*, and we have no authority to cede it.

"In addition, it is no secret that all the military experts rail against any thought of withdrawing from Yehuda and Shomron (Judea and Samaria). On the contrary: they emphasize repeatedly that the real danger to our existence comes from forsaking these areas and abandoning them to our enemies. How dare we commit such a grave offense against the Torah, one which we must not transgress even on pain of death, by claiming to save Israel and by clinging to the empty utterances of those who pursue peace with their mouths while lying in their hearts. They bring nothing but contemptible calamity *'upon the daughter of my people, saying 'Peace, peace' when there is no peace'* (Ezekiel 13:10)."

Sadly, in spite of this profound and stirring appeal, and other similar appeals made by other leading Torah giants, the State of Israel did withdraw from the Sinai Peninsula. And this first withdrawal, made to cement the 1979 peace agreement with Egypt, opened the gates to further withdrawals over the years.

⇛ THE HALAKHIC QUESTION OF BUILDING A SYNAGOGUE
ON THE TEMPLE MOUNT

One of the climaxes of the Six Day War was the liberation of the holiest Jewish site in the world, the Temple Mount, the location of the two Temples.

In June 1967, when the IDF paratrooper liberators alighted on the

Mount, they declared with great emotion: "The Temple Mount is in our hands!" Nevertheless, from that moment until today the Temple Mount has essentially been in the hands of Muslims, the only group permitted to pray there. Many observant Jews who would simply like to visit this holiest of sites do not do so because of our halakhic status of ritual impurity. This is because we are all assumed to have come in contact with death and are unable to be purified until a Red Heifer can be sacrificed.

However, there are places on the Mount that we *can* visit, even in our impure state. Rabbi Cohen, seeking to strengthen the connection of the Jewish people to their holiest shrine, followed the lead of his brother-in-law, Rabbi Goren, in this matter. Immediately after the Six Day War, Rabbi Goren initiated pioneering research as to the exact location of the Temple and the Holy of Holies on the Mount. On that basis, Rabbi Shear Yashuv published an article specifying the precise areas that Jews are halakhically permitted to access. His goal was, *inter alia*, to initiate the construction of a synagogue on the Temple Mount so that Jews would be able to pray there once again.

Rabbi Cohen's articles, as well as general fears that the 1979 Peace Treaty with Egypt would undermine Jewish sovereignty over the Temple Mount, led to the establishment of a movement known as *El Har Hashem* ("To the Mount of the Lord"), headed by a prominent academic, Professor Yoel Elitzur (b. 1949). The movement's aim was to persuade the rabbinic establishment to overcome its reservations about dealing with Temple Mount issues. One of the rabbis most identified with this movement was none other than Rabbi Moshe Segal (see Chapter 4 above), who had been Rabbi Cohen's commander in the Brit HaHashmona'im Youth Movement during the British Mandate period.

El Har Hashem published a manifesto entitled "Appeal to the Chief Rabbis," which was signed by seven of the foremost Israeli rabbis of the day, headed by Rabbi Cohen himself, as well as Rabbi Dov Lior (b. 1933), Chief Rabbi of Hebron and Kiryat Arba; Rabbi Yehuda Amital (1924–2010), Rosh Yeshivat Har Etzion; and Rabbi Yosef Kapah (1917–2000), head of the Yemenite community and a renowned expert on Maimonides.

The seven rabbis appealed to the Chief Rabbinate to give an authoritative ruling on the precise areas of the Temple Mount which Jews are permitted to access and the degrees of holiness of the different parts of the Mount. They also asked that a synagogue be built in the permitted area. This is the text of the letter:

> "At present the prevailing situation on the Temple Mount, '*God's footstool*' (Chronicles 1 28:2, Lamentations 2:1), is that non-Jews behave there as if it were theirs, and comport themselves as they

would in their own homes. In addition, the only Jews who come through its gates are non-observant tourists who walk all over it, trampling its holiness underfoot, as they are oblivious to the requirements of Halakha. As a result, the Temple Mount is today regarded, both in Israel and in the world at large, as an exclusively Muslim site in which Jews and Judaism have no legitimate role.

"This state of affairs constitutes nothing less than a desecration of God's name and contempt for that which is holy. We now run the very real risk of losing control of the entire Mount and even the rest of Jerusalem. We therefore appeal to the Chief Rabbinate to encourage *Am Yisrael* to ascend once more to the site of our Temple by clearly defining the precise areas of the Temple Mount which we are permitted to enter, with all the relevant specifications and parameters, so that it will be possible to establish a permanent place of prayer for the Jewish people on the Temple Mount. Those visiting and praying there, in accordance with all the applicable Jewish laws, will then do so with full confidence that it is completely permitted."

Although Rabbi Cohen repeated this appeal to the Chief Rabbis of Israel on several occasions, and it made a deep impression on the Israeli public, the Chief Rabbinate refused to discuss the issue. Instead, it continued to cite the precedent of the original ruling signed by Rav Kook and other great Torah scholars of the time (when the exact locations and measurements were unknown), prohibiting Jewish entry to the Temple Mount.

In practice, Rabbi Cohen himself also does not permit access to the Temple Mount due to the prevailing ruling by most Torah scholars. The situation can only be altered, he states, when the rabbis convene to discuss the matter and issue a new ruling, allowing access to those parts of the Temple Mount that are deemed halakhically suitable. In an article he published, Rabbi Cohen explained the fear he felt was the underlying reason that the Chief Rabbinate declined to discuss the issue:

"In my opinion, the real reason is that we are afraid of the monumental jolt that this will give to our religious system . . . We are still not ready for this. Regarding *aliyah* to the Land, we needed the students of the Vilna Gaon and the Baal Shem Tov to take the first steps and change the Diaspora *Galut* mentality. What the students of these two Jewish giants managed to do was to suspend the long-held view that we must wait for the arrival of the Messiah in order to make *aliyah* to *Eretz Yisrael*. The students of the Vilna Gaon and the Baal Shem Tov instilled the concept that the very phenomenon of *aliyah* itself hastens the much-awaited redemption of our people.

"Today, too, we must undergo a complete change of heart regarding the Temple Mount. Most of us are simply not prepared for the mental, psychological and spiritual upheaval necessary for this novel religious approach. For thousands of years we have prayed for a specific thing, and when our prayer is finally answered, we find it hard to adjust to the new reality.

"We don't seem to realize that even here in Israel many of us are still carrying the baggage of our *Galut* mentality with us. This ongoing situation is symbolized by the fact that we currently pray only at the *Kotel*, the remains of the Western Wall of the Temple compound, and not at or near, the site itself on the Temple Mount."

In the wake of public interest and the religious and halakhic questions that were generated, the Chief Rabbinate appointed Rabbi Cohen to chair a newly-established Temple Mount Commission. However, the Commission has not yet managed to persuade the Chief Rabbis or the Chief Rabbinate to come to any decision on this question.

OPPOSITION TO THE OSLO ACCORDS

On 13th September 1993, the Israeli Government signed the Oslo Accords with the Palestine Liberation Organization (PLO). Since 1964 (long before the Six Day War and the repossession of Judea and Shomron), the stated aim of the PLO had been an all-out assault against the Jewish people in general, and Israel in particular, leading to the murder of many Jews.

As part of the Oslo Accords, Israel undertook to hand over many cities and areas in *Eretz Yisrael* to the proposed interim self-governing body of the PLO – the Palestinian National Authority (PNA, later the PA). Not surprisingly, there was a great deal of opposition to the Oslo Accords, including sharp responses from many rabbinic leaders. At a rabbinical conference held in Jerusalem after the signing, Rabbi Shear Yashuv Cohen stated: "Anyone who casts doubt on the right of the Jewish people to *Eretz Yisrael* is a heretic who denies the very basis and foundation of the Jewish faith."

At another conference, he declared: "Any government that is willing to entertain the idea of uprooting Jewish communities from *Eretz Yisrael* is not a legitimate government."

On 26th July 1994, Rabbi Cohen sent a letter to the Chief Rabbi, Israel Meir Lau, asking him to convene the Chief Rabbinate Council and publicize a definitive legal ruling asserting the absolute rights of *Am Yisrael* over the Temple Mount, the Machpelah Cave in Hebron, Joseph's Tomb in Shechem (Nablus), and the other holy sites.

Because of his stance, Rabbi Cohen suffered a great deal of criticism from the left wing of the Israeli spectrum. This even included appeals to the Minister of Religions to suspend him from office as Chief Rabbi of Haifa and Religious Court President for voicing "political" opinions. Rabbi Cohen countered that it was not a question of politics, but rather his religious duty as Chief Rabbi to publicize his legal rulings on matters pertaining to *Eretz Yisrael*. Rabbi Cohen has continued to oppose any talk of ceding Israeli territory to the Arabs.

THE *HITNATKUT*: THE DISENGAGEMENT FROM GUSH KATIF AND GAZA

A decade after the signing of the Oslo Agreement, Prime Minister Ariel Sharon, one of its most outspoken opponents, publicized his own withdrawal plan which he called the Disengagement. It comprised a unilateral eradication and uprooting of the flourishing Jewish communities of the Gaza Strip and North Samaria – handing these areas over to the Palestinian National Authority, in return for . . . essentially nothing.

When the Disengagement was announced in late 2003 it aroused strong opposition among many of Israel's foremost Torah scholars and rabbis leading to acute tension between the religious leadership and the Prime Minister. The plan came on the heels of ten years of opposition by the various governments of Israel to the establishment of communities in many of the newly reacquired parts of Israel. Many of Israel's religious Zionist leaders now began to analyze and question their relationship to the State of Israel.

Several months before the implementation of the Disengagement, Rabbi Cohen spoke at the Ariel Rabbinical Conference in Eilat, and laid down the parameters of the Jewish People's correct halakhic attitude to the State of Israel. He drew a line between the intrinsic value of the State and its political institutions. He published his position in a number of articles in the media, such as this one:

> "*Medinat Yisrael*, the State of Israel, is not the supreme value in our lives as a goal unto itself. There are more important values that take priority, and the State came into being to protect and preserve these values under all circumstances. Our core values are values of holiness, regarding which the existence of the State and its institutions is merely a tool by which to bring these values to

fruition. There is no intrinsic holiness in State institutions even if we view the State as 'the first flowering of our redemption.'

"We, the Jewish people, were vouchsafed three intrinsic and sacred values, which we have been commanded to observe and preserve. These three values are *Torat Yisrael*, *Am Yisrael*, and *Eretz Yisrael* – Torah, People, and Land. The State of Israel arose out of the ashes of the Shoah, in order to safeguard and protect *Am Yisrael*, to serve as a vehicle by which our people would gradually be restored to their rightful home in *Eretz Yisrael*, eventually engendering an inner spiritual return – *teshuva* – of the entire house of Israel to *Torat Yisrael*, as our prophets prophesied.

"This is the reason for the existence of the State of Israel. If she no longer preserves the above core values, she is betraying her mission, and there is no reason for her existence. Let us be crystal clear: Without these three fundamentals, the State is betraying her sacred mission, as well as the vision of her founders, as expressed in Israel's Declaration of Independence. This begins with the following words: '*In the Land of Israel, the Jewish people came into being . . .*' i.e., *Eretz Yisrael* preceded *Medinat Yisrael*. A government that sets about dismantling and eradicating areas of Jewish residence in *Eretz Yisrael* destroys with its own hands the entire justification for the State's existence, Heaven forbid."

Rabbi Cohen's words provoked an outcry among religious Zionist rabbis, and gave rise to the question: "Is it conceivable that there could be a break in this process of our third Redemption if it turns out that the State of Israel is not fulfilling its role?"

As a result of the outcry, Rabbi Cohen explained that he was not advocating that we should stop praying for the welfare of the State or reciting Hallel with a blessing on Yom HaAtzma'ut. He clarified that a distinction should be made between a day when we offer general thanks to God, and a day of total joy:

"We will no longer be able to rejoice if, God forbid, the Disengagement process of dismantlement and expulsion is underway. We will also have to weigh carefully whether we should say that Israel is '*the beginning of the flowering of our redemption*' in our prayer for the welfare of the State; perhaps the time has come to add the words, '*May it come about that the State will be the beginning . . .*'"

When asked whether Israeli soldiers should refuse to carry out orders to uproot fellow Jews from their homes, another controversial issue related to the Disengagement/expulsion plan, Rabbi Cohen published his opinion that such orders should not be carried out, but not in the form of an outright refusal, but rather in the sense of: "I am simply not capable of doing this."

➔ THE PLAN TO INTERNATIONALIZE THE THREATENED JEWISH COMMUNITIES

Once Prime Minister Sharon had completed his political deals, crossed all the parliamentary hurdles, and succeeded in getting the Disengagement Law passed by the Knesset, it was feared that it would actually be carried out. Rabbi Cohen devoted a considerable amount of time to an initiative to have the Jewish communities remain in place, under international auspices. This would mean that the Israeli government would not have to tear up Gaza's flourishing Jewish communities with its own hands and uproot the people living there.

"If the goal of this plan is simply peace with the Palestinians, what is the problem with leaving the communities under international auspices, even as Israel withdraws from the area?" asked Rabbi Cohen.

To advance his plan, Rabbi Cohen engineered a meeting of rabbis and PA Muslim religious leaders to be held at the home of the United States ambassador to Israel, Dan Kurtzer (b. 1949). The meeting was called to explore ways of allowing the Jewish communities to continue living in the threatened areas under PA control. This meeting was initiated and organized by Rabbi Menachem Froman, rabbi of the Gush Etzion community Tekoa, who believed in effecting peace first by agreement between the sides' religious leaders. Unfortunately, however, the meeting was cancelled at the last minute.

A few months before the Disengagement/expulsion was finally implemented, Rabbi Cohen proposed his solution at the Ariel Conference in Eilat before two former Chief Rabbis of Israel, Rabbis Israel Meir Lau and Mordechai Eliyahu, as well as the Chief Rabbis of Rehovot and Ramat Gan, Rabbi Simcha HaCohen Kook and Rabbi Yaakov Ariel. These four key rabbis were authorized by many of their colleagues to convey Rabbi Cohen's original proposal to Prime Minister Sharon: "The Jewish communities in Gush Katif should continue to remain in place under international auspices."

In an open letter addressed to the Prime Minister and publicized in the media, Rabbi Cohen wrote:

"Government policy is based on the axiomatic assumption that Jewish residence on the soil of *Eretz Yisrael* depends on Israeli sovereignty. However, this assumption is erroneous. Jews dedicated their lives for the right and privilege of living in the Holy Land for hundreds of years before it had ever occurred to anyone to establish a Jewish State . . . It is self-evident that it is a religious duty, laid down in the Torah, for Jews to reside in *Eretz Yisrael*, construct houses there, plant trees, sow the soil, etc . . . Conversely, dismantling and uprooting Jewish communities in this Land constitutes a cardinal violation of the commandments of the Torah . . .

"The question begs to be asked: Why should we uproot the communities? Why can they not carry on living in a Palestinian state, and continue to observe the mitzvah of living in the Holy Land, just as our fathers and forefathers did for generations? . . . It is inconceivable that the only place in the world in which it is forbidden for Jews to live is their own ancestral home."

At that time the Prime Minister was refusing to meet with rabbis, but he had a unique and personal relationship with Rabbi Cohen. This dated back to the 1973 Yom Kippur War, when Rabbi Shear Yashuv served as the IDF chaplain of Sharon's division at the Suez Canal (see the end of Chapter 8). Therefore, following Rabbi Cohen's letter, staff from the Prime Minister's Bureau invited him in for a meeting.

This meeting took place in Jerusalem and lasted for over an hour. The Prime Minister rejected Rabbi Cohen's proposal on the grounds that he had no faith in Arab assurances or even the ability of the international community to protect Israeli citizens in Gaza and Shomron. He was afraid that if they were not evacuated, the Jewish residents would be butchered by the incoming Arabs. "I don't trust the Arabs. There would be a catastrophe," he explained to Rabbi Cohen, who countered, "And uprooting Jewish residents from their homes is not a catastrophe? I am afraid of what God will do to anyone who behaves in this way."

Rabbi Cohen recalls that when he said this, "Sharon's eyes welled up and he said, 'There's simply nothing I can do differently.'" Rabbi Cohen said that the discussion was very emotional; he continues to keep parts of it secret. But his proposal to save the Jewish communities in Gush Katif was shelved.

A few weeks later, during the summer of 2005 the government actually implemented the Disengagement Plan. The IDF uprooted the Jewish residents of Gaza and North Shomron from their homes, and eradicated any sign of their former lives there. Rabbi Cohen was distraught. The evening before the first soldiers went in to implement the plan Rabbi Cohen gave a lecture in Haifa and said:

> "He who uproots Jewish communities in *Eretz Yisrael* and, God forbid, brings about the destruction of synagogues and the uprooting of graves, will never be absolved of their crime, either in this world, or in the world to come . . . This is the highest form of wickedness and cruelty imaginable."

A bit later, while the plan was being carried out, he said:

> "I cannot conceive of an act more cruel and vicious than what, in one fell swoop, the Government of Israel has perpetrated this week in Gush Katif. The very act of bursting into a synagogue in order to drag out people gathered inside is unheard of among the nations of the world . . . There is no sin greater than this."

⇒ THE STRUGGLE TO SAVE THE SYNAGOGUES OF GUSH KATIF

In 2004, over a year earlier, IDF Chief Rabbi Israel Weiss (1949–2006) had published his ruling on synagogues that might be destroyed during the uprooting of civilian outposts in Judea and Shomron. His view was that if it proved impossible to dismantle the synagogue structures beforehand for future reconstruction, they should be demolished.

Rabbi Weiss' ruling fell into the hands of Rabbi Shear Yashuv, causing him "great pain," to use the very words with which he began his subsequent letter to Rabbi Weiss. He was particularly concerned that the ruling would be used as a precedent if and when the synagogues in Gush Katif faced a similar plight.

Rabbi Cohen sharply attacked Rabbi Weiss' ruling which paved the way for the destruction of synagogues in Judea and Shomron. He cited the Gemara in *Megilla* 28a: "*If synagogues have fallen to ruin . . . their holiness remains even when they are desolate.*" In other words, synagogues must never be treated disrespectfully, no matter what their condition. He continued:

> "Without entering in any way into political considerations or discussing the prohibition against uprooting Jewish communities in *Eretz Yisrael*, there is no doubt whatsoever that it is a cardinal sin to demolish any synagogue. It is our duty to demand guarantees

With Rabbi Ovadia Yosef

that their sanctity will be preserved, at least as respectfully as Israel treats the mosques and other non-Jewish religious sites that have fallen into her hands since the War of Liberation. [Consider, for example, the mosques on the Tel Aviv beachfront, and on Strauss Street in Jerusalem between the Histadrut Building and Isaiah Street. Haifa has many mosques and even when luxury high rise apartments have been built in their vicinity, a concrete barrier is erected around them for protection and preservation. There are many other examples as well.]

"In my opinion we must demand international guarantees regarding our holy places. God forbid that we should demolish even a single synagogue. The sanctity of a building built for prayer and Torah study is permanent and does not disappear following the forcible removal of those who live in the area; it is forbidden to damage the building in any way.

"The honored rabbi [Rabbi Weiss] may, if you wish, present this opinion of mine to the Minister of Defense and the IDF Chief of Staff, in whose power it is to prevent the demolition of synagogues and yeshivot in Gush Katif, or anywhere else in *Eretz Yisrael . . .* I am convinced that were [former IDF Chief Rabbi] HaGaon Major-General Shlomo Goren still alive he would have forcefully intervened against the demolition of synagogues in *Eretz Yisrael* and also against the demolition and transfer of yeshivot and of the Jewish communities in Gush Katif and in North Shomron."

A few months later, just before the implementation of the Disengagement, Rabbi Yishai Bar-Chen, the Rabbi of Elei Sinai in Gaza, asked Attorney Michael Corinaldi to initiate legal procedures to prohibit the IDF demolition of the Gush Katif synagogues.[1] International law experts had already opined that the demolition of these synagogues would set a dangerous precedent. They pointed out that the demolition of holy sites is illegal in international law and could endanger synagogues around the Jewish world. Since Rabbi Bar-Chen held rabbinic jurisdiction in a Gush Katif community he was requested to lodge a petition against the Israeli government.

Corinaldi entrusted his son Gilad with the mission of taking on the judicial struggle to prevent the razing of the synagogues. To build his case against the government Gilad mobilized rabbinic personalities of the highest rank, such as Rabbis Abraham Shapiro, Mordecai Eliyahu, Ovadia Yosef, Sholom Yosef Elyashiv, Zalman Nechemiah Goldberg, Shlomo Amar, as well as many academics. The government's justification was that demolition was essential in order to prevent their desecration by Arab mobs.

Rabbi Cohen and Rabbi Simcha HaKohen Kook were recruited to support Gilad's legal struggle, abandoning most of their other duties in order to devote their full attention to this matter. They decided to work for an emergency meeting of the Chief Rabbinate Council of Israel on the topic, given that the majority of the foremost Torah scholars had expressed their views on it. Rabbi Cohen wrote the following letter to Chief Rabbi Yona Metzger while the Disengagement was in the course of being carried out in Gush Katif:

> "When policemen and soldiers burst into the synagogues of Gush Katif to remove the residents it made a terrible impression of desecration of sanctity all around the world. We all remember how the IDF waited an entire month out of respect for a holy site, before entering the Church of the Nativity in Bethlehem to which Arab terrorists with blood on their hands had fled.
>
> "If, God forbid, our synagogues are razed by the IDF, this will be a terrible desecration of God's name. Their actions will reverberate throughout the Jewish world and bring international shame

---

1. Corinaldi's Hebrew work *Mishpat Ne'ilah* (2009, Bnei Brak) is the source for much of the following.

and disgrace on the religion of Israel . . . I repeat my request of six months ago which has not yet been answered, that the Chief Rabbinate Council convene a special meeting on the future of the synagogues and cemeteries in Gush Katif. . . . While the security forces should be given the opportunity to express their position, at the same time the authorized body to make the decision is the Chief Rabbinate Council."

On Thursday, 25th August, in response to the huge public outcry, Chief Rabbi Metzger at last decided to convene the Council. After a debate, the Council publicized its majority vote decision:

"The destruction of synagogues is strictly forbidden. We therefore rule that it is prohibited to raze any synagogue . . . Destroying synagogues would entail severe implications for the future of the many thousands of synagogues throughout the Jewish world. The Chief Rabbinate Council appeals to the Government of Israel to halt the plan of razing synagogues and places of learning in Gush Katif and North Shomron. In line with our policy toward places of worship of other religions, we appeal to the government to take immediate steps to protect and maintain our own holy places.

"The Chief Rabbinate Council calls on the government and the Prime Minister to take the lead in an international move to have the great powers, already involved in the negotiations, ensure that the Palestinian Authority protect and safeguard our synagogues. This is anchored in a number of U.N. and international conventions in which it was established that the prevention of the desecration and destruction of all holy sites, including synagogues, is obligatory and enshrined in international law."

The Chief Rabbinate Council also appointed Rabbi Shear Yashuv Cohen, Rabbi Simcha HaCohen Kook and Rabbi Yehuda Deri, Chief Rabbi of Be'er Sheva, to co-chair a committee for the protection of the synagogues in North Shomron and Gush Katif. And so on 30th August, the three rabbis set out on an emotional tour of the now destroyed Gush Katif. The aim of the tour was to ascertain which synagogues could be dismantled and rebuilt elsewhere and which not. Having completed their survey the three rabbis called upon the government, in the name of the Chief Rabbinate of Israel, not to raze those synagogues that could not be relocated.

At the same time, a suggestion was made by Rabbi Israel Rosen (b. 1941), Director of the Zomet Institute dealing with Jewish Law and technology, that the synagogues in Gush Katif be sealed up and filled with concrete. In this way they would be preserved as memorials of the synagogues they had once been. Rabbi Cohen concurred with this proposal and put it to the relevant authorities. However, the Ministry of Defense rejected the proposal. Rabbi Cohen continued his battle, speaking before the Knesset Judicial Committee and before the Supreme Court as part of his petition to have the Court order the government not to raze the synagogues in Gush Katif.

The Supreme Court refused to intervene in the government's decision, but as a result of all this activity and pressure, the government stepped back at the last moment and ordered the IDF not to demolish the synagogues. The two Chief Rabbis, accompanied by members of the Committee for the Preservation of Synagogues, attended the government session at which this last-minute decision was made. When government ministers asked the rabbis why the IDF should not raze the synagogues to prevent them from being vandalized by Arab rioters, Rabbi Cohen threw their question back at them:

> "And if our forefathers had known in advance, 2,000 years ago, that the wicked Titus was going to destroy our Temple, would it have entered their heads to destroy it with their own hands so that it wouldn't fall into the hands of the enemy?"

His response touched a nerve and the government voted not to destroy the synagogues after all.

Just before dawn on Monday, 8th Elul (12th September), the IDF forces left the Gaza Strip. A PLO rabble immediately stormed Gush Katif and set about desecrating and burning its synagogues. The Palestinians thus demonstrated to the whole world the barbaric way they treat holy sites. From that day on, many Jews mark 8th Elul as a time of solemn memorial and reflection, including sessions dealing with the sanctity of synagogues.

⇒ YOM HAATZMA'UT (INDEPENDENCE DAY) 2006

Six months after the Disengagement/expulsion was carried out against the Jewish communities of Gush Katif and North Shomron, the government inflicted another blow on the settlement enterprise of Judea and Samaria. This time it targeted Amona, a small outpost near Ofra in the Binyamin area of Shomron, where nine homes were deemed illegal and designated for destruction, even though the government itself had originally encouraged, and had actively assisted in, their construction. The destruction was accompanied by brutal violence on the part of the police. Hundreds of civilians were injured and only a miracle prevented actual bloodshed.

Israel Independence Day 2006 took place just three months later, and was inevitably accompanied by intense debate among religious-Zionist rabbis. What was the real meaning of "Yom HaAtzma'ut," given this recent series of severe blows inflicted by the government against the historic mission of *Am Yisrael* to live in their own land?

There was no consensus on this question. In line with his unwavering opposition to the Disengagement, Rabbi Shear Yashuv Cohen now proposed a change in the wording of the Prayer for the Welfare of the State of Israel. From now on, he suggested, Israelis should add a few new words: Instead of stating that Israel is the "flowering of our Redemption," he suggested that the prayer read, *"May it come about that the State of Israel become the beginning of the flowering of our Redemption."* However, he emphasized that the essence of the day should not be altered and that the Jewish people should continue to thank God for the great miracles He continues to perform by providing us with a political location in which to enjoy independence to this very day.

Rabbi Cohen's suggested innovation was based on a conversation with Chief Rabbi Herzog some 55 years earlier, shortly after Rabbi Herzog and his colleague, Sephardi Chief Rabbi Uziel, jointly published a prayer for the peace and well-being of Israel. The prayer opened with the following words: *"Our Father in heaven, Rock of Israel and her Redemption, bless the State of Israel, the beginning of the flowering of our Redemption."* As related in greater length in Chapter 8 above, Rabbi Cohen asked Rabbi Herzog for his source in determining that Israel is the actual beginning of the long-awaited Redemption. Rabbi Herzog quoted the Talmudic passage in *Sanhedrin* 98a, based on Ezekiel 36:8, which states that the abundance of fruits and agricultural growth is a clear sign of the People's return to their Land. However, after the implementation of the Disengagement, Rabbi Cohen said: "When we ourselves witness houses destroyed and trees uprooted, we are no longer so certain . . ."

THE BATTLE FOR THE TEMPLE MOUNT

The rise to power of the Hamas terrorists in Gaza was followed in the summer of 2006 by the Second Lebanese War. It was widely believed that the Hizbullah attacks were empowered by Israel's retreat from Gaza. Nevertheless, the Israeli political leadership continued to work toward various treaties and arrangements that would include handing over large tracts of the Jewish homeland to the Arabs.

As part of this "peace process," the United States organized an international conference to which they invited leading representatives of Israel and the Palestinian Authority, as well as of other countries. The conference took place in Annapolis, Maryland in late November 2007 shortly before Chanukah. One of the burning issues was the Palestinian Authority's demand that any future diplomatic agreement should include a clause giving full control over the Temple Mount to the Authority.

A month before the Annapolis Conference, United States Secretary of State Condoleezza Rice (b. 1954) visited Jerusalem. She held a private meeting with Rabbi Cohen, members of the Chief Rabbinate Council for Inter-Religious Relations, and representatives of the Muslim and Christian communities. The purpose was to discuss the future of the holy places in Jerusalem in advance of the Annapolis Conference, and to hear the arguments from the Jewish, Christian and Muslim points of view. The Muslim representatives claimed that the Jews wanted to destroy the Al Aksa Mosque, and also denied that the Jews had ever had a Temple on the Temple Mount. Rabbi Cohen responded:

> "Let's not forget that King David purchased the Temple Mount; King Solomon built the First Temple on the site; and then Ezra the Scribe rebuilt it. All who came after them must acknowledge the rights of those who preceded them. I do not propose that we should destroy the mosques on the site. But Muslims need to remember that they are there solely thanks to our merit."

Rabbi Cohen also reminded those present that in the past when Muslims ruled the area, they themselves built a synagogue on the Temple Mount in which the Jews prayed. He made it crystal clear that he rejected any concessions over Jewish control of the Temple Mount, the site of the Temple.

Secretary Rice, who had convened the meeting, said that she completely understood his words as she herself was both the daughter and granddaughter of Christian clergy and was well aware of what the Bible states. She added that as a result of this and previous meetings she understood that the core issue emerging was that the problem was essentially religious. If the religious issue wasn't resolved, nothing would be resolved she concluded.

Shortly afterward, the Chief Rabbis of Israel and Rabbi Cohen were invited to a conference in Washington held by the newly-established "Council of Religious Institutions of the Holy Land." Also in attendance at the three-day event was a team of White House public relations specialists, representatives of the Chief Rabbinate of Israel, the Muslim *Waqf* (which controlled Muslim sites on and around the Temple Mount, including the Al Aksa Mosque, as well as other sites in Jerusalem), Christian organizations, and a joint organization working for Jews, Muslims and Christians in Israel.

Attempts were made during these meetings to win over the rabbis to the idea of agreeing to divide the Holy Places: only the *Kotel* would remain Israeli while control over the entire Temple Mount would be transferred to the Muslims. The rabbis rejected this proposal out of hand and refused to agree to cede Israel's sovereignty over the Old City of Jerusalem in general and over the Temple Mount in particular.

After this meeting Rabbi Cohen wrote to Prime Minister Ehud Olmert (b.1954), setting out the position of the Chief Rabbinate and its strong stand even in the face of the heavy pressures exerted upon them in Washington. Olmert responded with the following Prime Ministerial commitment:

> "The Temple Mount is the site of the *Akeda* [the binding of Isaac by Abraham: Genesis 22], the site that King David purchased from Aravna the Jebusite (Samuel II 24 and Chronicles I 21) and the site of the First and Second Temples. There is no holier site for the Jewish people than the Temple Mount. Through the ages countless generations of Jews have stood facing this site whenever they recited the words of the *Amidah*, 'May our eyes behold Your return to Zion' and there they direct their hearts.
>
> "Forty years ago, when we were privileged to return and stand once more at the foot of His Holy Mount, we vowed that never again would we forsake it; nor would we relinquish Mount Moriah, the Temple Mount. The oath we took then is still in force now. The *Kotel*, the Western Wall, a remnant of the ancient wall that surrounded the Mount, is of course no substitute for the Temple Mount itself. Therefore, it is not our intention now, nor is it the intention of anyone who speaks in the name of the Government of Israel, to concede or relinquish our sovereignty over the Temple Mount. The issue is altogether not on our agenda."

A Light unto the Nations

The question of how far we should go in inter religious dialogue compels us to draw a fine line and walk with great care. On the one hand we seek 'rapprochement', to get close to the 'other' through 'paths of pleasantness' and 'ways of peace'. On the other hand, we have to step back in order to emphasize our own distinctiveness. We need constantly to be aware of the distinction between what is holy and what is not holy and between Israel and the other peoples. God forbid that we should overstep the mark, religiously speaking. Anyone involved in inter religious relations needs to set out beforehand a clear set of parameters, so that both parties know from the outset what is distinctive to our own religion and what is part of our 'mission' toward the wider world. In other words, we have to be clear about the difference between yichud *[distinctiveness] and* yi'ud *[mission].* Yichud *stresses that which differentiates between our holy faith and other religions. As we read in Deuteronomy 32:31: 'For their rock is not as our Rock.' On the other hand,* yi'ud *is best described by the vision of our prophet, Zephaniah 3:9: 'For, I will then turn the peoples toward a new language, that they will all proclaim God's Name' – the climax of which will happen, with God's help, during the days of Redemption, speedily in our days.*

We can see these two different approaches at work together in our very ancient prayer, Alenu, *which we recite three times a day during our daily services. This famous core prayer of ours describes two stages or approaches:*

disassociation and connection. On the face of it, these two
approaches appear to contradict each other. However, on
a deeper level, they can be easily reconciled and, in fact,
complement and supplement each other.

At the start of the Alenu *prayer, we emphatically*
declare our gratitude to God "Who has not made us like
the nations of the other lands, and not placed us like the
other families of the earth. He has not assigned our portion
as theirs, nor our fate like that of their multitude." These
words depict the first stage or path of our dialogue journey.

The second stage or path is described in the following
lines of the prayer's second paragraph: "We therefore
place our hope in You, o Lord our God, to see speedily the
strength of Your glory . . . to repair the world through the
kingdom of the Almighty, and all mortals will call in Your
Name . . . and come to know and internalize that to You
alone every knee will bend and to You alone every tongue
will swear allegiance . . . As is written, 'The Lord will then
be King over the whole earth; on that day the Lord will be
One and His name will be One.'"

Those of us who live in Eretz Yisrael have sensed
the huge change in attitude toward us, the Jewish People,
as well as toward Judaism, which has taken place among
other religions. We note especially that, since the Holocaust
and the establishment and flourishing of the State of Israel,
a revolution in thinking has taken place, particularly
within the Roman Catholic Church. We would like to
believe that these huge changes in attitude can be inter-
preted as a sign that we are now approaching the period
in our history known as 'the End of Days,' as described in
the second part of Alenu, *cited above. And it is thus with a*
profound sense of hope in our hearts that we approach the
subject of interfaith dialogue – with no feelings of inferiority
to our partners in dialogue, but with great caution, as one
who walks the narrow road between fire and water.

From a lecture by Rabbi Cohen: "Between Israel and the
Nations of the World: Dialogue and its Parameters"
Rabbinical Conference, France, Shevat 5766 (February 2006)

A Light
unto the Nations

⇒ THE ROMAN CATHOLIC CHURCH REPENTS

Rabbi Cohen has been involved for many years in interfaith dialogue, partly thanks to his extensive knowledge of world affairs and language skills. As far back as 1948 when he was taken captive as a Jewish soldier and incarcerated in a Jordanian POW Camp, he entered into dialogue with the Arab officers in order to request permission for his fellow prisoners to celebrate Jewish festivals and traditions. Later, as Deputy Mayor of Jerusalem, and especially after the 1967 reunification of Jerusalem, Rabbi Cohen was in constant dialogue with the many members of other religions who lived in Jerusalem. In addition, as Chief Rabbi of Haifa, a city with a sizeable Arab minority, he regarded dialogue activity with other religions as an essential part of his remit.

For close to 2,000 years one of the main tenets of Christianity has been that the Jewish people continue to suffer in *Galut* (exile) as punishment for not acknowledging the divinity of the Christian Messiah – and of course, for having killed Jesus, as accused. Christianity has long maintained that God rejected the Jewish people, and replaced them with the Christian Church, which already by the end of the second century it called *Verus Israel* (the true Israel). This Christian approach became known as "replacement theology," the tenet according to which God has replaced "the recalcitrant Jews" of the flesh with the Christian Church of the spirit.

The Christian world has never stopped blaming Judaism in both word and deed. During the long years of exile in the Diaspora Christian priests and clergy constantly preached to their flocks on the so-called "evil" represented by both Jews as a people and Judaism as a religion. Generations of Christian priests have encouraged their flocks to afflict and persecute the children of Israel. Millions of Jews have been burned at the stake by the religion of "faith, hope and charity." The Christian world has felt that it was thereby expressing its own superiority as "the *new* chosen people," after God, it said, "abandoned" the people of Israel in favor of *Verus Israel*, the Christian Church.

However, in recent decades a change took place within the Roman Catholic Church. The guilt feelings that Roman Catholics experienced in the face of the suffering experienced by the Jewish people during the Shoah, when they chose to stand idly by as "bystanders," not lifting a finger to intervene or prevent the murder of millions of their Jewish brothers and sisters, gave them pause for thought. In addition, the establishment of *Medinat Yisrael*, together with its victories in battle, refuted the Roman Catholic prototype of the "*galut* Jew," which they had preached for so long. All these factors brought about a change, a revolution even, in their mind-set.

The dialogue began with Pope John XXIII (1881–1963), who became Pope in 1958. He organized the Second Vatican Council which lasted from 1962 until 1965. His successor, Pope Paul VI (1897–1978), succeeded him as Pope in 1963 and continued his predecessor's good work.

On 26th October 1965, Pope Paul oversaw the publication of the declaration known as "*Nostra Aetate*" ("*In Our Time*"). This document, initiated by Pope John XXIII stated, *inter alia*, that the Jews of today are not responsible for the death of the Christian Messiah. It also condemned any manifestation of anti-Semitism. Pope Paul himself led the way by making changes to the liturgy, eradicating prayers of an anti-Semitic or missionary flavor.

The *Nostra Aetate* created a revolution in the way the Roman Catholic Church related to the Jewish people. Until 1965, the Church had been vehemently opposed to Zionism in general and to the State of Israel in particular, since their existence completely negated the Church's doctrine that the Jews were to remain in Exile until the "end of days," as a punishment for killing the Christian Messiah.

> The "stiff-necked" Jews had not only allegedly murdered the Christian Messiah. In addition, throughout the 2000-year history of Christianity, they had also stubbornly persisted in refusing to acknowledge the Christian Messiah as the Jewish Messiah. They preferred to die at the stake and the rack, through flaying and disembowelment, with the words of belief in the One God on their lips, rather than recognize what they considered to be a false Messiah.

Pope Paul VI's successor, Pope John Paul II (1920–2005), who came to office in 1978, went even further, and revolutionized Roman Catholic-Jewish relations more than any other Pope in history. On 13th April 1986, he stated that the Jewish people were to be regarded by Roman Catholics as "our older brother" and as the "chosen people," because, as it states in the Bible, the Lord had made a covenant with the Jewish people which could never be abrogated. Of course, he added, this does not contradict the fact that Christians are also "chosen."

Thus, the stance of the contemporary Roman Catholic Church is in total contrast to many centuries of persecution and murder. Today the official stance of the Roman Catholic Church is that the Jewish people are not required to accept the Christian faith. Starting in the 1970s, during the Papacy of Paul VI, the Roman Catholic Church no longer carries out missionary work among the Jews. On the contrary, Roman Catholics are now encouraged to find out as much as possible about their Jewish brothers and sisters, in order to increase understanding between the two religions, and not for ulterior motives.

This fundamental revolution in Christian understanding opened the door in the 1970s to the first attempts at interfaith encounters. Various Chief Rabbis of Israel, such as Rabbi Shlomo Goren and Rabbi Eliyahu Bakshi Doron, participated in these meetings as did, later, Chief Rabbi Israel Meir Lau, together with other leading Israeli rabbis. The aim of these encounters was to enhance the view that the Patriarch Abraham was the common ancestor to all three monotheistic religions, and that these have many fundamentals in common that can contribute to the establishment of peace and justice between nations and religions.

Progress was also made on the political front and closer ties were established between Israel and the Vatican. On 30th December 1993, the "Normalization Accord" was signed by the two parties and on 19th January 1994, the State of Israel and the Vatican exchanged ambassadors for the first time.

The next stage in this positive revolution was not long in coming. Not only did the Church condemn anti-Semitism, but on 16th March 1998, the Vatican published an official document entitled: *"We Remember: A Reflection on the Shoah."* In this ground-breaking document, the Church acknowledged her responsibility for nearly 2000 years of preaching anti-Semitism and contempt as a result of her mistaken ideology of which she now repented.

For the first time, therefore, the Roman Catholic Church took responsibility for the link between its theology and its role in the Shoah. The leaders of the Church called upon itself to embark on a period of repentance, confession, and atonement. Toward the end of the 20th century ceremonies were held at interfaith dialogue conferences in Spain and Portugal (where persecution of the Jews had been particularly disastrous during the Inquisition and the Expulsion from both countries, starting in 1492), in which they asked the Jewish people to forgive them for the behavior of the Church in hunting them down, forcing them to give up their faith, and murdering them.

For their part, the Israeli rabbis responded that they were not authorized to offer forgiveness on behalf of the myriads of Jews murdered by Roman Catholics throughout the ages. However, dialogue continued between the rabbis and the Vatican, for the purpose of publicizing joint declarations and acting to promote shared values. Within these parameters, Rabbi Cohen has taken part in many interfaith conferences around the world.

⇒   BETWEEN *YICHUD* (DISTINCTIVENESS)
     AND *YI'UD* (MISSION)

In the year 2000 Pope John Paul II visited Israel and met with the two Chief Rabbis, Rabbi Lau and Rabbi Bakshi Doron. He suggested that an official dialogue commission be established between the Chief Rabbinate of Israel and the Vatican. The obvious choice to lead the Israeli delegation was Rabbi Shear Yashuv Cohen, and he was asked to do so by the two Chief Rabbis. His Vatican counterpart was to be Cardinal Jorge Mejia.

Before assuming his new role, Rabbi Cohen researched the entire subject of interreligious dialogue from the halakhic point of view. He called his enquiry *Between Yichud and Yi'ud*, alluding to the fact that in Jewish tradition there are two approaches that seemingly contradict each other but which can in fact be reconciled, as explained at the beginning of this chapter.

On the one hand it is important to emphasize the distinctiveness of the Jewish people and religion. On the other hand, the mission of the Jewish People is to engender worldwide recognition and acknowledgement of the One true God. Our national task, therefore, is first to maintain our "distinctiveness" and only then to turn to the nations and fulfill our "mission."

Rabbi Cohen pointed out that the Patriarch Abraham, the forefather of our people and nation, encompassed these two attributes in his own personality. On the one hand, he symbolized separation from other peoples and distinctiveness in his religious vision of God as One, to which he stubbornly adhered against all odds. On the other hand, he sought out empathetic engagement even with idol worshippers, bringing them closer to the Holy One, Blessed be He.

Rabbi Cohen feels that the time is now ripe, given the miraculous establishment of *Medinat Yisrael* and the revolution in relations between the Roman Catholic Church and the Jewish people, for us to reach out to the entire world in the hope that they too might come under the wings of the *Shekhinah*. In other words, today there is a real possibility of acquainting the entire world with the basic principles and core values of Judaism.

As a basis for the work of the Bilateral Commission of the Chief Rabbinate and the Vatican that was established after the visit of Pope John Paul II to Jerusalem, Rabbi Cohen laid down two fundamental conditions. The first was that their dialogue sessions should not contain any debates or disputes on the core principles of each other's faiths. In other words, there should be no attempt to convince the representatives of the other religion of the truth of one's own faith. As a prerequisite, the Vatican leadership signed a special document committing itself never to engage in missionary activity of any kind against Jews.

The second of Rabbi Cohen's principles, a correlate of the first, was that the dialogue should deal only with shared values, such as: the sanctity of life; the promotion of world peace; preventing bloodshed and the rejection of suicide; the denunciation of the sexual exploitation of women, human trafficking, and the increasing secularization of society; a joint struggle against homosexuality; and promoting deeds of justice, charity and loving-kindness to all, including a commitment to preserving the life and property of our fellow human beings, as part of our shared religious ethos.

⟹   DIALOGUE WITH THE CHURCH OF ENGLAND AND THE ANGLICAN COMMUNION

In subsequent years, these principles provided the basis for dialogue with other Christian churches as well. In September 2006 a historic meeting took place in Jerusalem between the Chief Rabbis of Israel and the Archbishop of Canterbury, Dr. Rowan Williams (b. 1950, appointed 2002–12). Dr. Williams' advisor on interreligious affairs, Canon Guy Wilkinson CBE (b. 1948, appointed 2005–10), played an instrumental role in establishing this dialogue and has done more than anyone in the Church of England to encourage her positive engagement with Israel.

The joint declaration between the Church of England and the Chief Rabbinate included these words reflecting the principles mentioned above:

"We consider that the purpose of this and future meetings is to provide new opportunities for dialogue between us. Dialogue has profound value in its own right and its purposes are mutual understanding and respect of each other's traditions and beliefs; the sharing of common concerns; the development of personal human relationships . . . and in all these things an openness to God's initiative. Neither evangelism nor conversion has a place amongst the purposes of the dialogue and we emphasize the importance of respect for each other's faith and of rejecting actions intended to undermine the integrity of the other."

➤ THE BILATERAL COMMISSION OF THE CHIEF RABBINATE AND THE HOLY SEE

As stated above, Rabbi Cohen describes the dangers of dialogue with other religions, and especially with Christians, as "treading the fine line between fire and water." He approves of engaging in dialogue only in an official capacity as delegates of the Chief Rabbinate of the State of Israel. At the same time:

"It is important nowadays to sustain good relations with Christians, in order to fight together against our joint enemy, extremist Islam. Because, if we don't do this, then Edom (Christianity) and Ishmael (Islam) will end up uniting against us and who knows what might happen then."

After the two conditions: avoiding missionary work and religious debate and working on topics of joint interest, were accepted by both sides, the Bilateral Commission convened for the first time. The Pope chose three cardinals and two archbishops to represent the Church. Rabbi Cohen, representing the Chief Rabbinate, chaired the Israeli side which included also Rabbi Ratzon Arusi (b. 1944), Chief Rabbi of the Yemenite community and Kiryat Ono (a suburb of Tel Aviv); Rabbi Yosef Azran (1941–2010), Chief Rabbi of Rishon LeZion; Rabbi David Brodman (b. 1936), Chief Rabbi of Savyon; and Mr. Oded Wiener, Director-General of the Chief Rabbinate. Rabbi David Rosen (b. 1951), former Chief Rabbi of Ireland, and Mr. Shmuel Hadas (1931–2010), the first Israeli Ambassador to the Vatican (from 1994), were also present in an advisory capacity.

Subsequent to this first historic meeting, members of the Commission took part in a number of conferences at which they delivered lectures on a variety of topics. Occasionally, Chief Rabbis Shlomo Amar and Yona

Metzger attended these meetings. The Commission also published joint declarations on contemporary issues. Some of the topics discussed were the resurgence of manifestations of global anti-Semitism; violence, hatred and terrorism; struggles against world poverty; protests against assisted suicide; and opposition to "gay pride" parades in Jerusalem.

As a result of all his hard work on behalf of the Bilateral Commission, Rabbi Cohen was asked by the Chief Rabbinate to chair its Commission for Dialogue between Judaism and Islam, and to represent the Chief Rabbinate at global interfaith meetings.

ADDRESSING THE VATICAN SYNOD

The hard work of the Bilateral Commission bore fruit in October 2008, when Rabbi Cohen was the first Jew in history to be invited to address the Synod of cardinals at the Vatican. Before this invitation, tensions had been mounting between the Chief Rabbinate and the Vatican. After the death of Pope John Paul II in 2005, his successor, Pope Benedict XVI (b. 1927: appointed 2005, resigned 2013), retracted much of his predecessor's good work in terms of the relations between the Roman Catholic Church and the Jewish people.

Pope Benedict opened negotiations to cancel the secession from the Church of a splinter group that objected to the progress made at the Second Vatican Council of 1965. Among their number was an Englishman, Bishop Richard Williamson, who publicly reiterated his reactionary views that the Shoah had never actually taken place. He also said that the Jews were "the enemies of Christ," and professed his approval of the anti-Semitic libel known as *The Protocols of the Elders of Zion*.

Pope Benedict's second backward step was his stated intention to reintroduce an offensive prayer which had been removed from the litany by Pope Paul VI. This prayer explicitly calls on the whole world, including the Jewish people, to repent and convert to Christianity, "the one true religion." In other words, while the Popes immediately before him had stated categorically that Judaism was to be regarded as a religion in its own right, the "older brother" of Christianity, and that the Jewish people were not to be cajoled into taking on the Christian faith, Pope Benedict was intimating that the only true religion is Christianity, even for Jews.

This whole affair caused much anguish among the Jewish community worldwide, as well as further afield. For the Chief Rabbinate of Israel, these developments came as an especially severe blow. In an attempt to defend Pope Benedict's restoration of the above prayer, the Church explained that the newly-reinstated prayer was not relevant for our own times, but only for the "End of Days." The Vatican took pains to reiterate that the Church still regarded Judaism as the "older brother" of Christianity, and that there was therefore no ambition to convert the Jewish people to Christianity. They also added for good measure that they regarded anti-Semitism as a grievous sin. As part of the conciliation process the Vatican invited Rabbi Cohen to address the cardinals in the Vatican, during the Synod of October 2008.

Rabbi Cohen accepted on condition that he would be allowed to speak his mind and express exactly what he felt. He insisted on delivering his speech not in a church setting, but in an auditorium. Moreover, he received assurances that all crosses would be removed, except for those worn by the cardinals.

These are the words spoken by Rabbi Cohen to the Vatican Synod on that historic occasion which took place on Monday, 6th October 2008, in the presence of more than 200 cardinals, archbishops, and heads of monasteries, who had gathered together in Rome from all over the world:

> "It is indeed a privilege and a rare honor to be invited to this Assembly as a special guest representing the Jewish faith and the Chief Rabbinate of Israel. I believe this is the first time that a Rabbi has been invited to address a plenary session of the Synod of Bishops. We certainly very much appreciate what the gesture implies. There is a long, hard and painful history of the relationship between our people, our faith, and the Roman Catholic Church leadership and followers – a history of blood and tears. I deeply feel that my standing here before you is very meaningful. It begins with a signal of hope and a message of love, co-existence and peace for our own generation, and for generations to come.
>
> "Indeed, this continues the approach initiated by the late Pope John XXIII, which reached a climax in the life and work of the late Pope John Paul II during his historic visit to the Holy Land. We see in your invitation to me to lecture here today, a declaration that you intend to continue this policy and doctrine that refers to us as your 'Older Brother' and 'God's Chosen People' [here the Pope made a sign of approval with his hand] with whom He entered into an everlasting covenant. We deeply appreciate this declaration."

Rabbi Cohen then gave a detailed description of the Jewish Scriptures, their role in the synagogue and their influence and use in contemporary Israeli society. He ended his address with the following words, which he wrote together with the Israeli Ambassador to the Holy See:

"I feel I cannot conclude my address without expressing our deep shock at the terrible and vicious words of the President of a certain state [Iran] in the Middle East in his speech last month at the United Nations General Assembly. The false and malicious accusations, the threats and the anti-Semitic incitement, have brought back to us the painful memory of the tragedy of our people, the victims of the Shoah, which we hope and pray will never happen again. We hope for your help as religious leaders and for that of the entire free world, to protect, defend and save Israel from the hands of its enemies."

Speaking to the Reuters news agency in Rome, Rabbi Cohen said:

"He [the President of Iran] says that he wants to annihilate and destroy Israel. The problem in the days of the Second World War was that people didn't believe that Adolf Hitler really meant to fulfill what he said. Unfortunately, we had the Shoah and we do not feel that enough was done by the leadership of the religions in the world and other powerful leaders to stop it at that time. We expect them to do it today."

He also told the journalists that he might have turned down the Vatican invitation to give a speech to the Synod, had he been informed in advance that this historic address would coincide with ceremonies to honor Pope Pius XII (1876–1958: appointed 1939–58) who had been the Pope during World War II. The date he had been invited to speak, 6th October 2008, also happened to be the 50th anniversary of that war-time Pope's death. It was therefore a natural occasion for those who wished, to begin the procedure for the former Pope's canonization as saint of the Roman Catholic Church.

"We feel that the late Pope should have spoken up much more strongly than he did . . . He may have helped in secrecy many of the victims and refugees but the question is: could he have raised his voice and would it have helped? We, as the victims, feel that the answer is yes. I am not empowered by the families of the millions of deceased to say, 'We forget, we forgive.' . . . I did not know that [the anniversary commemorations] happened during the same meeting. If I had known . . . I might have refrained from coming because we felt that the pain is still here.

"I have to make it very clear that we, the rabbis, the leadership of the Jewish people, cannot, as long as the survivors still feel pain, agree that this leader of the Church in a time of crisis should be honored at the present time. It is not our decision. It pains us. We are sorry it is being done."

Rabbi Cohen concluded with a quote from the prophet Ovadiah (1:11), which aptly sums up the pernicious role of the "bystanders" during the Shoah: *"On the day you stood aloof . . . you became one of them."* It appears that Rabbi Cohen's words in Rome helped delay the canonization of the war-time Pope Pius XII, though the process began soon after that historic occasion.

With the installation of Pope Benedict's successor, Pope Francis (b. 1936: appointed 2013), the jury is still out on whether the positive Roman Catholic moves made toward the Jewish community in the second half of the 20th century and at the beginning of the 21st century by Pope John XXIII and Pope John Paul II will bear fruit. Pope Francis has said, "We hold the Jewish people in special regard because their covenant with God has never been revoked."

In any event, there is no doubt that Chief Rabbi Shear Yashuv Cohen of Haifa can be credited as being the leading Israeli rabbi of distinction to hold out the flag of dialogue to the Christian world, thus sanctifying God's name before an even wider public.

The Vistas

The Hebrew edition of this book ends with Chapter 14. Most of the material for this added chapter was amassed in the United States by Rabbi Aaron Reichel, a nephew of Rabbi Shear Yashuv Cohen. Rabbi Reichel interviewed dozens of people* and wrote a comprehensive manuscript for publication. Unfortunately, not enough space was available for the inclusion of all of the written and oral contributions that had been assembled, so this chapter is an abridged version. We apologize to all those people who have not been cited, and we hope that they understand. The supplementary thoughts from two Chief Rabbis of the United Kingdom, the former Head of the Church of England and the latter's Secretary for Inter-Religious Affairs were obtained by the book's translator.

*The names of the people interviewed orally or in writing for this chapter (not all of whom were quoted by name, and not all of whom responded orally; some responded in writing): Rabbi Hy Arbesfeld; Dr. Adena Berkowitz; Rabbi Saul Bernstein; Dr. Rivka Blau; (Rabbi) Zev Brenner; Rachel Chaifetz (daughter of Shragai Cohen), Rabbi Zevulun Charlop (grandson of Rabbi Yaakov Moshe Charlap, who spelled his name differently), Chana Cohen (widow of Shragai Cohen), Judah Cohen, Esq. (son of Rabbi Jack Simcha Cohen), Dr. Rabbanit Naomi G. Cohen, Rabbi Shear Yashuv Cohen, Natalio Fridman, Rebbetzin Blu Greenberg, Rabbi Rafael Grossman, Rabbi Baruch Jacobson (son of Rabbi Gershon Jacobson of the Algemeiner Journal), Rabbi Yaakov Kermaier, Lawrence Kobrin, Esq., Rabbi Simcha Krauss, Dr. Irene Lancaster, Rabbi Haskel Lookstein,

Cantor Joseph Malovany, Rabbi Itzhak Marmorstein, Naomi Mauer (Associate Publisher of The Jewish Press and daughter of Rabbi Sholom Klass), Daphne Merkin, Mrs. Jennie Michael, Rabbi Aaron I. Reichel, Esq. (the interviewer of virtually all but the British interviewees); Rabbi Bernard Rosensweig, Rabbi Sol Roth; Chief Rabbi Emeritus Jonathan Sacks; Ephraim Savitt, Esq., Rabbi Allen Schwartz, Rabbi Dr. Jacob J. Schacter, Evy Shechter, Rabbi Arthur Schneier, Rabbi Fabian Schonfeld, Canon Dr. Andrew Shanks, Rabbi Nisson Shulman, Barbara Lehman Siegel, Esq., Rabbi Elazar Teitz, Mrs. Shirley Weisberger, Rabbi Avi Weiss, R. Bernice Weiss, Canon Guy Wilkinson, Former Archbishop of Canterbury Lord Rowan Williams, Rabbi Lawrence Zierler, Yoni Zierler. A special thank you to Rabbi Mark Dratch of the Rabbinical Council of America.

The Vistas

How did it come about that Rabbi Cohen has had such an impact outside of the State of Israel? Born, raised and educated in Jerusalem, Rabbi Cohen seemed unlikely to make an indelible mark on the City of Haifa. Subsequently serving Haifa for about 35 years as Chief Rabbi, and then as Emeritus Chief Rabbi, he would have seemed an unlikely choice to make an unprecedented impact on the international community. Yet, that is exactly what he did.

Rabbi Cohen's first trip abroad was in 1949 as a military hero, fresh from a POW camp in Jordan, with his focus on fundraising and seeking medical attention for his war injuries. So successful was he as a speaker in his primary communal missions, however, that he was consequently recruited on a regular basis to make trips throughout the world on behalf of Israel Bonds and the United Jewish Appeal.

During these missions, however, his personal charisma, credentials and energy led to much more than exercises in fundraising. He also inspired Jews throughout the Diaspora to a deeper and more passionate appreciation of Judaism and Zionism, generating good will in a world that historically has not always treated Jews or Israelis with kindness and respect. He lectured, developed and encouraged many projects, and in general represented the embodiment of the best that Judaism and *Medinat Yisrael* had to offer. He was "a leader who combined traditional Torah learning with real service to the State," according to prominent Rabbi, Jacob J. Schacter.

Rabbi Dr. Samuel Belkin, the intellectual prodigy who went on to become President of Yeshiva College and then turned it into the educational empire now known as Yeshiva University, famously quipped, tongue in cheek, that as President of the University charged with building and funding such a huge educational enterprise, he was "a rabbi who does not preach and a teacher who does not teach." By contrast, Rabbi Cohen managed to raise funds for Israel and various institutions in addition to remaining not just a rabbi, but a Chief Rabbi, who never ceased to preach to people of many faiths, and an educator who never missed an opportunity to educate people in many disciplines.

Rabbi Cohen's wife, Rabbanit Dr. Naomi Cohen, commented that when raising money for the United Jewish Appeal and Israel Bonds, her husband was the star, the guest speaker, and was not involved in actual fundraising *per se*. But, when he started getting involved in fundraising for Ariel he immersed himself in the challenge and was very directly involved.

RAISING FUNDS FOR ARIEL

Over the years, Rabbi Cohen observed that many prominent rabbis made a difference, not just by strengthening existing institutions, but by building new ones. The various important roles of Machon Harry Fischel in terms of research and scholarship on the highest level in the "Yeshiva world," has already been discussed at length above. The Machon started publishing and editing manuscripts when virtually no other Yeshivot were doing so, and it trained judges for the religious courts in a special training program when virtually no other Yeshiva had such a program. But the Machon could only go so far and Rabbi Cohen could not raise money for it as a practical matter, since anyone approached for money would have said that this was the job of the Harry Fischel Foundation, because it had been the aim of its Founder that the Machon should be self-funding.

Gradually Rabbi Cohen came to the conclusion that if he were free to raise money in line with other heads of academies and universities, he could do more to establish many creative programs. One rabbi who set an example for him and served as an inspiration was his father-in-law, Rabbi Herbert S. Goldstein, the epitome of the innovative rabbi and fundraiser.

Rabbi Cohen therefore set up "American Friends of Ariel" to support the autonomous Ariel Institutes that he founded as an independent affiliate of Machon Harry Fischel. He saw to it that annual dinners were held in New York, drawing the "crème de la crème" of the Orthodox philanthropic society, as noted by the legendary talk show host Zev Brenner, and "the Orthodox aristocracy," as described by Rabbi Jacob J. Schacter. "American Friends of Ariel" was headed by community activists such as Larry Kobrin, Samuel Shechter and Natalio Fridman.

A table at the Ariel dinners was usually designated for members of the Rabbinical Council of America (RCA), who supported Rabbi Cohen and Ariel and encouraged their congregants to attend. Among those rabbis at the table at one time and/or another were Rabbis Saul Berman,

Louis Bernstein, Jack Simcha Cohen, Irving Greenberg, Rafael Grossman, Haskel Lookstein, Joseph Polak, Emanuel Rackman, O. Asher Reichel (a brother-in-law of Rabbi Cohen), Shlomo Riskin, Fabian Schonfeld, Arthur Schneier and Avi Weiss. Rabbi Cohen was obviously held in high esteem by the members of the RCA and routinely addressed their conferences whenever his schedule permitted.

The "American Friends of Ariel" were really friends of Rabbi Cohen, nurtured in the course of his many visits to America and who were, in turn, hosted by him and his wife during their visits to Israel. At the milestone 80th birthday celebration of Rabbi Cohen on behalf of Ariel in NYC, Rabbi Cohen even said as much, noting almost apologetically that he had expected the dinner on behalf of Ariel to center more on Ariel than on himself.

The Ariel dinner took place virtually every year, and was a highlight in the Jewish calendar for many of the leading American Jewish community leaders and activists. The list of guests of honor or keynote speakers over the years would be the dream team for any organization: Prime Minister Yitzchak Rabin, Nobel Laureate Elie Wiesel, refusenik-turned-Jewish-Agency Head Natan Sharansky, Prime Minister Binyamin Netanyahu and others. Their only common denominator seemed to be their leadership role on behalf of the Jewish people and their joint admiration for Rabbi Cohen.

At Rabbi Cohen's 80th birthday celebration hosted by Ariel, Rabbi Grossman observed, albeit with a bit of poetic license, that there is no city in the world with a significant Jewish population that has not been impacted by a person who studied at Ariel.

TRAINING RABBIS

At Ariel, rabbis were not just educated; they were trained. Rabbi Joseph Polak, who was destined to rise to prominence in America, had studied at the Machon on the recommendation of Rabbi Norman Frimer, the Head of the International Hillel House. Polak was particularly impressed by the way Ariel did not stop at graduation but continued to nurture its rabbis, as we have seen above.

Rabbi Cohen also led by example. Rabbi Fabian Schonfeld recalled:

> "We had a conference of European rabbis in Switzerland about 25 years ago. Some of the rabbis were on the cautious side [a euphemism if there ever was one] regarding Israel, critical of Israel in a good sense, that it was too secular, too nationalistic, and too militaristic. Rabbi Cohen stood up and told them what it meant

to be a supporter of Israel. He showed what you can do instead of castigating and name calling."

GUEST SPEAKER AT SYNAGOGUES

Rabbi Cohen spoke at synagogues on both sides of Central Park in order to raise funds, share insights, educate, and inspire. Cantor Joseph Malovany recalled that over the years Rabbi Cohen addressed the congregants of the Fifth Avenue Synagogue on a number of occasions. His talks ranged from explicating Midrashim, to the deepest philosophical thoughts of Rav Kook and those of Rabbi Cohen's noted father, Rabbi David Cohen, *HaRav HaNazir*. Cantor Malovany observed: "He never repeated himself. He always offered new insights on the Torah reading of the week. He often quoted the Kabbalah at its most simple level so that regular worshipers would understand."

On Shabbat, Rabbi Cohen would lay the groundwork for his most effective fundraising and follow up on this during the week. When he wasn't based at a hotel on the Upper East Side, he often slept over as a guest on the Upper West Side. In between these two influential neighborhoods gleamed New York City's showpiece Central Park, with some of the only real estate in Manhattan untouched by bulldozers. The park contains a maze of different routes for pedestrians, joggers, cyclists, romantic horse-drawn carriages and of course, cars. As beautiful and breathtaking as this park may be it can be dangerous at night, and even by day, in some of its more secluded sections. Two park incidents highlight the character of Rabbi Cohen.

One Shabbat, when Rabbi Cohen's nephew was entrusted with accompanying his uncle from the Upper West Side to the Upper East Side, the young guide proudly took a circuitous scenic route through the relatively (by Manhattan standards) fresh air of the park, rather than the direct route full of air-polluting cars. However, when they emerged on the other side, they discovered, to their consternation, that they had veered a few blocks south of their desired destination. This extra walk was not good for the rabbi's leg, and for the event they arrived later than planned. The nephew braced himself for a deserved tongue lashing. It never came. The intent had been positive and the nephew obviously suffered upon realizing what had happened so the rabbi saw no need to rub it in or to say anything at all on the subject.

On another occasion while walking through a secluded area of the park, a man approached who seemed up to no good. The opportunity for foul play was there, and in fact, the man "asked" for money. Since it was Shabbat, however, the rabbi did not have any. Things could have gotten ugly and the rabbi could have easily become another "statistic," God forbid. Here is how the noted New York criminal attorney Ephraim Savitt, a relative of the rabbi, recalled hearing what happened. Sounding more like a rabbi or even a novelist than a lawyer, Savitt noted:

> "There were no bike riders, joggers, or police [at that time and place] in Central Park . . . Just a Jerusalem rabbi and a would-be mugger intent on getting free souvenirs from the rabbi, who had no money on him that day, with only his life and limb available to satisfy his stalker.
>
> "Rabbi Shear Yashuv, calling on his combination of military experiences as a Haganah fighter in the Old city of Jerusalem during Israel's War of Independence, his months in captivity as a prisoner-of-war in Trans-Jordan, and his diplomatic skills as a Jerusalem Deputy Mayor, turned to face his attacker in the deserted park, greeted him with a "good day" salutation, and asked him if he could be so kind as to provide directions to the [other side of the park] where he was headed to synagogue prayers. Completely disarmed, the would-be attacker pointed the Rabbi in the right direction. The man then asked the Rabbi where he was from. When Rabbi Shear Yashuv responded "Jerusalem, Israel," the now-friendly fellow was overawed that he had been stalking a rabbi from the Holy City. He told Rabbi Shear Yashuv that his intentions had "not been good," and asked the rabbi for forgiveness, which the rabbi gladly offered, with a great deal of relief.
>
> ". . . Rabbi Shear Yashuv's combination of rabbinic wisdom, diplomatic skills, and survival instincts as an old combat soldier bridged gaps between different sectors of Israeli society and different religions worldwide, but on this occasion bridged the gap on a cold winter day in an isolated stretch of Central Park, between the profane and the holy."

As we have seen, Rabbi Cohen's destination on the East Side of Manhattan was often the Fifth Avenue Synagogue and his host for lunch after the services was a leading pillar of the Jewish community, Herman Merkin and his wife Ulla. Among the other congregants at the Fifth Avenue Synagogue was Elie Wiesel, one of many leading Jewish personalities whom Rabbi Cohen considered a personal friend and who was the principal speaker at one of the Ariel dinners.

Another prominent congregant was the incredibly bright and multi-talented Rabbi Dr. Manfred Lehmann, an international businessman whose contacts included people as far away as in Central Africa. These ties proved invaluable to Israel when she carried one of the most dramatic rescues in the history of the world at an airport in Entebbe, Uganda, on the Fourth of July in 1976, eclipsing the American celebrations of its bicentennial. In addition, Lehmann was a bibliophile and a collector of rare Judaica. Rabbi Cohen rarely missed an opportunity to serve as a catalyst for creative good works. So when Rabbis Cohen and Lehmann realized how they could combine their resources, Rabbi Cohen arranged for the publication by Ariel of a volume of rare annotated manuscripts in the Ohel Hayyim catalogue in memory of Jamie Lehmann, Dr. Manfred Lehmann's brilliant son who had passed away at an early age, but who had still managed to write many creative works on Jewish topics.

As an honorary member of the family of the Fifth Avenue Synagogue, Rabbi Cohen was once given the honor of *Kriat Hashem* at a ritual circumcision, announcing the name of the youngest child of the Rabbi of the Synagogue, Rabbi Yaakov Kermaier. Rabbi Cohen commented that he did so with particular satisfaction, as a great-grandfather of the newly-named Netanel Kermaier had been a student of Rav Kook, early in the 20th century.

Rabbi Cohen spent many weekends at different congregations all over the world. A single example: Rabbi Fabian Schonfeld recalled that Rabbi Cohen and his wife were his guests one Sabbath in Kew Gardens, Queens, New York. "It was a very wonderful and pleasurable Shabbat for us. It was a pleasure to be with him and to talk with him. To be in his presence was a real *nachas ruach* (soothing for the soul). We invited him to speak at our synagogue and in the Touro College nearby."

⮑   GUEST LECTURER AT RABBINICAL ACADEMIES

Wherever Rabbi Cohen went he was asked to speak. Whenever he visited Yeshiva University he was invariably asked to deliver a lecture, whether to the highest level of post-graduate rabbinic students or to a wide range of rabbinic students. So recalls Rabbi Zevulun Charlop, a grandson of Rabbi Cohen's own early mentor, Rabbi Yaakov Moshe Charlap. Rabbi Zevulun Charlop served as Dean of the Rabbinical School affiliated with Yeshiva University for many years.

There was no lack of invitations to lecture at Yeshiva University nor at the Yeshiva of Touro College founded by Rabbi Bernard Lander who had earlier been Dean of the Bernard Revel Graduate School of Yeshiva University. Rabbi Shear Yashuv accepted these happily.

But the decision to accept an invitation to speak at the Yeshiva

Chovevei Torah Rabbinical School was far more complicated. Chovevei was known to be on the fringes of Orthodoxy, maintaining an Orthodox self-identity, but implementing so many innovations that quite a few mainstream modern Orthodox leaders wanted nothing to do with it. Some even sought to ban its founder, Rabbi Avi Weiss, from the mainstream Orthodox Rabbinical Council of America. Although Rabbi Cohen's primary ties in America remained with Yeshiva University and its leading rabbis, he also built bridges with rabbis who were on the 'left' of modern Orthodoxy.

Rabbi Avi Weiss recalled: "Throughout the early years of the founding of Yeshivat Chovevei Torah Rabbinical School, Rabbi Shear Yashuv Cohen was a constant source of encouragement. What made him stand out was his ability to rise above the political fray and with great courage, assess and make decisions based on the merits of Chovevei."

When Rabbi Cohen lectured there, "his talk was of great Torah depth," recalled Rabbi Weiss. "But what stands out for me was his warmth and his ability to so powerfully connect to our students."

Rabbi Weiss made a point of visiting Rabbi Cohen every time he was in Israel. There was even some discussion of having Chovevei students study at the Ariel Institutes in Israel. It didn't happen, though the fact that it entered the serious discussion stage is in itself significant.

Rabbi Weiss referred to Rabbi Cohen as "a Rav of great depth and halakhic commitment, but with an openness that profoundly touched my soul and I know he has touched the souls of tens of thousands more."

⇥ CONSULTATIONS BASED ON RABBI COHEN'S SCHOLARSHIP

Rabbi Cohen would routinely be consulted by the cream of America's Orthodox rabbinate whenever they were looking for a "rabbi's rabbi" of the rare category they could respect, look up to and relate to. Top American rabbis who could have relied on the advice of the best rabbis and rabbinical courts that America has to offer would seek out Rabbi Cohen to deal with complex and sensitive cases, often involving the ultra-sensitive and complex areas of marriage and divorce where many rabbis fear to tread.

The *Av Bet Din* of the highly sophisticated city of Boston, Rabbi Joseph Polak, provided this recollection:

"It had been a long day in Rabbi Shear Yashuv's Cohen's visit to Boston, somewhere in the middle of the first decade of the 21st century. He had traveled here partly in response to an invitation extended by the Boston Jewish community in a twin-city cultural exchange with Haifa, and partly because I had invited him to deliver the *Nachum Glatzer Memorial Lecture* at the Boston University School of Law during that visit.

"The lecture, as I recall, which was held in the School of Law's Barrister's Hall, was well-attended and the Rabbi and his wife, Dr. Naomi Cohen (who herself had delivered a separate lecture earlier in the day), happily ensconced in the back of my car, were travelling to my home following this lecture. At the time, I was the rabbi at Boston University and a longstanding member of the Boston *Bet Din*.

"My cell phone rang in the car. It was a *sheyla* (question on religious law), as it emerged, coming from deep in the heart of Texas, from one of my alumni. He and his wife were earnestly looking for children to adopt and a situation had just presented itself that just might make another adoption possible. Twins, no less, had been born to a gentile Caucasian mother somewhere in the Texas panhandle and my former *talmid* and his wife (married in a wedding I had performed some years earlier) were excited at the new possibility.

"Is there a *michshol* (a significant problem), I asked? Maybe, came the reply. These twins were the product of an incestuous liaison between a father and daughter and don't we need to establish whether the concept of *mamzerut* is applicable in cases of incest among gentiles?

"I smiled. The answer was hardly in my head and I said into the phone that I need to consult *sfarim* (Jewish legal books) to deal with this question, but I 'just happen to have' the Chief Rabbi of Haifa in the car here and let's see if he is willing to risk a *psak* (ruling) off the top of his head.

"I laid the question gently to him; the irony of the situation was lost to neither of us. He looked at me and said, in Yiddish: 'It has to be O.K. This is exactly what happened between Lot and his daughters, and at the end of the line, generations later, we got King David.'

"I looked at him and smiled. '*Kevod HaRav* (the Rabbi) is undoubtedly correct but is he willing to base a *psak* of this gravitas on such a *midrash*?' He smiled back at me, and said, 'Of course not.' In my study, some minutes later, we took out the *Even HaEzer* and swiftly reached a legal resolution.

"In the end, even before hearing the *psak*, my *talmid* and his wife changed their mind about the adoptions, having been warned by their doctor about the genetic repercussions of such babies. But what I learned from the episode amongst many other things, is the reliability of the intuition of a *Godol HaDor* (a leading rabbi of a generation), who is a *Godol HaDor* precisely because he does not go by intuition alone, however reliable. I can tell you a great deal about the process of *hora'ah* (directive), but from HaRav Cohen's *derekh* (approach), I can tell you even more about its integrity."

Another very sophisticated rabbi, Rabbi Lawrence Zierler, was:

> "reminded of a time when we were together at a specially arranged meeting . . . where I was seeking his guidance in a complex case of an *agunah* . . . Not wanting to disregard the authority of his American colleagues, he asked me to compose a *sheyla* detailing the uniquely compelling circumstances, and he would then appeal to a reputable American *Bet Din* to consider the matter of upend-ing the original *kiddushin* (marriage) based on what was clearly a *mekach ta'ut* (decision to marry based on false pretenses). We deliberated over the evidence long and hard during that meeting. His pain for the woman's plight was more than manifest, Rav Shear Yashuv lent his ear and heart to the predicament and was bent on helping me resolve it by whatever available means."

SUPPORT FOR COURT TO FREE AGUNOT (CHAINED WOMEN)

Rabbi Cohen was not merely consulted by individual rabbis. As recently as in the summer of 2014, an international *Bet Din* was set up under the leadership of Rabbi Simcha Krauss, a former President of the Religious Zionists of America, with the explicit intention of finding halakhic means to resolve the plight of *agunot* who were denied the right to remarry under traditional Jewish law.

Many rabbis had attempted to solve this problem, but without success. In this instance, however, the particular reason for optimism was that, in addition to the composition of the court – among its members are former RZA (Religious Zionists of America) President Rabbi Yosef Blau and Rabbi Ronald Warburg – two prominent Israeli Orthodox rabbis gave the court their public blessings. One of the judges, incidentally, was the aforementioned Rabbi Joseph Polak.

The court's formation was announced by none other than Blu Greenberg, founder of JOFA, the Jewish Orthodox Feminist Alliance. She noted that, in the course of creating this court:

"the *Av Bet Din*, Rabbi Simcha Krauss and the *Av Bet Din* Emeritus of Boston, Rabbi Joseph Polak, visited Rabbi Cohen to ask for his intellectual and spiritual support. While several other rabbis gave support, but said they did not want their names mentioned publicly, Rabbi Cohen was not afraid to openly stand up for what he believed was right, the elimination of *iggun* (chains) through halakhic means. In many other matters, he took this same position, standing up for the rights of the downtrodden and disenfranchised."

Rabbi Krauss noted the significance of the public endorsement by Rabbi Cohen. "He is one of the great rabbis and *poskim*; he is open-minded and fair; traditional but not closed-minded; he knows the world and has a mastery of other *poskim*."

Another prominent rabbi who openly supported this court was Rabbi Zalman Nechemia Goldberg, former *Av Bet Din* of the Rabbinical High Court in Jerusalem, and one of the most important *Roshei Yeshiva* of Ariel.

Rabbi Zevulun Charlop, referred to above, recalled engaging Rabbi Cohen in many a conversation about Jewish law before and after his presentations at the rabbinical school affiliated with Yeshiva University. One such discussion stood out in particular. It occurred shortly before Rav Shear Yashuv was scheduled to leave for the airport and return to Israel. Rabbi Charlop told him of a ruling by the Rogachover Rebbe about a conditional marriage involving Boaz and Ruth in the Bible, which supported a controversial position taken by Chief Rabbi Goren. Rabbi Cohen, the latter's brother-in-law, realized that this ruling could be helpful to him, as he was being pressed by other prominent rabbis on this issue. Despite various difficulties, Rabbi Cohen was able to have the ruling faxed to him at the airport and was able to deliver it to Rabbi Goren.

➤   HARRY AND JANE FISCHEL FOUNDATION

After the establishment of *Medinat Yisrael*, when air travel was not nearly as common as it is today, Rabbi Cohen nevertheless used to visit the United States on an annual basis. After he married into the Fischel family and was appointed to the Board of the Fischel Foundation, he made it his business to coordinate his visits with the annual meetings of the Board. Over time he became a driving force on the Foundation and eventually became the Chairman of its Board. Such was the respect for him that his views generally carried the day.

The current Administrator of the Foundation recalls having once proposed a resolution in America. In advance of the official vote, he garnered the unanimous consent of all the Americans on the Board (who dominated in terms of numbers) to either support the resolution or abstain. However, when Rabbi Cohen was told of the resolution, he very diplomatically made his opposition known, giving his reasons. The result was that every single expression of original support for the resolution melted away. Even the proponent of the resolution had to concede that the resolution had been defeated in an honorable and respectable way, with no hard feelings.

On another occasion, Rabbi Yitzchak Marmorstein of *Bet HaRav Kook* and Rabbi Gregory Wall (who at the time made his principal living as a clarinetist) proposed that the Fischel Foundation should sponsor a unique multimedia concert tour throughout America. The idea was to put to music the poetry and philosophy of the great Rav Kook and his disciple, the *Nazir* of Jerusalem, Rabbi Cohen's father.

Not only did some members of the Board deem this idea to be overly radical and impractical, but the sum needed for this multi-city tour was greater than the sum normally allotted to projects beyond the fixed commitments of the Foundation. Nevertheless, when Rabbi Cohen arrived with a cassette of a concert recorded in Israel, the resolution carried the day. The tour took place in the same American and Canadian cities originally visited by Rav Kook on his only trip to North America in 1924. Needless to say, few concerts have ever reached heights of such intellectual and poetic passion, culminating in the sounding of the *shofar*.

Rabbi Cohen was clearly receptive to new ideas, and ready to implement them.

⇥ IMPACT ON PEOPLE'S LIVES

It seems that wherever the rabbi went, whatever he did, his antennae were always up. He was always looking to help his fellow human beings, whether on a broad communal scale or on an individual local scale.

A family friend, Mrs. Kenneth (Jenny) Michael, recalls traveling by car from Haifa to Efrat with Rabbi Cohen and his wife, a very good friend of hers. The whole time the Rabbi was on a cell phone trying to convince rabbis at the other end to allow skin to be removed from a corpse in order to save the lives of soldiers who had been terribly burned in a tank.

Rabbi Cohen could captivate the imagination of people of all ages. Here is the story of someone who, as a young boy, became so captivated by the rabbi, that he viewed him as his "hero." Not only that, but when this young boy himself grew up to be a prominent rabbi in Teaneck and Senior Rabbinic Fellow at the Shalom Hartman Institute in Jerusalem,

Rabbi Lawrence Zierler, he says that "everybody in my immediate family knew this, and I said as much to Rabbi Cohen every time I met him." In his words:

"My first exposure to Rabbi Shear Yashuv Cohen occurred in 1972 when I was twelve years old. I happened to catch an interview with him carried on a Jewish Cable TV program in Toronto. I was then studying in a Yeshiva that was somewhat haredi, and my exposure to such a Torah luminary with such open views on society and participation in dialogue with non-observant Jews was rare, even though I grew up in a very open-minded home. I was taken both by his ideas and his manner of speech. In soothing tones he described his outreach work within the Greater Haifa community where he served for many years as Chief Rabbi. His commitment to *Klal Yisrael* and his extensive involvement in addressing the needs of a very diverse population was breathtaking . . .

"Hoping to one day to actually meet and engage with this creative and forward-thinking rabbinic mind, I received the opportunity years later at an RCA convention in the mid-1990's. Rabbi Shear Yashuv's warmth and approachability were palpable. In his address to that convention he touched on many points that underscored his world view. Noting that the Divine Presence is not independent of *Olam Hazeh* (This World), he reminded us that the real mission of a Torah scholar is to bring the presence of the Almighty wherever the other person is . . . In these comments one heard a proof text and basis for Rabbi Shear Yashuv's *modus operandi* in his expansive understanding of the role of communal rabbinic leadership.

"Rabbi Cohen's love and interest in all Jews, in all places of identity and religious engagement, was manifest in yet another part of his address to this rabbinic group. He noted that there are three words for 'friendship' as seen in the verses of Leviticus (19:16–18). These words represent three different levels of affinity for the 'other' and carry with them, respectively, three levels of engagement . . . in ascending order of magnitude. Apropos friendship, the Torah first simply states: '*Do not despise your brother in your heart.*' This is a simple, one could say generic, concept around the human experience. We are not to live with hatred for our fellow humans.

"Then there is the requirement of '*You should surely rebuke your colleague or comrade.*' The implication here is that one is operating on a different relational level, with more of a connection. The person is known to you and therefore you can and must, given your level of interpersonal involvement, rebuke him when he errs, and set him straight when he is off course, knowing that there will be receptivity for this, since it comes from a good and caring place.

"Finally, when the Torah commands us with the familiar words: '*Love your neighbor as yourself,*' it is speaking to the highest level of friendship. It is referring to a relationship that is deep-seated and long-established. With your 'neighbor' you are expected to be able to appreciate his yearnings, woes and needs. You can truly *love* him, for you know him at the deepest level. And with this intensity of involvement, the Torah can reasonably expect from us true love and affinity for that other individual. Even rebuke must be communicated constructively and with love.

"Rabbi Shear Yashuv's genuine concern for all is reflected in this nuanced understanding of the Torah's use of these three designations for friendship and relational contexts. It needs to be noted that his love of humankind has been extended to all created in the image of the Divine, as evidenced in his seminal inter-religious efforts, always carried out with propriety in a balanced and measured way."

To sum up, Leviticus describes three levels of friendship. These are, in ascending order, the level of not bearing grudges; the closer level of being able to tell someone off in a loving way; and the third level of loving your fellow human being in an empathetic way, as described elsewhere in this book. Rabbi Cohen epitomized all three levels, and knew when each approach was appropriate to his own "neighbor."

ALMOST CHANGING A LIFE

Sometimes, Rabbi Cohen *almost* changed a person's life. Rabbi Rafael Grossman had many occasions to refer to his first cousin, Chaika Grossman, a former leader of the Bialystoker uprising against the Nazis and a leader of the left-wing *HaShomer HaTzair* movement, mentioned above in Chapter 7. Chaika had several opportunities to interact with Rabbi Cohen and once commented that: "If all rabbis were like Rabbi Shear Yashuv Cohen, I might possibly have become religious."

This view is widespread in the non-observant Jewish community of *Medinat Yisrael*.

⇒   MUTUAL RESPECT TOWARD HIS REMARKABLE WIFE

Few husbands have a wife as gifted in so many ways as Dr. Naomi Cohen. Even fewer husbands, especially of the "old school" have the self-assurance to be comfortable with such a wife.

Rabbi Avi Weiss could not help noticing that Rabbi Cohen's wife was also quite remarkable, holding her own in a discussion about Philo with Chovevei's Rosh Yeshiva, Rabbi Dov Linzer, described by Rabbi Weiss as "not only a brilliant *Talmid Chacham*, but well-read in just about everything." But what made the greatest impression on Rabbi Avi Weiss was the memory of Rabbi Shear Yashuv gazing with admiration as his wife engaged in this give and take:

> "Without necessarily agreeing with every position his wife took on the role of women in Jewish Law and Judaism, Rabbi Cohen did not insist she had to agree with him publicly on every nuance, but he was clearly proud of the positions she took."

A similar position seemed to have been taken by the iconic Modern Orthodox Rabbi and Rabbanit who preceded Rabbi Weiss in Riverdale, New York. Rabbi Irving "Yitz" Greenberg and his wife Blu have been on the cutting edge of Modern Orthodoxy for decades.

Rabbi Greenberg was known as a leading thinker at Yeshiva College, the main guiding light of the nationwide student organization *Yavneh* during its formative and most vibrant years, and a co-founder of *CLAL*, among many other positions of leadership. His wife Blu has been a leading Orthodox feminist and has over the years, shared many views and platforms with Rabbi Cohen's wife. But the relationship and the dynamics between the couple also caught her attention and elicited her admiration. Blu Greenberg recalls:

> "Rabbi Cohen was stately and well-spoken and as the office of the rabbinate requires, politic and judicious in his comments. Naomi was spontaneous and thoroughly honest. She did not filter anything but spoke her mind; nothing she said was inappropriate, but neither was it cautious. Her comments were honorable yet refreshing and down to earth. Often she would say something and then give a little laugh afterwards as if she [had] let go of a thought that she might have held onto a little longer. What impressed me was that Rabbi Cohen never seemed to worry about the dignity of the office, but fully appreciated her candor. He respected her and her words. It was not that he tolerated her speech, nor that he

tried to silence it as some other people in his position might have done; rather, he listened to what she had to say with ... genuine ... respect.

"Both Rabbi Cohen and Naomi were very open-minded, very committed to Orthodoxy and *halakha*, not afraid of being at the forefront for the best ethical values in Judaism, and to us they represented the model par excellence of what rabbinic leadership should be. They have contributed so much to Jewish life during the last 50-plus years and continue to do so with genuine modesty and dedication. It has been a great privilege to call them friends."

REPRESENTATIVE OF THE JEWISH PEOPLE

We have seen the role Rabbi Cohen played on the world stage in the area of ecumenical discussions. Here is a comment by another prominent participant on that stage, Emeritus Chief Rabbi of the United Kingdom and the Commonwealth, Jonathan Sacks:

"Rabbi Shear Yashuv Cohen has always made a powerful impression on me as a figure of immense open-mindedness and generosity of spirit. Such figures are sadly far too few in the rabbinate today. We spent four days together in Amritsar, North India, with Sikhs, Hindus, Muslims and the Dalai Lama, as part of an encounter organized by the Elijah Foundation. His gracious manner and old-world courtesy were a *Kiddush Hashem* (Sanctification of God's Name) on that occasion as so often. He is a man who understands the delicacy of the halakhic process and the need on the part of its decisors to understand the human situation of their questioners. His role as the presiding influence of the Ariel Institutes is a major factor in its success and relevance to the contemporary Jewish world. I studied there for some months before becoming Chief Rabbi, in 1990–1991. He is a scholar of great breadth and erudition and one of the most sympathetic religious leaders I have ever met."

Incidentally, as stated in the Translator's Introduction, Rabbi Sacks' successor, Chief Rabbi Ephraim Mirvis (formerly Chief Rabbi of Ireland) also studied at Ariel. Chief Rabbi Mirvis delivered his Rosh HaShanah 2013 installation sermon before the Prince of Wales, the Leader of the Opposition, other members of Parliament, rabbinical court judges, fellow Chief Rabbis, representatives of other religions and the judiciary. He stated there that as "a passionate supporter of Israel," he was extremely proud of being the only Chief Rabbi of the United Kingdom to have been ordained in Israel – and at Ariel to boot.

In Chapter 14, it is noted that Rabbi Cohen took some of the first steps toward rapprochement with the Vatican, the seat of the Roman Catholic Church. This positive relationship is highlighted by the photograph seen around the world showing a previous Pope and Rabbi Cohen meeting one to one, wearing similar white *kippot*.

Rabbi Cohen also took the first step in rapprochement with the 80-million strong Church of England and its leaders. The Archbishop of Canterbury is the senior Bishop of the Church of England whose 'Supreme Governor' is the Monarch. Constitutionally, the Archbishop of Canterbury is the second-most important person in the land, being given precedence over the Prime Minister of the day.

Archbishop Williams, now Lord Williams of Oystermouth, served as Archbishop of Canterbury from 2002 to 2012. He is generally regarded as the most distinguished thinker among the Archbishops of Canterbury in a millennium. Before being appointed Archbishop he had lectured in theology at Cambridge University and become Lady Margaret Professor of Divinity at Oxford University. He is presently Master of Magdalene College Cambridge. This is what Dr. Williams has to say about Rabbi Cohen:

> "The work of an Archbishop of Canterbury brings a good many unexpected graces and gifts in terms of the people encountered, and I would emphatically include Chief Rabbi Shear Yashuv Cohen among those who have brought grace, inspiration and enlightenment.
>
> "When the Chief Rabbinate of Israel and the Church of England, together with its sister Anglican churches across the world, agreed [initially in 2006] to the holding of regular meetings for serious and sustained discussion, not only of current affairs but of focal issues of religious understanding, all agreed on the importance of seeking members and contributors of the highest intellectual and spiritual credibility. We were fortunate indeed that, from the first meeting in 2007 Chief Rabbi Cohen was part of these conversations.
>
> ". . . Chief Rabbi Cohen represented a style of Jewish reflection which was not often encountered in the blandness of so much 'interfaith' discourse. It was impossible to ignore the sheer depth of a mind formed in the most rigorous traditions of exegesis and scholarship; but even more important was the ethical and spiritual integrity animating that scholarship.

"The Chief Rabbi is, quite simply, a wise man, one who exemplifies the picture offered in the third chapter of Proverbs, where the person obedient to the Torah of the Almighty finds that the commands of the Lord are *'life to your soul and a graceful ornament to your neck . . . When you lie down you will not fear; you will lie down and your sleep will be pleasant. You will not fear sudden terror nor the holocaust of the wicked when it comes. For HASHEM will be your security, and He will guard your feet from entrapment'* [Proverbs 3:22–26, the Stone Edition, edited by Rabbi Nosson Scherman]. [*Translator's note:* This ArtScroll traditional Jewish translation was actually provided in the original statement by Dr. Williams.]

"These are words that are not merely academic these days; we know that 'sudden terror' and the fear of the wicked are all around in a climate of mindless violence and what often seems an intensified anti-Semitism. Rabbi Cohen brings to this situation a mind and heart profoundly rooted in faith, and is able to discuss the painful crises of our day with a perspective that is not dominated by headlines or the urge to please a religious or a secular public.

"We have been privileged to have so deep and serious a mind as part of our conversations. It has not meant that we have agreed about everything. Much more importantly, though, it has meant that we Anglicans . . . have learned an intense respect for the lucidity and honesty, the care and devotion, out of which Rabbi Cohen's convictions come. It has been an enormously important experience, and I am very glad indeed that we shall have a thorough chronicle of this remarkable life available in English, thanks to this translation by Dr. Irene Lancaster."

Canon Guy Wilkinson CBE, formerly the Archbishop of Canterbury's Secretary for Inter-Religious Affairs and National Adviser to the Church of England (2005–2010) provided additional context: ". . . I was responsible for national and international dialogues and for advising the Archbishop and the Church of England nationally on relations with leaders and communities of other faiths." Regarding Rabbi Cohen, the Canon had this to say:

"It has truly been said that Chief Rabbi Shear Yashuv Cohen has earned the huge respect of world religious leaders, heads of state and public figures. This is in no small degree because he is a man of true hospitality: he welcomes with warmth those of other religions whom he has not previously met and whose community he may have had antecedent reasons to mistrust.

"His hospitality therefore includes a certain humility: he sets aside any reservations he may have and awaits the encounter with patience and respect . . .

"In speaking on the sanctity of life, Rabbi Cohen highlighted the life-giving attributes of God as the source of all vitality that demands that everything possible be done to affirm the inalienable sanctity of human life. Perhaps it is this God-given vitality which gives the sparkle to his eyes.

"The theme of hospitality was explicit in the second meeting between the Chief Rabbinate of Israel [headed by Rabbi Cohen] and the Church of England . . . in 2008.

"In the course of the discussions, Chief Rabbi Cohen referred to the hospitality of Abraham who even set aside his prayers to offer hospitality to his angelic guests; this, he said, was as a model for both Christians and Jews, speaking of the symbolic nature of Abraham's tent, with its open sides as a sign of the open hospitality of God to all.

"Rabbi Cohen's hospitality includes not only humility, but also a strong sense of humour which runs through all conversations with him and comes out not only in his smile, but in gentle comments and asides. Awaiting the rather long drawn-out preparations for an evening meal in Canterbury [England], he commented that Jewish people had learned about patience and that Anglican-Jewish relations might need time to mature . . ."

All this acclaim from Christians did not in any way diminish Rabbi Cohen's firm values as an observant Jew. Rabbi Fabian Schonfeld, one of the Presidents of the Rabbinical Council of America, and highly respected by his peers, commented that Rabbi Cohen was "a true example of what it means to be a haredi in a positive sense," a truly pious person, "with the good qualities of haredim, without getting involved in miniscule or unnecessary activities. He was really *frum* (pious); he knew what it means to represent *Eretz Yisrael, Am Yisrael* and *Torat Yisrael.*"

Lawrence Kobrin, who has held many positions of leadership in the Jewish community over the years, including Chairman of the Board of the Jewish Week (New York) and the President of American Friends of "Ariel," said:

"It is regretful that he did not in fact become the Chief Rabbi of the State of Israel. His impeccable halakhic credentials, combined with openness to, and understanding of, the contemporary non-religious world, would have immeasurably aided in bridging the gaps between them. These gaps are those with which we now suffer."

Chief Rabbi Shear Yashuv Cohen is the embodiment of an outstanding personality. Over the years he has demonstrated that he has the will to survive, the will to persevere, the will to defend his country against all the odds, and the will to make herculean efforts to seek out viable halakhic solutions to thorny contemporary halakhic problems as they arise, solutions that are within the rabbinic consensus, and finally, the will to reach out to the whole world.

Afterword

In the Babylonian Talmud *Baba Metzia* 84a, we find a description of Rabbi Yohanan as "*a figure full of ancient beauty: the only person of this caliber to be left in Jerusalem.*" This is how we ourselves feel about the figure of Chief Rabbi Shear Yashuv Cohen who irradiates everything he touches. We in Haifa have benefitted tremendously from having a person of his great gifts living among us here for so many decades.

Rabbi Cohen grew up to be a Torah and Talmudic scholar of the highest distinction, nurtured within the very heart of the great religious Zionist circles of Jerusalem. The giants whom he knew at very close range included the legal expert and mystic, Rav Kook, the first Chief Rabbi of *Eretz Yisrael* under the British Mandate. Then there was Rav Kook's son, Rabbi Tzvi Yehuda Kook. Another great teacher and rabbi was Rabbi Yaakov Moshe Charlap. And last, but certainly not least, was Rabbi Cohen's own father, the Nazir of Jerusalem, Rabbi David Cohen. So, for someone of Rabbi Shear Yashuv Cohen's caliber to have been living among us is truly a privilege of the highest order.

Through close proximity with these Torah giants and by internalizing their profundity of thought and practice from a very early age, Rabbi Cohen imbibed three very important core principles. These three core principles have continued to inform Rabbi Cohen's entire *halakhic*, philosophical and Torah approach to learning and life.

The first core principle of Rabbi Cohen's philosophy of life is an ardent and uncompromising love for the very ground on which we walk in this Holy Land. He has exhibited, and continues to have, a readiness to give even his life for its revival, as well a perpetual desire to take part in its rebuilding – and especially of the Holy City of Jerusalem. He feels acute pain at every desecration, and has long taken active part, in terms of both Torah guidance and practical application, in the struggle to preserve its wholeness.

The second core principle that Rabbi Cohen learned from his rabbis and teachers is the love of the Torah of Israel with all his heart, soul and might. The desire to "increase and glorify Torah" that pulsates in his heart is manifest in his establishment of many Torah institutions. The countless Torah classes that he has given in Israel and around the world attest to his commitment to the dissemination of Torah as widely as possible. His halakhic research and Jewish thought are set out in his many books and articles, some of which are still to be published.

And now we come to the third core principle, the most important of all, which is Rabbi Cohen's *Ahavat Yisrael* – love of the people of Israel. Rabbi Cohen is gifted with the amazing ability to put everyone at ease and to treat everyone at their own level. His love of "neighbor" is that great rarity: love for its own sake. Everyone who knows Rabbi Cohen, whether friend, acquaintance, admirer, or student, can attest to this unique quality of his. He manages to find something in common with the whole religious spectrum, whether Hasidim, Mitnagdim, Sephardim, or Ashkenazim.

However, Rabbi Cohen has taken these teachings even further. He has built on the specifically Jewish trilogy of love of land, learning and people to reach out in a very personal capacity to all the peoples and religions of the world, seeing this as one of his key missions in life.

For how often does one see a Torah and Talmud scholar of the highest order debate and even negotiate politically with leaders of world religions and heads of state, always in their own language? It is only a very rare person indeed who can do this, and even manage to improve (and sometimes even to completely *change*) the attitude of these religious and political world leaders towards the Jewish people and their country, Israel.

Rabbi Cohen's noble, aristocratic, bearing, which he inherited from his rabbis and teachers, goes together with his genuinely-held view, as stated in the popular Mishnah (Sayings of the Fathers 3:18), *"Beloved is every single person who lives on earth, for they were all created in the image of God."*

Chief Rabbi Cohen has earned the deep respect of his fellow rabbis, world religious leaders, heads of state, public figures and his own flock in Haifa.

The last photo taken of Rabbi Shear Yashuv Cohen, as he receives the first
copy of his newly-published commentary on Shir HaShirim (Song of Songs).
At right: Editor Rabbi Yedidya HaCohen.
(Photo courtesy of Jhony Navarro, the Rabbi's caregiver.)

Further Reading

Suggested background readings

THE FOREWORD

Collins, Liat (7th December 2012). "Rabbi, Warrior, and Seeker of Peace, Shear Yashuv Cohen has not only witnessed more than 80 years of local history, he has taken part in it." *Jerusalem Post*. 80th Anniversary Supplement, p. 42. Retrieved at: *http://www.jpost.com/Jewish-World /Jewish-Features/Rabbi-warrior-and-seeker-of-peace*.

THE WORLD OF THE RABBI'S CHILDHOOD

Eisenstein, Chaim (December 2015). "Hearing the Sounds of the Divine." *Torah To-Go*. New York: Rabbi Isaac Elchanan Theological Seminary. Yeshiva University Center for the Jewish Future, 5–8 (the biographical information about the Nazir is inaccurate, but the *Nazir's* philosophical "Torah" is well expressed).

RABBI KOOK

Raz, Simcha (2003). *An Angel Among Men*.

Wein, Berel (2008). *Holy Man in the Holy Land*. 3 audio CD's. Lakewood, NJ: The Destiny Foundation.

Mirsky, Yehudah (2013). *Rav Kook: Mystic in a Time of Revolution*. New Haven: Yale University Press.

IN THE TENTS OF THE TORAH

Yoshor, Moses (1986). *The Chafetz Chaim*. Brooklyn, New York: Mesorah Publications.

Finkelman, Shimon (1989). *The Chazon Ish*. Brooklyn, New York: Mesorah Publications.

Cohen, Shear Yashuv (1991). "Chief Rabbi Herzog – Master Jurist and Gaon." Jewish Law Association Studies, Atlanta, GA: Scholars Press, 5, 9–20.

Freedman, Dr. Shalom (2006). *Rabbi Shlomo Goren: Torah Sage and General*, Jerusalem and New York: Urim. (Information about the military rabbinate).

THE BATTLES FOR JERUSALEM AND FOR ISRAEL'S PHYSICAL SURVIVAL 1948, 1967 AND 1973

Collins, Larry, and **Lapierre**, Dominique (1972 and later editions). New York: Simon & Schuster: *O Jerusalem.*

Phillips, John (1977). *A Will to Survive.* New York: Doubleday. (In 1948, Phillips photographed the fall of the Old City of Jerusalem. He returned in 1967, located the people he had photographed in 1948 and photographed them again, adding thumbnail biographies. Rabbi Cohen features at the very end of the book – on a stretcher – as the last person to be taken out of the Old City. The book contains a Foreword by Golda Meir and an Afterword by Teddy Kollek.)

Oren, Michael B. (2003*). Six Days of War – June 1967 and the Making of the Modern Middle East.* New York: Oxford University Press.

Rabinovich, Abraham (2004. Revised 2012). *The Yom Kippur War: The Epic Encounter That Transformed the Middle East.* New York: Schocken Books/Random House.

MUSICAL ACCOMPANIMENT TO RABBI COHEN'S *SHABBAT SHALOM YERUSHALAYIM* PRAYER

http://www.youtube.com/watch?v=TbZOBYdNgsU

Musical notes: http://www.unisyn.org.il/UploadFiles/unisyn/1451-2152009 _A_Prayer_For_Jerusalem.pdf

UNDERSTANDING ISRAEL

Eban, Abba (1972). *My Country: The Story of Modern Israel.* New York: Random House.

Peters, Joan (1984). *From Time Immemorial— The Origins of the Arab-Jewish Conflict over Palestine.* New York: Harper & Row. (Controversial landmark book which argues that the Arab population in pre-Mandate and Mandate Palestine increased in direct proportion to the growing

Jewish presence. It also argues that UNRWA continues to perpetuate the refugee status of Arabs displaced during the War of Independence.)

Gilbert, Martin (2007). *Churchill and the Jews.* New York: Simon & Schuster. (Confirms *inter alia* the views of Joan Peters, mentioned above.)

Avner, Yehuda (2010). *The Prime Ministers: An Intimate Narrative of Israeli Leadership.* Jerusalem: The Toby Press.

Halevy, Yossi Klein (2013*). Like Dreamers: The Story of the Israeli Paratroopers who Reunited Jerusalem and Divided a Nation.* New York: Harper Collins.

MACHON HARRY FISCHEL AND THE ARIEL INSTITUTES OF HIGHER TORAH LEARNING

Fischelfoundation.org (internet entry).

Harry Fischel Institute for Research in Talmudic Jurisprudence (internet entry)

Machon Harry Fischel: See under *Fischelfoundation.org.*

FOR INFORMATION ON ARIEL

Ariel Institutes on Facebook

Fischelfoundation.org, click on tab for affiliates.

POPULAR ARIEL PUBLICATIONS IN ENGLISH (SELECTION)

Chigier, Rabbi Dr. Moshe (Hebrew: 5744/1984. English: 5745/1985). *Husband and Wife in Israeli Law.* Jerusalem: Harry Fischel Institute for Research in Talmud and Jurisprudence. (Rabbi Chigier was a Fellow of the Harry Fischel Institute and later legal advisor to the Ministry of Religious affairs.)

(1989). *Torah from Zion: Rabbinic In-Service Studies, Selected Papers Presented before Ariel Rabbinic Study Sessions.* Jerusalem: Ariel.

Frank, Yitzhak (1991. Revised and expanded edition, 1997). *The Practical Talmud Dictionary.* Jerusalem: Ariel.

Frank, Yitzhak (1991. Revised and expanded edition, 1997). *Grammar for Gemara, an Introduction to Babylonian Aramaic.* Jerusalem: Ariel.

FAMILY

Goldstein, Herbert S., editor (1928). *Forty Years of Struggle for a Principle, The Biography of Harry Fischel* (compiled from Harry Fischel's daily diary, newspaper clippings and addresses). Bloch Publishing Company.

Goldstein, Herbert S., Reichel, Aaron, editors (1928, 2012); *Harry Fischel, Pioneer of Jewish Philanthropy, Forty Years of Struggle for a Principle and the Years Beyond*, augmented edition of *Forty Years of Struggle* (preceding entry), including also the diary of Harry Fischel for the years 1928–1941. Ktav. (Also available as an e-book from Kodesh Press.)

Reichel, Aaron I. (1984. 2nd edition 1986). *The Maverick Rabbi, Rabbi Herbert S. Goldstein and the Institutional Synagogue – A New Organizational Form*. Norfolk: Donning.

INTERFAITH DIALOGUE

Nostra Aetate (28th October 1965). Declaration by Pope Paul VI. Pope John Paul II's statement which includes the words that Jews are "our older brother", and to be regarded by good Roman Catholics as the "Chosen People." *http://www.vatican.va/archive/hist_councils/ii_vatican_council /documents/vat-ii_decl_1965-1028_nostra-aetate_en.html*

Normalization Accord (30th December 1993). Vatican and Israel agree to exchange ambassadors for the first time.

"We Remember: A Reflection on the Shoah" (16th March 1998). The Roman Catholic Church repented for 2,000 years of preaching anti-Semitism, culminating in the Shoah. In a cover letter dated 12th March 1998 (addressed to Edward Idris, Cardinal Cassidy, President of the Commission for Religious Relations With the Jews), the Pope describes his "sense of deep sorrow [regarding] the sufferings of the Jewish people during the Second World War" and reiterates his view that "the Shoah remains an indelible stain on the history of the century." He further expresses his hope that this document will "help heal the wounds of past misunderstandings and injustices" and go some way to create "a future in which the unspeakable iniquity of the Shoah will never again be possible."

"Joint Declaration" (5th September 2006/12th Elul, 5766). Anglican Communion establishes Anglican Jewish Commission. *http://nifcon .anglicancommunion.org/media/111580/Agreement-between-The-Chief -Rabbis-of-Israel-and-The-Archbishop-of-Canterbury.pdf*

Cohen, Shear Yashuv (2008). "Jewish Leadership and Interfaith Dialogue," West Side Institutional Synagogue, NYC, inaugural Rabbi Herbert S. Goldstein Memorial Leadership Lecture.